THE PRAISE OF FOLLY

Folly Lectures Her Followers

DESIDERIUS ERASMUS

THE PRAISE OF FOLLY

Translated with an introduction and commentary by
CLARENCE H. MILLER

NEW HAVEN AND LONDON
YALE UNIVERSITY PRESS

Designed by Thos. Whitridge and set in monotype Bembo.
Printed in the United States of America by The Vail-Ballou Press, Binghamton, N. Y.

Library of Congress Cataloging in Publication Data

Erasmus, Desiderius, d. 1536.
  The praise of folly.

  Translation of Moriae encomium.
  Bibliography: p.
  Includes index.
  1. Folly. I. Miller, Clarence H. II. Title.
PA8514.E5 1979   260   78-13575
ISBN 0-300-02373-1 (pbk.)

Erasmus' Letter to Martin Dorp has been translated from *Opus Epistolarum Des. Erasmi* edited by P. S. Allen and H. M. Allen (12 vols. 1906–1947) by permission of the Oxford University Press. Frontispiece: Anonymous drawing, probably from Leiden, ca. 1520–30, Nationalmuseum, Stockholm.
Illustration on p. 7: By Hans Holbein the Younger, a marginal drawing in a copy of *Moriae encomium* (Basel, 1515, sig. X4^r), Kunstmuseum Basel, Kupferstichkabinett.

23 22 21 20 19 18 17 16 15 14 13 12

CARO MAGISTRO

AC

PIO AMICO MEO

MAURITIO BASILIO McNAMEE

SOCIETATIS JESU

Editor and publisher wish to express
their esteem for and debt to the
International Council for an Edition of
the Complete Works of Erasmus, the Royal
Netherlands Academy of Arts and Sciences,
and North-Holland Publishing Company for
sponsoring and publishing the definitive
edition of Erasmus's *Encomium Moriae*.

CONTENTS

INTRODUCTION

Fortunately Erasmus himself has given us some detailed information about the genesis, composition, and publication of his masterpiece (see below, p. 1). In the summer of 1509 he was on his way to England from Italy, where he had been stimulated by his contact with Italian humanism, disgusted by secular and ecclesiastical corruption, and exhausted by his prodigious labors on the *Adagia*, an enormous, profusely annotated collection of Greek and Latin proverbs published by Aldus at Venice in 1508. Riding on horseback over an Alpine pass, he conceived the notion of writing a mock-encomium on folly—Folly's oration in praise of herself—partly because he was thinking of his friends in England, particularly of his closest friend there Thomas More, whose family name resembles the Greek word for folly. After a journey of about two months, he arrived at More's house in London, the Old Barge in Bucklersbury, where he was confined for a while with a kidney ailment. Whether he was delivered of a kidney stone we do not know, but he did bring Folly into the world, smiling and eloquent from her first breath. When he had written part of Folly's speech, he showed it to his English friends to let them share the fun, or (as we can easily imagine) he read them what he had written, taking on the role of Folly himself. Thoroughly delighted, they urged him to go on with it. Within about a week, Folly, though not quite full grown, was essentially complete and ready to begin her brilliant career as one of the most popular and controversial prima donnas of Western literature.

From somewhere in the English countryside, probably in June of 1510, Erasmus wrote a letter dedicating his *Moria* (as he usually called the work) to More. This preface is an integral part of the work and was always printed with it during Erasmus' lifetime. Erasmus said he did not originally intend to publish the *Moria*; but since the explanations and defenses in the preface are clearly intended for a general audience, we can safely assume that by the time the preface was written he was no longer unwilling to see the work printed, even under his own name and not (like his daring attack on Pope Julius II) anonymously. Nevertheless, when it was first printed at Paris, almost certainly in 1511 and certainly before August of that year, it was seen through the press and corrected (very badly) not by Erasmus, though he happened to be in Paris at the time, but by a young English scholar, Richard Croke. This shabby first edition was twice reprinted (in Strassburg and Antwerp) before the first authorized edition was issued on 26 July 1512 by the Ascensian press at Paris.

That *Folly* was conceived on the great watershed of Europe, poised between the urbanity of the Italian Renaissance and the earnestness of Northern Humanism, has seemed significant to some critics in moments of lofty speculation. That it was written in More's house and dedicated to him may suggest affinities with the genial wit of the author of *Utopia*, but it should also serve to remind us that during an earlier stay in London in 1505 and 1506 More and Erasmus had collaborated and competed in translating from Greek to Latin some dialogues of Lucian, whose caustic and brilliant satire provided one important model for the *Folly*. That it was composed in England also has a broader significance in that it was only after his first visit to England in 1499 that Erasmus finally fixed his sights firmly on the great goal of his life: to edit, translate, and annotate the Greek New Testament—a work which he largely executed in England, especially during his five years at Cambridge (1509–14), and which finally appeared in print at Basel in 1516. Finally, that the *Folly* was first printed in Paris may seem fitting, since the Sorbonne was the very stronghold of the reactionary theologians whose hairsplitting arrogance and exegetical ineptitude are so often the butts of Folly's wit.

In fact, no other brief, integral work of Erasmus condenses the humanists' program for educational, religious, and theological reform better than the *Folly*, especially if we read it in conjunction with Erasmus' defensive letter to Dorp and More's even longer, more profound defense of the *Folly* and Erasmus' projected Greek New Testament (both composed in 1515). During the three centuries before Erasmus wrote, logic had gained a commanding position in the university arts curriculum, casting the pale survivals of grammar and rhetoric, the dominant studies during classical antiquity, into the shade. The enormous and intricate structure of scholastic philosophy and theology rested on the revival (about 1200) of Aristotle's logical works, the *Organon* or great "instrument" of human learning, and on the subtle, dazzling (not to say dizzying) refinements of them made by medieval logicians, especially Peter of Spain (about 1250). The humanist revival, which gained increasing momentum during the fifteenth century, especially in Italy, might be simplistically described as an attempt to regain and restore the rightful roles of grammar and rhetoric. Grammar was no longer to be the mere mastery of the ordinary rules of Latin syntax but the establishment and explication of sound texts through linguistic and historical studies, a movement which culminated in nineteenth-century classical philology. Grammar in this larger sense was made possible and necessary because of the rediscovery of many works by ancient Greek and Latin writers. Rhetoric was no longer to be lists of ornamental figures of speech, the medieval flowers and "colors" of rhetoric, but the art of speaking and writing Latin persuasively, with coherence and fluency, articulation and copiousness. The new rhetoric was based largely on the rediscovered rhetorical works of Aristotle, Cicero, and Quintilian—especially the last two. We should remember that the new grammar had as its province not merely what we think of as literature, but also philosophy (especially Plato, Cicero, and Seneca), history, politics, medicine, law, geography, astronomy, architecture, and even military strategy. And the new rhetoric was not merely an academic pursuit or the elegant entertainment of a leisured elite, but the key to many important ecclesiastical, governmental, and diplomatic posts.

Needless to say, the pillars of the educational and ecclesiastical establishment, especially the old-fashioned theologians and monks, were not very eager to be reformed. It is hard for us to conceive of a time when anyone could deny that the New Testament should be studied in the original Greek and explicated in the light of the Greek and Latin fathers. But Erasmus' *New Testament* was repeatedly and bitterly attacked, and so was his *Folly*, especially after the Lutheran outburst dashed the hopes of moderate reformers and Erasmus found himself caught between Scylla and Charybdis, between the protestant revolt and the catholic reaction. As Erasmus' prefatory letter shows, he fully expected the *Folly* to be attacked. In the preface, in his letter to Dorp, and in three of his letters written in 1517 and 1518, he defended the *Folly* on primarily grammatical or literary grounds: the nature of the genre, its precedents, the scope of the subject matter, the moderation of tone. The long commentary which was added to the *Folly* in 1515 by Gerard Listrius (but which was partly written by Erasmus himself) tries to elucidate the ironical genre to which the *Folly* belongs, the paradoxical encomium, and to defend daring passages, often by appeals to literary decorum. Most of Erasmus' additions to the commentary after 1515 are also defensive. Later assailants of the *Folly*—Edward Lee (1518), Diego López Zúñiga (1522), Pierre Cousturier (1526), and Alberto Pio (1529 and 1531)—ignored the literary character of the work entirely. They picked various sentences out of their context and labelled them blasphemous or heretical. A flagrant example is Cousturier's contention that Erasmus was blasphemous because he made Folly claim that the invention of sciences was due to her: "for God is the lord of sciences, but Erasmus attributes the invention of them to Folly, therefore he has blasphemed against God." With increasing weariness, Erasmus answered point by point, over and over again. But his chief difficulty was that too often he tacitly seemed to agree with his opponents' assumption that Folly expressed Erasmus' own opinions; he denied it occasionally, but he implicitly granted it by defending Folly's remarks because of their precision and restraint. In 1543 the Sorbonne officially condemned the *Folly*. From then until the end of the century it was included in at least fourteen indices of forbidden books, in France, Spain, and Italy. The opprobrium heaped on the *Folly* by Erasmus' enemies shows that they took it anything but lightly.

Erasmus, of course, knew that the *Folly* was a glorious *jeu d'esprit* and that his opponents were racking a butterfly on a wheel. But his continuous revisions show that he also considered it a serious and important book: not merely foolish, not merely wise, but foolishly wise (*morosophos*). During his lifetime it appeared in thirty-six editions from the presses of twenty-one printers in eleven cities, including Paris, Lyons, Strassburg, Venice, Florence, Basel, Cologne, Deventer, and Antwerp. He augmented and revised it in seven major editions: 1512 (Paris), 1514 (Strassburg), 1515, 1516, 1521, 1522, and 1532 (all in Basel). All but one of the long additions were first printed in 1514; together with the passage added in 1516, they make the work about eighteen percent longer than the first edition. The passages added in 1514 clearly heighten the religious dimension of the work. Two were added to the satirical exposé of theologians and monks in Folly's long survey of her followers. Others add new citations and arguments to Folly's virtuoso attempt to show that Christianity as it is revealed in the Scriptures is based on Folly. With prickling particularity, they illustrate the quibbling questions debated by theologians, the stupid fascination of the monks with ceremonies and superstitious practices, the outrageously irrelevant introductions to the friars' sermons, and the scholastic theologians' citation of Scriptural tags taken out of context and wrenched to serve some dialectical subtlety or paradox. They ridicule some of the same follies exposed in Erasmus' and More's letters to Dorp: a refusal to go beyond the Vulgate to the Greek of the New Testament, and a false stress on hypersubtle dialectic to the neglect of the new "grammar" as a way of advancing theology by a richer understanding of Scripture and the fathers. In later revisions, apart from many smaller stylistic improvements, Erasmus corrected a few places where he had lapsed into speaking in his own person rather than under the persona of Folly. He also qualified and mitigated the sweeping condemnations of certain groups in the earlier editions and added a few words to make the paradox of Christian folly more guarded and less open to the charge of blasphemy.

One reason why the *Folly* was persistently misunderstood and attacked was the novelty of its literary form. It was a spectacular revival of a classical genre which had been practically extinct for a thousand years, the paradoxical encomium. Arthur Pease has defined such an encomium as a declamation "in which the legitimate methods of the encomion are applied to persons or objects in themselves obviously unworthy of praise, as being trivial, ugly, useless, ridiculous, dangerous, or vicious."[1] Among the precedents for the *Folly* cited by Erasmus in his preface (p. 3) are a number which do not strictly belong to the genre. But when Folly herself, with involuted irony, defines the form she is following by dissociating herself from it, she mentions only examples which fit the genre exactly: many orators, she says, "have spent sleepless nights burning the midnight oil to work out elaborate encomia of Busiris, Phalaris, the quartan fever, flies, baldness, and other dangerous nuisances" (p. 12). The form was continuously cultivated in both Greek and Latin from the fifth century B.C. to the fourth century after Christ and included among its practitioners such luminaries as Plato, Isocrates, and Lucian, but very few examples have survived from classical times. Since classical rhetoricians taught that the paradoxical encomium could be "much freer in its arrangement than the more strictly logical forms of eloquence,"[2] we should not be surprised that Hoyt Hudson's detailed outline of the *Folly* according to the oratorical structure laid down by Quintilian and Walter Kaiser's analysis according to the plan of the Aphthonian encomium do not reveal the pattern of Folly's speech in a fully satisfying way. The third-century rhetorician Menander, one of the most important sources of our knowledge of the rules for eulogies, mentions a kind

1. "Things without Honor," *Classical Philology*, 21 (1926), 28–29.
2. Pease, p. 36. See also Theodore C. Burgess, *Epideictic Literature* (Chicago, 1902), 157–66.

of speech which, though it has no set structural pattern, seems close to the spirit and style of the *Folly*: λαλιά is a "name given to a style rather than to a topic. It is noticeable for the absence of fixed rules. Several topics of the epideictic circle might be treated in the style of the λαλιά, which was more free and easy, sometimes conversational, yet abounding in sweetness, spirited narrative, pictures, skilful turns, proverbs, quotations. . . . It may be sportive in character, praising or censuring something."[3]

Classical sources for the arguments, allusions, sayings, and proverbs in the *Folly* are numerous indeed, as the footnotes will testify. Few have been able to savor its finer bouquet without the help of notes, to catch the wit on the wing rather than in the taxidermy of annotation. As Sir Thomas Chaloner, the first English translator (1549), remarked, Erasmus turned out his whole scholarly knapsack for the *Folly*, and it was crammed full in 1509 because he had just finished listing and commenting at length on 4,500 Greek and Latin proverbs and sayings in his *Adagia*. Tags from Virgil and Homer are sprinkled generously, especially in the first part, to lend a dash of mock-heroic elevation. Horace is frequently cited and quoted throughout to provide a comfortable aura of urbane common sense. Gellius and Pliny are exploited for useful anecdotes or "scientific" evidence. With sophistical ease, Folly often distorts, almost unnoticeably, the classical authorities she cites to support her arguments. At one point she even boasts of her sophistical prowess in distorting evidence (p. 38). Since Plato was among the most important and influential of the Greek writers rediscovered by the humanists, it might be helpful to notice how she uses (and abuses) him.

The major ideas drawn from Plato are: (1) the distinction between two kinds of madness, modelled on Plato's distinction between two kinds of love (p. 57); (2) the Sileni of Alcibiades (p. 43); (3) the myth of the cave (pp. 72–73, 133–34); and (4) the higher kind of love leading from the impermanent world of flux to the stable realm of the one, true, and beautiful (p. 136). The distinction

---

3. Burgess, p. 111.

between the two kinds of madness is structurally important because it allows Folly to describe various beneficent obsessions (hunting, building, gambling, and so on). But her analogy between madness and love, however convenient, is merely superficial and sophistical. She exploits the myth of the cave in two quite inconsistent ways. In the first part, when she is trying to prove that foolish illusions enable us to lead a happy life, she praises the fools who contentedly watch the shadows in the cave and contemptuously dismisses the wiseman who perversely insists on seeing the reality outside. But in the third part, when she claims as her own devout Christians who reject the world and the flesh for the things of the spirit, she praises this same wiseman as an exemplary Christian fool. Moreover, she uses Plato's image of the Sileni to prove a skeptical or Pyrrhonist viewpoint, quite contrary to Erasmus' own explication in the *Adagia*.[4] She is certainly not a consistent Platonic philosopher—she even rejects him completely more than once (pp. 37, 40). She uses Platonic ideas with the same inconsistent nonchalance as she exploits quite different philosophies—Aristotelian, Epicurean, Pyrrhonist, even Stoic when it suits her purposes (though the Stoics are usually her favorite straw men).

The ironical complexity of the *Folly* becomes more evident if we compare her shifting use of Platonism with Erasmus' own straightforward use of it in the *Enchiridion*. Erasmus himself invited such a comparison in his letter to Dorp: "In the 'Folly' I had no other aim than I had in my other writings, but my method was different. In the 'Enchiridion' I propounded the character of a Christian life in a straightforward way. . . . And in the 'Folly,' under the appearance of a joke, my purpose is just the same as in the 'Enchiridion' " (pp. 142–43). The same general purpose, well and good. But the different method, the appearance of a joke, in a word, the irony of the *Folly* makes all the difference. In the *Enchiridion*, the analogy of the Sileni is used in a straightforward way to highlight the spiritual sense of Scripture and to divide it rather sharply from the crude literal sense. Plato's myth of the cave is used only in the second of Folly's ways,

---

4. Margaret Mann Phillips, *Erasmus on his Times: a Shortened Version of the 'Adages' of Erasmus* (Cambridge, 1967), pp. 77–97.

and Platonic notions of love from the *Phaedo* are cited to make a sharp division between body and soul, matter and spirit, which Erasmus himself accepts and propounds.[5] But when Folly uses similar ideas of Platonic love to describe and praise the Christian fool, her inconsistent and contradictory use of Plato should remind us that we are not justified in accepting Folly's view as identical with Erasmus' even though it closely resembles what Erasmus says in the *Enchiridion*. From start to finish Folly is simplistic and sophistical. Folly, but not necessarily Erasmus, defines Christianity narrowly as the irrational pursuit of mystical ecstasy and the utter repudiation of the material world. The last part of Folly's speech is completely inconsistent with the first part, but it is equally ironical. When she argues that folly is the only source of comfort, joy, and happiness, our first reaction is "certainly not," but we are gradually forced to admit "yes, too often." When she argues that the true Christian must act like a fool in the eyes of the world, we are forced to admit "yes, certainly," but we find ourselves continually wishing to interject "no, there's more to it than that." The experience of the book is to play off one irony against the other, not to imagine that Erasmus is simply propounding straightforward Platonism.

Two ancient mock-encomia ought to be mentioned because they are the only classical examples of a decisive feature of the *Folly*, that the subject of the speech is also its speaker. In Aristophanes' *Plutus* (lines 507–610) Poverty delivers an encomium of herself, and in the first of Lucian's paradoxical encomia of Phalaris, the tyrant speaks his own praises. But Erasmus' most brilliant stroke has no classical precedent: he chose a topic which makes his encomium both self-affirming and self-negating. As Walter Kaiser has pointed out, "Erasmus' great originality, then, was to make Stultitia both the author and the subject of her encomium, to conceive of 'Moriae' as being simultaneously both objective and subjective genitive."[6] Folly's praising Folly leads into a maze like that of the Cretan liar: Folly is being praised and therefore is praiseworthy, but what Folly praises can hardly be praiseworthy. What is said often seems right,

5. *Enchiridion*, pp. 105, 133, 68, 103.
6. *Praisers of Folly* (Cambridge, Mass., 1963), p. 36.

but if we consider the source, we know it must be wrong. The precedents for making Folly speak as a dramatic character and for the dual conception of the fool as either an irresponsible sinner or a victor over the supposed wisdom of the world are to be found not in classical sources but in the literary and social heritage of the middle ages.

Sebastian Brant's *Ship of Fools* (1494), which is too often mentioned as a forerunner of the *Folly*, is actually pervaded by a single-minded notion of the fool as sinner. On the other hand, in the widespread Latin dialogue *Marcolf and Solomon*, the folk-fool Marcolf defeats the worldly wisdom of Solomon himself. Both roles were combined in the licensed court fool, to whom Folly lays special claim (pp. 55–56). Among the many licensed fools Erasmus must have encountered in his travels were those kept by Henry VII, Henry VIII, and Thomas More. Some of the most famous, especially in Italy, were women, and some were noted for their parody of ecclesiastical men and manners. In his Colloquy "The Well-to-do Beggars," Erasmus presented the licensed fool as an irresponsible sinner whose peculiar garb protects him from the consequences of his rash words and deeds, but he also suggested that such fools may be wiser than some theologians and princes.[7] The most famous literary embodiment is the fool in *King Lear*. In defending the *Folly*, Erasmus often appealed to the tradition of the licensed fool in ancient and modern times.

Another precedent for the topsy-turvy values of Folly was the Feast of Fools, which flourished, in spite of ecclesiastical prohibitions, from the twelfth to the sixteenth centuries. At Christmastime the lower clergy at many cathedrals and other principal churches chose a bishop, or abbot, or even pope of fools to lead a rowdy parody of the hierarchical and liturgical pomp of the ecclesiastical establishment. The celebration varied from place to place, but it sometimes included a burlesque sermon. Thomas More mentioned "an abbote of mysrule in a Christemas game that were prykked in

7. *Coll.*, p. 212.

blankettes, and then sholde stande vp and preche vppon a stole and make a mowynge sermon."[8]

Erasmus must have been familiar with the foolery of Fasching and carnival in Germany and the Low Countries, but even closer to the subject and manner of the *Folly* were the dramatic performances produced by the *sociétés joyeuses* in France, especially in Paris and Dijon, from the end of the fifteenth century to the middle of the seventeenth. Under the leadership of a "Prince of Fools" or "Mother Folly," they presented such satiric skits as the *sottie* and the *sermon joyeux*. The *sottie* was a sort of roll-call of fools recited before a performance to attract spectators and usually followed by a sermon, a morality play, and a farce.[9] In its simplest form (before 1500), two or three fools met and exchanged nonsense with each other. The costume was the fool's cap with ass's ears and the fool's scepter; Mother Folly herself appears in many of them. The principal theme was that everyone from the highest to the lowest obeys the lordship of Folly. The motto of the *société joyeuse* at Dijon was "The number of fools is infinite," a text cited by Folly herself (p. 119) and one of her main points. In his letter to Dorp, Erasmus was probably thinking of the *sotties* when he claimed for the *Folly* "the same freedom which the uneducated allow in popular comedies. In them how frequent and free are the insults hurled at kings and priests and monks and wives and husbands—indeed who is safe? But yet, because no one is attacked by name, everyone laughs and either frankly admits to his fault or prudently dissembles it" (pp. 148-49).

The *sermon joyeux* was a brief mock-sermon delivered before a serious sermon, morality play, or saint's life.[1] They were in praise of a whole host of saints such as Saint Herring, Saint Onion, or Saint Chitterling, but they also preached on women, drunkards, and various other more or less disreputable subjects. The form

8. *The Confutation of Tyndale's Answer*, ed. L. Schuster, R. Marius, J. Lusardi, and R. Schoeck (New Haven, 1973), p. 42.

9. Emile Picot, "La Sottie en France," *Romania*, 7 (1878), 236–326.

1. Emile Picot, "Le Monologue drammatique dans l'ancien théatre Français," *Romania*, 15 (1886), 358–422; 16 (1887), 438–542; 17 (1888), 208–75.

flourished in the late fifteenth century, when Erasmus was in France, though few early examples have survived. Only a few have been preserved which have fools as their subject matter, but the headings under which Emile Picot lists the corpus of *sermons joyeux* suggests affinities with the *Folly*: (1) the lives of various "saints" or humorous persons; (2) love, women, and marriage; (3) drinkers and taverns; (4) various subjects; and (5) sermons of fools. Both the *sottie* and the *sermon joyeux* were preludes to serious plays or sermons—an arrangement which may have suggested Folly's startling shift to religious folly in the last part of her "sermon."[2] In the preface to his translation (1549), Sir Thomas Chaloner, who had traveled in France, remarked that Erasmus imagines that Folly speaks "before all kyndes of men assembled as to a sermon."[3]

This enormous mélange of foolery, classical and medieval, was available to other writers besides Erasmus (though few had his imperial command of the ancients). But he was the first to shape it into a literary masterpiece. We do not have to read very far into Brant's *Ship of Fools* to recognize that Erasmus' superiority springs from his dramatic persona and the literary form of her speech. What we still lack for a full appreciation of Folly as a persona is a stylistic analysis of the very texture of her language. But the introduction to a translation is hardly the place to make even a beginning of this difficult task. Suffice it to say that she is not only a splendid entertainer—coy and urbane, modest and boastful, suave and outrageous—but also a consummate sophist. She uses the weapons of the logicians against them, and much of her argumentation could be analyzed according to the Aristotelian categories of sophistical argumentation which had been refined for centuries and were regularly taught in the universities. At one point she deliberately displays her sleight of hand by enveloping a scriptural quotation in an obviously false syllogism:

2. Holbein's last illustration in a copy of Froben's 1515 edition shows Folly descending from a pulpit. See Betty Radice, "Holbein's Marginal Illustrations to the Praise of Folly," *Erasmus in English*, 7 (1975), 11.

3. Ed. Clarence H. Miller, Early English Text Society No. 257 (Oxford, 1965), p. 3.

What should be concealed is more valuable than what is left
exposed and unguarded. (Hence the Aristotelian proverb "The
waterjug is left lying in the doorway.")
Folly should be concealed whereas wisdom should be openly
displayed (*Ecclesiasticus* 20 : 33).
Therefore folly is more valuable than wisdom. (pp. 121–22)

In this syllogism, directed against those infatuated by Aristotelian
logic, the use of an Aristotelian proverb to support the major is not
without malice aforethought. The syllogism is also a glaring example of one of the standard fallacies discussed by Aristotle: it argues
from a proposition which is true only *secundum quid* (that is, as it
applies to personal, portable property) to a conclusion *simpliciter*.
The outrageous and seemingly incredible false division of "devita"
into "de vita" (pp. 126–27) is actually an obvious example of one
of the less common and less important Aristotelian fallacies "in
dictione," the "fallacia accentus."

As for the literary structure of Folly's speech,[4] most critics have
begun to take a tripartite plan as their starting point:

(1) Folly provides the illusions necessary to render life in this
world tolerable or even pleasant (pp. 1–76).

(2) Folly makes the professional leaders of church and state blind
enough to be happy in their vicious irresponsibility (pp. 76–115).

(3) Folly enables the Christian fool to renounce the world in favor
of Christian joy in this life and the beatific vision in the next (pp.
115–37).

The second section, a survey of academic and social classes, is
adapted from a medieval genre, the satire of estates. Erasmus'
survey is more intellectual than medieval satire of estates usually
is, but it displays a similar sense of hierarchical cohesiveness.
Society is made up of the body politic and the mystical body, the
state and the church, each with distinct and various groups con-

---

4. On this point I have borrowed a few paragraphs from my article "Some
Medieval Elements and Structural Unity in Erasmus' *Praise of Folly*," *Renaissance Quarterly*, 27 (Winter, 1974), 499–511.

tributing diversely to the harmony of the whole. Folly herself is aware that her survey does not entirely fit the pattern of the encomium, for she brings it to a close by remarking: "But it is no part of my present plan to rummage through the lives of popes and priests, lest I should seem to be composing a satire rather than delivering an encomium. . . . " (p. 115). The mixture of genres is related to a question answered variously by the critics: in the survey does Erasmus abandon his persona and let us hear him directly rather than ironically?

The first and third sections propound seemingly incompatible paradoxes which deal with how individual aspirations toward success and fulfillment are related to the requirements of society at large. The first section is devoted to the ironical thesis that the happiest life is a fool's life. The wise man is not only inept and ineffective in the practical affairs of everyday living, but his harsh truths would also destroy the illusions and deceptions necessary to keep up the stage play of life. Sexual pleasure, the propagation of the human race, the pleasures of the table, friendship and marriage, the glories of warfare, the investigations of science, the inventions of technology, the harmony of civil society all depend on illusions, self-deception, and vainglorious aspirations. Natural fools are among the happiest of men. Even madness, as long as it is not violent, can make people far happier than wisdom. Protected by benevolent euphoria, fanatics of all sorts—hunters, gamblers, alchemists, superstitious worshippers of saints—can maintain the illusion of happiness. Self-love and flattery oil the wheels of society and keep it running smoothly. All life is dual, like the Sileni of Alcibiades—ugly or beautiful according to the viewer's angle of vision. The comedy of life is a play that can be entertaining only so long as its basic illusion is kept up. To strip away disguises ruins the play and leads only to disillusionment, futility, despair, or even suicide. The ironic double vision of this first part has been most frequently analyzed, admired, and related to the outlook of other great writers of the Renaissance, such as Ariosto, Rabelais, Cervantes, or Shakespeare. As in the *Utopia* the reader is piquantly poised between seemingly contradictory views; with a laugh, or a smile, or a sigh he is forced to admit that what seems absurd is sometimes, often, very often, almost always true.

The third section is based on a paradox which seems directly opposed to the first part: the folly of Christian fools throws them out of step with society at large. This sort of folly does not integrate men into their social surroundings; it separates them from the world and its values. Such folly may lead to ridiculous eccentricity, mental alienation, a kind of ecstatic madness in which even ordinary sense perceptions may be lost. Indeed, this folly seems to be oriented toward the final, perfect alienation of the beatific vision. Folly caps her argument with a brilliant and daring pun: ecstasy, the alienation of a mind drawn out of itself into union with God, is "Moriae pars," Folly's portion, "which shall not be taken from her by the transformation of life, but shall be perfected" (p. 137).

Placed between these two contradictory paradoxes, the middle section is essential to the impact of the whole work. It agrees with the first part in that both find the establishment quite foolish and even the happier for its folly. Would not grammarians and schoolteachers be among the most miserable of men, tyrannizing futilely over a wretched and filthy pack of cowed schoolboys, if they were not puffed up by arrogant and foolish delusions of grandeur? The almost incredible self-deception of quibbling theologians lets them imagine that by their petty labors they support the whole church, like Atlas holding the world on his shoulders. If a king considered his responsibilities, would he not be most miserable?

But these happy fools in the middle section also differ from the fools in the first part. However beatific folly may be for individual academic and social leaders, it has a disastrous effect on society as a whole. The fools in the first part are not usually presented in responsible roles; they are alchemists, hunters, gamblers, fortune-hunters, lecherous old men and women, thick-skulled soldiers. Even the gods indulge in folly in their off-duty hours, as it were, when they have finished settling quarrels and hearing petitions (p. 76). In the first part the ineptness of wise men in public affairs might be borne (we are told) if they were not such awkward and cantankerous bores at parties, dances, plays (p. 39). One important reason why Folly is able to carry off the ironical paradox of the first part is precisely that she does not sort out people according to their social functions but rather treats private vices or depicts large, indiscriminate swarms of mankind. The fabric of society is presented as essentially unreal, a pageant or a play which can be maintained only by hiding reality and accepting disguises.

But the very wise men who would disrupt the play of life in the first part comprise the intellectual, political, and ecclesiastical leaders included in the survey of the second part. And their individual happiness consists precisely in avoiding the responsibilities of their roles. Thus, in the first part, the robes of a king are only one of the costumes necessary to keep up the illusions of life: "Now the whole life of mortal men, what is it but a sort of play, in which various persons make their entrances in various costumes, and each one plays his own part until the director gives him his cue to leave the stage? Often he also orders one and the same actor to come on in different costumes, so that the actor who just now played the king in royal scarlet now comes on in rags to play a miserable servant. True, all these images are unreal, but this play cannot be performed in any other way" (pp. 43–44). In the second part, however, the trappings of a king are symbols of his responsibilities: "Then put a gold chain around his neck, a sign of the interlocking agreement of all the virtues. Next give him a crown set with precious gems to remind him that he is supposed to excel everyone in the exercise of all the heroic virtues. Give him a scepter to symbolize justice and a heart completely fortified against the assaults of corruption. And finally, give him a scarlet robe to represent an extraordinary love of the commonwealth. If a prince should compare these accouterments with his own way of life, I cannot but think that he would be thoroughly ashamed of his splendid apparel and would be afraid that some clever wit might make a laughing stock of all this lofty costume" (p. 108). Because the medial survey is more direct and less ironical than the other two parts, we are not surprised to discover that the same allegorical significance of the royal costume is presented in a straightforward way in Erasmus' *The Education of a Christian Prince* (1516).[5]

5. *Educ. Chr. Pr.*, pp. 152, 186–87.

The medial survey not only leads us out of Folly's first paradox, but also prepares us for the Christian paradox of the third part. Here, the whole fabric of society is again dissolved. The world and all its ways are rejected by Christian fools. They refuse to love even their country, parents, children, and friends except insofar as they reflect the goodness of God. The survey agrees with this view in that it too rejects the foolish establishment—the academics, politicians, and ecclesiastics who fail to fulfill their functions. Society as it has degenerated under their management is indeed the very world which is rejected by Christian fools. We can accept the final ironic paradox of the Christian who is absurd and foolish in the eyes of the world because that world has already been presented as vitiated by another less basic ironic contrast: the rulers of the world remain happy by ignoring their duty to regulate and purify the world.

The second part, whatever problems it may present about Erasmus' use of his persona, is clearly a necessary and integral part of the work. Even Folly could not have carried off a direct leap from the first part to the third, and no critical view of the *Folly* can be adequate if it does not take the medial survey into account. The reader's (or better, listener's) task is to remember all of Folly's speech, to consider it as a whole—a task in which Folly (not Erasmus) does her best to defeat him. Through vivid immediacy she tries to hide her shifting inconsistencies. For her prowess in the world she gives more credit to Selflove and Flattery than to her other handmaidens, but for her own sophistry the prime place must be given to Forgetfulness. At the end of her speech she claims—and we may be allowed to doubt her claim—that she cannot provide an epilogue because she docs not remember what she has said. However much Folly may hate him for it, the reader must try to be a "listener with a memory." Only if he constructs the epilogue which Folly refuses to give can he hope to become not merely an initiate of Folly but an initiate of Erasmus' *Folly*.

BIBLIOGRAPHY
AND ABBREVIATIONS

The three annotated bibliographies by Margolin (see below) provide an abundance of scholarship and criticism on *The Praise of Folly* for the years 1936–70. In the footnotes, apart from the abbreviations I have given here, I have adopted common abbreviations for Latin and Greek works (as used, for example, in *The Oxford Classical Dictionary*, Oxford, 1949; *A Latin Dictionary*, ed. C. T. Lewis and C. Short, Oxford, 1951; and *A Greek-English Lexicon*, ed. H. Liddell and R. Scott, Oxford, 1925). All unidentified translations are my own.

I. EDITIONS, COMMENTARIES, TRANSLATIONS OF
The Praise of Folly

Bibliotheca Belgica: Bibliographie générale des Pays Bas, ed. F. van der Haeghen, Ghent, 1898–1923. Vol. 13, which is devoted entirely to Erasmus, appears in vol. 2, 271–1048, of the reissue, ed. Marie-Thérèse Lenger, 6 vols., Brussels, 1964–70.

Éloge de la Folie, tr. Pierre de Nolhac, comm. Maurice Rat, Paris, 1936. Latin with facing translation. Includes Erasmus' letter to Dorp. Some original material in the commentary.

Hudson. See *The Praise of Folly,* below.

Moriae encomivm, id est Stulticiae laudatio . . . Jerome Froben and Nikolaus Bischoff, Basel, 1532. The last edition revised by Erasmus. Contains both the text and the Lister commentary in their final form.

ΜΩΡΙΑΣ ΈΓΚΩΜΙΟΝ sive Laus Stultitiae, ed. Wendelin Schmidt-Dengler, tr. Alfred Hartmann, Ausgewählte Schriften, Darmstadt, 1975.

Μωρcας Έγκωμcον Stultitiae laus, ed. I. B. Kan, The Hague, 1898. The second original commentary.

The Praise of Folie, tr. Sir Thomas Chaloner, ed. Clarence H. Miller, Early English Text Society No. 257, Oxford, 1965. The first English translation (1549).

The Praise of Folly, tr. and comm. Hoyt H. Hudson, Princeton, 1941. Contains some original material in the commentary and an analysis in terms of the classical oration.

Praise of Folly and Letter to Martin Dorp 1515, tr. Betty Radice, comm. A. H. T. Levi, Penguin Books, 1971.

Stultitiae laus . . . a facsimile of the Froben 1515 edition with marginal drawings by Holbein, ed. H. A. Schmid, Basel, 1931. The 1515 edition was the first to contain Lister's commentary.

Stultitiae laus, vol. 4, cols. 401–504, in *Opera omnia*, ed. Jean Leclerc, Leiden, 1703–06. Reprints the Lister commentary.

II. CRITICISM, INTERPRETATION, AND RELATED WORKS

Amsterdam ed. *Opera omnia Desiderii Erasmi Roterodami*, vol. 1 (parts 1–5), vol. 4 (part 1), Amsterdam, 1969–.

Bainton, Roland. *Erasmus of Christendom*, New York, 1969.

Burgess, Theodore C. *Epideictic Literature*, Chicago, 1902.

CCSL. *Corpus Christianorum: Series Latina*, Turnhold, 1954–65. Volumes numbered to 176, of which 49 have been published.

Chomarat, Jacques. "L' 'Éloge de la Folie' et Quintilien." *Information littéraire*, No. 2 (1972): 77–82.

Christian, Lynda G. "The Metamorphoses of Erasmus' 'Folly'." *Journal of the History of Ideas, 32* (1971): 289–94.

CSEL. *Corpus scriptorum ecclesiasticorum Latinorum*, 83 vols., Vienna, 1866–1971.

Curtius, Ernst. *European Literature and the Latin Middle Ages*, New York, 1953.

CW. See More, below.

Dorey, Thomas A., ed. *Erasmus*, Albuquerque, 1970.

Ep. obscur. vir. Epistolae obscurorum virorum, Latin text with an English rendering . . . by F. G. Stokes, London, 1925.

Erasmus, *Adag.* "Adagia," *Opera* (see *Op.*, below), Vol. 2.

———— See Amsterdam ed., above.

———— *Coll. The Colloquies of Erasmus*, tr. Craig R. Thompson, Chicago, 1965.

———— *Copia. On Copia of Words and Ideas*, tr. and ed. D. B. King and H. D. Rix, Milwaukee,Wisc., 1963.

———— *Corresp. The Correspondence of Erasmus*, tr. and ed. R. A. B. Mynors et al., vols. 1–4, Toronto, 1974–.

———— *Educ. Chr. Pr. The Education of a Christian Prince*, tr. Lester Born, New York, 1968.

———— *Enchiridion. Enchiridion militis Christiani*, tr. Raymond Himelick, Bloomington, Ind., 1963.

———— *Ep. Opus epistolarum Des. Erasmi Roterodami*, ed. P. S. Allen et al., 12 vols., Oxford, 1906–58.

———— *Erasmus on his Time: a Shortened Version of the Adages of Erasmus*, tr. Margaret Mann Phillips, Cambridge, 1967.

———— *The Essential Erasmus*, ed. John P. Dolin, New York, 1964.

———— *Julius Exclusus*, tr. Paul Pascal, ed. J. K. Sowards, Bloomington, Ind., 1968.

———— *Op. Opera omnia*, ed. Jean Leclerc, Leiden, 1703–06.

———— *Selected Letters. Erasmus and his Age: Selected Letters of Desiderius Erasmus*, tr. Marcus Haworth, S. J., ed. Hans J. Hillerbrand, New York, 1970.

———— *Selected Writings. Christian Humanism and the Reformation: Selected Writings of Erasmus with the Life of Erasmus by Beatus Rhenanus*, ed. John C. Olin, New York, 1965.

Gavin, J. Austin. "The Commentary of Gerardus Listrius on Erasmus' *Praise of Folly*: a Critical Edition and Translation with Introduction and Commentary." Unpublished doctoral dissertation, St. Louis University, 1973.

Gavin, J. Austin, and Walsh, Thomas M. "The *Praise of Folly* in Context: the Commentary of Girardus Listrius." *Renaissance Quarterly, 24* (1971): 193–209.

Kaiser, Walter. *Praisers of Folly*, Cambridge, Mass., 1963.

Kay, W. David. "Erasmus' Learned Joking: the Ironic Use of Classical Wisdom in *The Praise of Folly*." *Texas Studies in Literature and Language, 19* (1977): 247–67.

Könneker, Barbara. *Wesen und Wandlung der Narrenidee im Zeitalter des Humanismus: Brant-Murner-Erasmus*, Wiesbaden, 1966.

Kristeller, Paul O. "Erasmus from an Italian Perspective." *Renaissance Quarterly, 23* (1970): 1–14.

Lefebvre, Joël. *Les fols et la folie*, Paris, 1968.

Margolin, Jean-Claude. *Douze années de bibliographie érasmienne 1950–1961*, Paris, 1963.

———— *Quatorze années de bibliographie érasmienne 1936–1949*, Paris, 1969.

———— *Neuf années de bibliographie érasmienne 1962–1970*, Paris and Toronto, 1977.

Miller, Clarence H. "Some Medieval Elements and Structural Unity in Erasmus' *The Praise of Folly*." *Renaissance Quarterly, 27* (1974): 499–511.

More, Thomas. *The Correspondence of Sir Thomas More*, ed. E. Rogers, Princeton, 1947.

———— *CW*. The Yale Edition of the Complete Works of St. Thomas More. *CW 3: Translations of Lucian*, ed. Craig Thompson, New Haven, 1974. *CW 4: Utopia*, ed. Edward Surtz, S. J., and J. H. Hexter, New Haven, 1965.

———— *Selected Letters. St. Thomas More: Selected Letters*, ed. E. Rogers, tr. Marcus Haworth, New Haven, 1961.

Otto, August. *Die Sprichwörter und sprichwörtlichen Redensarten der Römer*, Leipzig, 1890.

Payne, John. *Erasmus: his Theology of the Sacraments*, Richmond, Va., 1970.

Pease, Arthur S. "Things without Honor." *Classical Philology, 21* (1926): 27–42.

PG. Patrologiae cursus completus, series Graeca, ed. J. P. Migne, 161 vols., Paris, 1857–66.

PL. Patrologiae cursus completus, series Latina, ed. J. P. Migne, 221 vols., Paris, 1844–90.

Rebhorn, Wayne A. "The Metamorphoses of Moria: Structure and Meaning in *The Praise of Folly*." *Publications of the Modern Language Association, 89* (1974): 463–76.

Rechtien, John. "A 1520 French Translation of the *Moriae Encomium*." *Renaissance Quarterly, 27* (1974): 23–35.

Rothschild, Herbert B. "Blind and Purblind: A Reading of *The Praise of Folly*." *Neuphilologus, 54* (1970): 223–34.

Schäfer, Eckart. "Erasmus und Horaz." *Antike und Abendland, 16* (1970): 54–67.

Schmidt-Dengler, Wendelin. Introduction to *Laus Stultitia* (Latin-German), Ausgewählte Schriften von Erasmus, 8 vols., *2* (Darmstadt, 1975), ix–xxix.

Smith, Preserved. *Erasmus: a Study of his Life, Ideals, and Place in History*, New York, 1923, rpt. 1962.

Sowards, J. Kelley. *Desiderius Erasmus*, Boston, 1975.

Stenger, Genevieve. *"The Praise of Folly* and its Parerga." *Medievalia et Humanistica*, N.S., No. 2 (1971): 97–117.

Swain, Barbara. *Fools and Folly during the Middle Ages and the Renaissance*, New York, 1932.

Sylvester, Richard S. "The Problem of Unity in The Praise of Folly." *English Literary Renaissance, 6* (1976): 125–39.

Thompson, Craig R. "Better Teachers than Scotus or Aquinas" in *Medieval and Renaissance Studies* (Southeastern Institute of Medieval and Renaissance Studies, No. 2, 1966), ed. John L. Lievsay, Durham, N. C., 1968, pp. 114–45.

Thompson, Sister Geraldine. "Erasmus and the Tradition of Paradox." *Studies in Philology, 61* (1964): 41–63.

—— *Under Pretext of Praise: Satiric Mode in Erasmus' Fiction*, Toronto, 1973.

Tilley, Morris P. *A Dictionary of the Proverbs in England in the Sixteenth and Seventeenth Centuries*, Ann Arbor, 1950.

Tracy, James. *Erasmus: the Growth of a Mind*, Geneva, 1972.

Trillitzsch, Winfried. "Erasmus und Seneca." *Philologus, 109* (1965): 270–93.

Walther, Hans. *Proverbia sententiaeque Latinitatis medii aevi*, Göttingen, 1963–69.

Welsford, Enid. *The Fool: his Social and Literary History*, London, 1935.

Willeford, W. *The Fool and his Scepter*, Chicago, 1969.

Williams, Kathleen, ed. *Twentieth-Century Interpretations of the Praise of Folly*, Englewood Cliffs, N. J., 1969.

A NOTE ON THE TEXT,
THE FOOTNOTES,
AND ERASMUS' REVISIONS

I have based this translation on the forthcoming Latin text I have prepared for the Amsterdam edition.[1] My Latin text is the first one derived from a complete collation of the thirty-six editions printed during Erasmus' lifetime (and of five major editions which appeared afterwards); it is also the first one which indicates Erasmus' additions and revisions and which fully incorporates the final stage of revision. For the Lister commentary, parts of which are by Erasmus, I have used the last edition revised by Erasmus (1532, Basel, Jerome Froben and Nikolaus Bischoff, E870).[2] The notes I give here are based on the work done for my fuller commentary on the Latin text for the Amsterdam edition. For Erasmus' defensive letter to Martin Dorp, I have relied on the text given by P. S. Allen.[3]

Whatever appears in italic type here is in Greek in the original. Whatever appears within single quotation marks is a proverb or a

1. See the bibliography.
2. "E" followed by three numbers refers to the *Bibliotheca Belgica* (see the bibliography). Occasionally I have corrected minor errors in the 1532 edition of the commentary from one or more of the ten earlier editions.
3. No. 337 in *Opus epistolarum* (see Erasmus, *Ep.*, in the bibliography).

well-known saying. The early editions, with a few trifling exceptions, contain no paragraphing; the paragraphing in the translation is my own.

After the first unauthorized edition (Paris, 1511, E838–9), Erasmus augmented and revised the *Folly* seven times:

1512, Paris, Jodicus Badius Asensianus (E841)
1514, Strassburg, Matthias Schürer (E843)
1515, Basel, Johann Froben (E846–7)
1516, Basel, Johann Froben (E848)
1521, Basel, Johann Froben (E860)
1522, Basel, Johann Froben (E862)
1532, Basel, Jerome Froben and Nikolaus Bischoff (E870)

The long additions to the text first appeared in 1514 and 1516: these I have indicated in the translation by enclosing the passages added in 1514 within single pointed brackets (⟨ ⟩) and by enclosing the additions of 1516 within double pointed brackets (⟪ ⟫). The year dates in the running headlines at the top of each page indicate when that page as a whole or any parts of it first appeared. In the footnotes I have also identified a few of the shorter additions and revisions from editions other than those of 1514 and 1516.[4]

4. I have not indicated the generally insignificant revisions in the letter to Dorp. The five Italian editions of the *Moria* published during Erasmus' lifetime (April 1515, August 1515, 1520, and 1525 at Venice, and 1518 at Florence) are all derived from the Strassburg edition of October 1512 and hence contain neither the Lister commentary nor any of Erasmus' additions and revisions.

ERASMUS' PREFATORY LETTER
TO THOMAS MORE

From Erasmus of Rotterdam, greetings to his friend Thomas More

Recently, when I was returning to England from Italy,[1] to avoid wasting the whole time that I had to ride on horseback in *crude* and illiterate talk, I decided to devote some of my attention either to the studies we share with each other or to the pleasure of recalling the most learned and charming friends whom I had left in this country.[2] Among them, my dear More, you were one of the first to come to mind, for I have always enjoyed you as much in my memory when we have been apart as I have delighted in your presence when we were together—and rest assured nothing in my whole life could be sweeter than your company. Therefore, since I thought I ought to do something at least, and since that time seemed hardly suited to serious thinking, I chose to amuse myself by composing an encomium of Folly. "How did you ever get that idea?"[3] you will say. First of all, it was suggested to me by your family name "More",

1. Erasmus left Rome early in July, 1509. See above, p. ix; *Ep. 1*, 19, 459–60, *Adag.* 1140; and below, p. 144.

2. Literally, "here" (hic). This word shows that this letter was written, or at least begun, in England.

3. Literally, "What Pallas put it into your mind?"—an allusion to Homer *od.* 21.1.

which comes as close to the Greek word for folly (Moria)[4] as you yourself are far removed from the fact of folly, and everyone agrees you are far from it indeed. Then too, I suspected that this jeu d'esprit of mine would be especially acceptable to you because you ordinarily take great pleasure in jokes of this sort—that is, those that do not lack learning, if I may say so, and are not utterly deficient in wit—and because you habitually play the role of Democritus[5] by making fun of the ordinary lives of mortals. On the other hand, though your extraordinarily keen intelligence places you worlds apart from the common herd, still the incredible sweetness and gentleness of your character makes you able and willing to be a man for all seasons[6] with all men. And so you will readily accept this little declamation[7] not only as a *memento*[8] of your friend, but also as an object of your patronage and defense,[9] since it is dedicated to you and henceforth is not mine but yours.

For there will probably be no lack of quarrelsome quibblers who will attack it unjustly, some as too light and frivolous for a theologian, some as more biting than is compatible with Christian moderation. They will cry out that I am reviving the Old Comedy[1] or imitating Lucian,[2] accusing me of ripping everything to shreds. As

4. This and other puns on More's name were not uncommon. See G. Marc'hadour, "Thomas More: les arcanes d'un nom," *Moreana* No. 2 (1964), pp. 55–70; and No. 5 (1965), pp. 73–88.

5. The philosopher Democritus (fifth century B.C.) was said to have laughed at the follies of mankind (Juvenal 10.28–30; Seneca *de ira* 2.10.5).

6. Suetonius *Tib.* 42; *Adag.* 286. In 1520 Richard Whittinton (*Vulgaria*, ed. Beatrice White, Early English Text Society, orig. ser. no. 187, London, 1932, pp. 64–65) applied the same Latin phrase to More and translated it "a man for all seasons."

7. Lister stresses that such a rhetorical exercise is not to be scrutinized with theological strictness. Cf. *CW 3*, part 1, xxxii–xxxiii.

8. Catullus 12.13.

9. In 1515 More wrote a long letter to Dorp in defense of the *Folly* and of the humanist program (*Selected Letters*, pp. 6–64).

1. Such comedy, represented primarily by Aristophanes, attacked individuals by name.

2. Lucian of Samosata (ca. 125–190) wrote witty, caustic dialogues, several of which were translated from Greek into Latin by More and Erasmus, working together, in 1505–06 (*CW 3*, part 1, xxii–xxx).

for those who are offended by the levity ⟨and playfulness⟩ of the subject matter, they should consider that I am not setting any precedent but following one set long ago by great writers: ⟨ages ago Homer amused himself with *The Battle of the Frogs and Mice*, as Virgil did with the Gnat and the Rustic Salad, and Ovid with the Walnut-Tree.⟩[3] So too Polycrates ⟨and his corrector Isocrates⟩ both wrote encomia of Busiris;[4] Glauco praised injustice;[5] Favorinus, ⟨Thersites and⟩ the quartan fever;[6] Synesius, baldness;[7] Lucian, the fly ⟨and the art of the parasite. Seneca amused himself by writing an *apotheosis* of Claudius.[8] Plutarch wrote a dialogue between Gryllus and Ulysses.[9] Lucian and Apuleius wrote comic tales about an ass, and some writer or other composed the last will and testament of the piglet Grunnius Corrocotta,[1] which is even mentioned by St. Jerome⟩.[2]

And so, ⟨if they wish,⟩ they can imagine that I was simply playing with pawns for my own amusement or, if they prefer, that I was riding a hobbyhorse like a child.[3] But surely, since we grant every other state in life its own recreations, it is quite unfair to allow students no amusement at all, especially if trifles lead to serious ideas

3. These four apocryphal poems parody the high style by applying it to low subjects.

4. These two Greek orators (fourth century B.C.) wrote mock-encomia of the mythical Egyptian tyrant Busiris (Isocrates *Bus.* 1–4).

5. According to his brother Plato (*rep.* 357a–62c).

6. According to Gellius (*NA* 17.12.2), the rhetorician Favorinus (died about A.D. 135) praised Thersites, the ugliest Greek at Troy (Homer *il.* 2.216–19), and the quartan fever.

7. This fifth-century bishop wrote his mock-encomium in reply to Dio Chrysostom's *Praise of Hair*. It was often combined with the *Folly* in early editions. See Genevieve Stenger, "*The Praise of Folly* and its Parerga," *Medievalia et Humanistica*, N.S., No. 2 (1971), pp. 97–117.

8. Seneca's *Apocolocyntosis* or "pumpkinification" of Claudius presents the emperor after his death, not deified but banished to the underworld.

9. Changed to a pig by Circe, Gryllus argues that it is better to remain an animal than to be restored to humanity (Plutarch *mor.* 985d–92e). See below, p. 53.

1. A school exercise of the third century after Christ.

2. *Comment. in Isaiam*, prol.; *CCSL 73A*, 465.

3. Horace *serm.* 2.3.248.

and if a frivolous subject is handled in such a way that a reader who has any sense at all can profit by it a good deal more than he can from the forbidding and showy subjects undertaken by some writers. Thus, one man praises rhetoric or philosophy in a speech he has patched together for years. Another sings the praises of some prince or other. Another urges war against the Turks. Another predicts future events. Another fabricates some trifling questions like 'whether goat's hair may be called wool'.[4] For just as nothing is more trivial than to treat serious matters in a trivial way, so too nothing is more delightful than to treat trifles in such a way that you do not seem to be trifling at all. Whether I have done so others will judge. But unless I am completely deceived by 'Selflove,'[5] my praise of Folly is not altogether foolish.

But now, to reply to the false charge that the work is too biting, men of wit have always been free to satirize with impunity the ordinary lives of men, as long as this freedom did not degenerate into furious rage. Hence I am all the more amazed how sensitive ears are nowadays: it seems they can hardly bear to hear anything except solemn titles. Then too, you can see some people so perversely religious that they can tolerate the gravest insults against Christ more easily than the lightest joke aimed at pope or prince, especially when *it concerns the pocketbook*.[6] But if someone writes a satire on the lives of men without censuring a single person by name, I ask you, can this be considered scurrilous? Surely it should be taken as judicious and instructive satire. Besides, I beg you to notice on how many counts I indict my own self. Then too, anyone who omits no category of men is clearly not angry at any individual but rather at all vices. Therefore if anyone cries out that he has been injured, he betrays his own bad conscience or at least his fear of exposure. In this sort of writing St. Jerome took far more liberties and was far more biting; sometimes he did not even refrain from mentioning names. As for me, I not only abstained from mentioning any names at all, but I also moderated my style so that any judicious

4. Horace *epist.* 1.18.15; and *Adag.* 253.
5. *Adag.* 292.
6. Aristophanes *nub.* 648.

reader will easily understand that I aimed at giving pleasure, not pain. Moreover, unlike Juvenal, I did not stir up that cesspool of secret vice; I took pains to survey funny rather than filthy vices. And then, if anyone is not satisfied with these explanations, he should at least remember this: it is an honor to be insulted by Folly. Since I made her speak as my persona, I had to preserve decorum by making her speak appropriately. But why am I saying all this to you?—you are such an extraordinary advocate that you can make a strong defense even if the case itself is weak. Farewell, most learned More, and defend vigorously this your *Moria*. From the country, June 9, [1510]⁷

7. In Froben's edition of July, 1522, the year 1508 was added for the first time to this prefatory letter. If Erasmus supplied that year date his memory was simply faulty, since he did not return from Italy to England till 1509. Since the letter was professedly written from England, not France (see p. 1, footnote 2, above), the most probable hypothesis is that Erasmus sent to More a copy of the *Folly*, with the dedicatory letter prefixed, from some residence in the English countryside in 1510.

THE PRAISE OF FOLLY

Folly Comes Down from the Pulpit

Stultitiae laus,
That is, the Praise of Folly,
A Declamation[1] by Erasmus of Rotterdam

FOLLY HERSELF SPEAKS:

Whatever mortals commonly say about me—and I am not unaware of how bad Folly's reputation is, even among the biggest fools of all—still it is quite clear that I myself, the very person now standing here before you, I and I alone, through my divine radiance, pour forth joy into the hearts of gods and men alike. Hence it is that as soon as I came out to speak to this numerous gathering, the faces of all of you immediately brightened up with a strange, new expression of joy. You all suddenly perked up[2] and greeted me with happy, congenial laughter—so much so that every last one of you here before me, wherever I look, seems to be high on the nectar of the Homeric gods, and on the drug nepenthe[3] too, whereas before you all sat there downcast and tense, as if you had just come back from the cave of Trophonius.[4] But when the sun first reveals his fair

1. Lister: "It was fitting for her to call it a declamation, to let you know that it was written as a witty exercise, for fun and enjoyment...." See above, p. 2, footnote 7.

2. *Adag.* 748.

3. An herb mentioned by Homer (*od.* 4.220) and Pliny (*HN* 21.91.159 and 25.5.12) which, mixed with wine, was said to drive away cares.

4. Anyone who consulted the oracle in this cave emerged gloomy (*Adag.*

golden face to the earth, or when a harsh winter yields to the balmy breezes of early spring,[5] everything suddenly takes on a new appearance, a new color, and a certain youthful freshness: so too, when you caught sight of me, your faces were transformed.[6] Thus, what these eloquent orators can hardly accomplish in a long and carefully thought out speech—namely, to clear the mind of troubles and sorrows—that very goal I achieved in a flash simply by making an appearance.

But now you shall hear the reason I have come forth today in this unusual costume,[7] if only you will be so good as to give me your attention—not the kind you give to godly preachers, but rather the kind you give to pitchmen,[8] low comedians, and jokesters—in short, lend me your ears, just as my protégé Midas did long ago to Pan.[9] For I now propose to play the sophist with you for a while—not the kind that nowadays crams boys' heads full of troublesome trifles and passes on the tradition of disputing with more than womanish persistence; rather, I shall follow in the footsteps of those ancient rhetoricians who avoided the infamous title "Sophi" (or "wisemen") and chose instead to be called "sophists."[1] Their aim

---

677. For an analysis of the first Latin sentence, which ends here, see Kaiser, pp. 41-42.

5. Reminiscences of Horace (*carm.* 4.5.6, 3.7.2, 1.4.1). On the traditional meanings, sacred and profane, of an opening description of spring, see F. J. E. Raby, *A History of Secular Latin Poetry in the Middle Ages* (Oxford, 1934), 2, 193, 238-39, 245, 249; and R. Baldwin, *The Unity of the Canterbury Tales*, Anglistica vol. 5 (Copenhagen, 1955), pp. 20-25.

6. In *Ecclesiastes* (*Op.* 5, 862D-72D) Erasmus explains to the Christian preacher several kinds of exordia, including the one Folly uses here, drawn from the immediate surroundings. He gives one similar to Folly's from Prudentius (*CSFL 61*, 420).

7. The cap and bells of the licensed fool, which both she and her followers wear in Holbein's marginal drawings (sigs. B1 and X4 in the facsimile edited by H. A. Schmid, Basel, 1931).

8. Lister points out that Erasmus had in mind Italian mountebanks, selling patent medicines or performing magic tricks in a public square.

9. Because he preferred the music of Pan to that of Apollo, Midas' ears were changed to those of an ass (*Adag.* 267).

1. Folly reverses the values assigned to the two meanings of "sophista." Applied to the ancient orators it had the pejorative connotations still pre-

was to sing the praises of gods and heroes in formal encomia. You shall hear, then, an encomium, not of Hercules, nor of Solon,[2] but rather my own of myself—that is, of Folly.

As for those wise men who teach that it is very foolish and improper for anyone to extol himself, I do not care this much for their opinion.[3] Even granting that it is as foolish as they claim, they cannot deny that it is in keeping with the principle of decorum. For what could be more fitting than that Folly herself should 'pat herself on the back' and *'blow her own horn'*?[4] Who can describe me better than I myself?—unless someone imagines that somebody else knows me better than I know myself. However that may be, I am convinced that my self-praise is considerably more modest than what the ordinary run of nobles and wisemen do: out of a certain perverse sense of shame, they procure some flattering orator or superficial poet (and pay him good money at that) so that they can hear someone else preach their praises—that is, sheer lies—and yet this shamefast nobleman preens himself like a peacock and ruffles his feathers while that shameless flatterer lifts a worthless nonentity to the level of the gods, while he sets him up as the perfect model of all virtues (an ideal from which the patron knows he is *'whole worlds'*[5] away), while he 'decks out a crow in borrowed feathers,'[6] *'whitewashes the blackest vices,'* and (to come to an end at last) *'makes*

---

served in "sophistical," but in the middle ages it came to be applied, with positive overtones, to academic professors of rhetoric.

2. Several encomia of Hercules are known. Although Solon, the Athenian lawgiver and one of the seven wisemen, was frequently praised, no formal encomium of him is known.

3. In the exordium of an oration, a pose of inadequacy was quite traditional. See Quintilian *inst.* 4.1.59–60, and Jacques Chomarat, "L' 'Éloge de la Folie' et Quintilien," *Information littéraire*, No. 2 (1972), pp. 78–79. Folly accompanies the phrase "this much" with a gesture of contempt.

4. Lister points out that this proverb, correctly used, applies to those who display their good character by their deeds. Here Folly misapplies it to those who boast about their deeds.

5. Literally, "two octaves." *Adag.* 163.

6. The crow who borrowed the peacock's feathers is best known from Phaedrus (1.3) and Horace (*epist.* 1.3.19), but Folly's language is closer to St. Jerome (*CCSL 20*, 103).

a silk purse out of a sow's ear.'[7] Finally, I follow that well known proverb which says that a person may very well praise himself if there happens to be no one else to praise him.[8]

Here I might add that I am amazed at the . . . ingratitude should I say, or is it rather laziness? . . . of mankind: they all cultivate me avidly and are very glad to benefit from my goodwill, but in all these centuries there has never been a single soul who has celebrated the praises of Folly in a thankful oration—though there has been no lack of speechwriters who have spent sleepless nights burning the midnight oil to work out elaborate encomia of Busiris, ⟨Phalaris,⟩ the quartan fever, flies, baldness,[9] and other dangerous nuisances. From me, therefore, you will hear an extemporaneous speech, unpremeditated but all the truer for that.[1] I say this because I wouldn't want you to think that I made it up just to show off my cleverness, as ordinary speechmakers generally do. For you know that such orators, even though they have labored over a speech for thirty whole years (and plagiarized some of it at that), will still swear that they dashed it off in a couple of days, or even dictated it, as a mere exercise. As for me, the method I like best of all is simply *'to blurt out whatever pops into my head.'*[2]

Clearly, then, none of you should expect me to follow the path worn by the common herd of rhetoricians, that is, to explain my subject matter—myself—by a definition, much less to divide it into parts.[3] Either technique would be an unpropitious beginning—to

7. *Adag.* 350 and 869.

8. Folly twists the proverbial notion (Walther 33291f) that a man who praises himself must have bad neighbors—that is, there is no one else to praise him.

9. See above, p. 3, footnotes 4, 5, and 6. Phalaris, the Sicilian tyrant, was praised by Lucian in two declamations. In the first, the tyrant, like Folly, praises himself.

1. Folly relies on the proverbial idea that a woman's snap judgment is likely to be more reliable than her reasoned advice. See Tilley W668.

2. *Adag.* 473.

3. The definition and division were technical parts of the traditional oration (Cicero *top.* 5.26–28, and Quintilian *inst.* 5.10.63 and 7.3.2). See Hudson, p. 129.

circumscribe within the narrow limits of a definition a person whose power extends so widely or to break up into separate pieces someone who enjoys the combined worship of all kinds of creatures. Besides, what good would it do to present a shadowy image of myself by means of a definition when you can see me with your own eyes, standing here before you face to face? For I am just what you see, the true *dispenser of divine gifts*[4] whom the Romans call "Stultitia" and the Greeks "*Moria.*"

But why even bother to give you my name, as if you could not tell at a glance who I am, 'prima facie' as it were, or as if anyone who might claim I am Minerva or Sophia could not be refuted by one good look at me, even if I did not identify myself in speech, 'that truest mirror of the mind.'[5] For I never wear disguises, nor do I say one thing and think another. I always look exactly like what I am, so much so that I cannot be concealed even by those who most jealously arrogate to themselves the character and title of wisemen, strutting around '*like an ape in the king's clothes*' or '*the ass in a lion's skin.*'[6] However hard they try to hide it, the tips of their Midas-ears[7] sooner or later slip out and betray them. An ungrateful crew if there ever was one: they are among my most loyal followers but are so ashamed of my name in public that they are always hurling it at the heads of others as a mark of the greatest opprobrium. Now I ask you, since these wretches are *most foolish* in fact but try to pass themselves off as wisemen and deep philosophers, what more fitting title could we find for them than "*foolosophers*"?[8]

4. Homer applies the phrase to the gods (*od.* 8,325) but not the goddesses.

5. Folly cites two proverbial ideas which are contradictory: in the first, a person's true nature may be judged merely from his appearance (*Adag.* 3817; Otto No. 717); in the second, from his speech (Walther 20342).

6. Both Lister and Erasmus (*Adag.* 610) mention that their contemporaries sometimes dressed their pet monkeys in fine clothes. The Cumaean ass, having found a lion's skin, posed as the king of the beasts until his disguise was revealed (*Adag.* 266).

7. See above, p. 10, footnote 9.

8. "Foolosophers" is from the first English translation (1549) by Sir Thomas Chaloner. The Greek word has the same elements as "sophomore" but in reverse order, "morosoph" as it were. The word pinpoints much of the irony

For in this point also I have seen fit to imitate the rhetoricians of our times, who are quite confident that they are all but divine if (like the horseleech)[9] they have two tongues. They think they have done a noble deed if they sprinkle some Greek tags in their Latin speeches, however inappropriate, like bright bits in a mosaic. In fact, if they don't have some esoteric expressions, they scrape together four or five obsolete words from some moldy manuscripts in order to baffle their readers. Thus, those who understand them will be all the more pleased with themselves, and those who do not understand will admire them the more, the less they understand them—for you are aware, I suppose, that among the pleasures I offer, one of the most refined is to value most highly whatever is most foreign. But if any of them are a little more ambitious, then they should smile and applaud and *wiggle their ears* like asses, so that everyone will think they understand perfectly. *So much for that.*[1]

Now I will take up where I left off. You know my name, then, gentlemen most . . . what epithet can I apply to you? What but "most foolish"? For what more honorable name could the goddess Folly apply to the initiates of her mysteries? But since there are not very many who know my lineage,[2] I will try (with the help of the Muses) to explain it. Neither Chaos, however, nor Orcus, nor Saturn, nor Japetus, nor any other of these worn-out, moldy old gods was my father.[3] Rather, it was *Plutus*,[4] the one and only *father*

---

of the work. More used the same Greek word in the *Utopia* (*CW* 4, 64/2). It also appears in Lucian (*Alex.* 40), Erasmus' *De copia* (*Op. 1*, 12C), and in *Adag.* (prol., *Op. 2*, 11E).

9. This idea about the leech probably arose from a misunderstanding of Pliny (*HN* 11.40 and 11.28) and from the allegorical interpretation of the *Book of Proverbs* 30: 15.

1. With two Greek tags (*Adag.* 335, and Aristophanes *Plut.* 8), Folly ends her condemnation of Greek tags.

2. Lister notes that Folly alludes to the parts of the formal encomium, which usually begins with the birth of its subject.

3. Chaos was the first thing to exist (Hesiod *theog.* 116–23); Orcus, an underworld god frequently identified with Pluto; Saturn, the father of Jupiter, Juno, Neptune, and the other gods; Japetus, a Titan and the father of Atlas, Prometheus, and others (Hesiod *theog.* 507–11).

4. The god of riches (Hesiod *theog.* 969–74).

of men and gods alike,[5] Hesiod and Homer and even Jupiter himself to the contrary notwithstanding. Plutus alone, as it is now and ever has been, has everything and everyone, sacred and secular alike, at his beck and call: he keeps the whole pot boiling. His decision governs war, peace, kingdoms, counsels, judgments, agreements, marriages, pacts, treaties, laws, arts, recreations, serious business—I'm running out of breath—in short, all the affairs, public or private, in which mortals engage. Without his help that whole crew of poetic divinities—I will go further, even the so-called "select" gods[6]—would either not exist at all or would eke out a miserable existence as *homebodies.*[7] Whoever is frowned on by him can never find enough help even from Pallas herself.[8] Conversely, whoever is smiled on by Plutus can afford to tell Jupiter himself to go to hell, thunderbolt and all. *Such is the father I can boast.*[9] And this great god certainly did not give birth to me from his brain, as Jupiter did to that sour stick-in-the-mud Pallas. Rather, he begot me on Neotes (Youth),[1] the fairest, the most charming nymph of all. Moreover, he did not do it within the forbidding bonds of matrimony, like the progenitor of that limping blacksmith,[2] but rather in a fashion not a little sweeter, *"mingled together in passionate love,"* as my friend Homer says.[3] But make no mistake, I was not begotten by Plutus as Aristophanes represents him,[4] his eyesight completely gone and one foot already in the grave, but rather when

---

5. A half-line frequently applied to Jupiter by Homer and Hesiod.

6. Among these twenty (sometimes twelve) chief gods discussed by Varro and Augustine (*City of God* 4.23.37, 7.2) are three Folly mentions: Orcus, Saturn, and Jupiter.

7. Lucian (*sacrif.* 9) remarks that without men's sacrifices the gods would eat poorly at home.

8. Goddess of wisdom, born from Jupiter's head, archenemy of Folly.

9. An imitation of a Homeric formula.

1. Sometimes said to be the cupbearer of the gods. Lister notes that riches and youth produce folly.

2. Vulcan, Jupiter's legitimate son by his wife, Juno.

3. Homer uses this and similar phrases to describe sexual intercourse, especially when it is illicit.

4. See below, p. 48, footnote 4.

he was young, sound, and hot-blooded, inflamed not merely by youth but even more by nectar, which on that occasion he had drunk at the banquet of the gods, perhaps in larger, stronger drafts than usual.

But if anyone wants to know my birthplace—since nowadays people seem to think one of the most important points of nobility is the place where a person gives out his first wails—I was brought forth neither in wandering Delos,[5] nor in the waves of the sea,[6] nor *in hollow-echoing caverns,*[7] but rather in the Isles of the Blest, where everything grows without effort—*they plough not, neither do they sow.*[8] In those isles there is no work, no old age, no disease. Nowhere in their fields do you see asphodel, mallows, sea onions, lupines, beans, or any such trash as that.[9] Instead, both sight and smell are gratified by moly, panace, nepenthe, amaracus, ambrosia, lotus, roses, violets, hyacinths, a veritable garden of Adonis.[1] Born as I was among all these delights, I certainly did not begin my life by crying, but rather immediately smiled at my mother.[2]

Far be it from me to envy *the mighty son of Cronos*[3] the goat which

5. Jupiter made this island stationary to be the birthplace of Apollo and Diana (Ovid *met.* 6. 333ff.).

6. From which Venus was born.

7. A formula in Homer and Hesiod. The one-eyed giant Polyphemus and the monster Echnida were born in hollow caves (*od.* 1.73, and *theog.* 297).

8. See below, p. 35 and p. 21, footnote 7. The Greek phrase is Homeric (*od.* 9.109) and was applied to the golden age by Lucian and Horace.

9. Folly scorns these plants as the ordinary fare of the common people. All of them have very practical uses as food or medicine.

1. All of these plants could be used as ingredients in perfumes, unguents, oils, and soporifics. Moly is probably not Homer's salutary plant (*od.* 10.305) but rather a form of nightshade, a soporific which could be fatally poisonous, called either "moly" or "morion." Pliny (*HN* 21.105.180) mentioned that morion has been wrongly praised by certain men. Hence, Folly in her praises mentions the "praised morion." On nepenthe, see above p. 9, footnote 3. Ambrosia was used to make a love potion. Lotus and hyacinth are associated with sexual passion. The gardens of Adonis, short-lived potted plants used to honor Venus' lover, were proverbial for fleeting beauty and pleasure (*Adag.* 4)

2. The allusion to Virgil (*ecl.* 4.60–63) anticipates Folly's arguments for her divinity.

3. A variant of a formula applied to Zeus by Homer.

gave him suck,[4] since I was nursed at the breasts of two most elegant nymphs: Methe (Drunkenness), begotten by Bacchus, and Apaedia (Stupidity), the daughter of Pan. You can see them both here among my other attendants and handmaidens. If you want to know the names of the rest of them, you'll not get them from me in any language but Greek. This one—you see how she raises her eyebrows —is obviously *Philautia*[5] (Selflove). The one you see here, with smiling eyes and clapping hands, is named *Kolakia* (Flattery). This one, dosing and half asleep, is *Lethe* (Forgetfulness). This one, leaning on her elbows with her hands clasped,[6] is *Misoponia* (Laziness). This one, wreathed with roses and drenched with sweet-smelling lotions, is *Hedone* (Pleasure). This one, with the restless glance and the rolling eyes, is *Anoia* (Madness). This one, with the smooth complexion and the plump, well-rounded figure, is *Tryphe* (Luxury). You also see two gods among the girls: one is called *Comos* (Rowdiness), the other *Negreton Hypnon* (Sweet Sleep).[7] This, then, is the loyal retinue which helps me to subject the whole world to my dominion, lording it over the greatest lords.

You have heard about my birth, upbringing, and companions. Now, lest my claim to divinity should seem unsubstantiated, listen carefully and I will show you how many benefits I bestow on gods and men alike and how widely my divine power extends. Consider, if that author (whoever he was) was not far from the mark when he wrote that the essence of divinity is to give aid to mortals,[8] and if the persons who taught mortals how to produce wine or grain or some other commodity have been justly elevated to the senate of the gods, why should I not rightly be considered and called the very *alpha*[9] of all the gods, since I alone bestow all things on all men?

4. Hidden away in Crete by his mother, Zeus was nursed by the goat Amalthea.

5. *Adag.* 292.

6. The Latin for the phrase "with her hands clasped" seems to fit the languor of Laziness, but it is ironical because its proverbial meaning is "with the greatest energy" ("with clenched fists," as it were). Otto Nos. 1044–45.

7. The phrase is Homeric.

8. Pliny (*HN* 2.5.18).

9. *Adag.* 1318, where Erasmus quotes Martial 2.57 and 5.26. *Revelations*

First, what can be sweeter or more precious than life itself? But to whom should you attribute the origin of life if not to me? For it is not the spear of *stern-fathered* Pallas or the aegis of *cloud-gathering*[1] Zeus which begets and propagates the human race. No, Jupiter himself, father of the gods and king over men,[2] whose mere nod shakes all Olympus,[3] even he must put aside that three-forked lightning bolt of his; he must dispense with that fierce Titanic countenance (with which he can, at his pleasure, terrify all the gods); clearly, he must change his role like an actor and play a humble part whenever he wants to do what in fact he is forever doing— that is, *make a baby*.[4] To be sure, the Stoics rank themselves only a little lower than the gods. But give me a man who is a Stoic three or four times over, a Stoic to the nth degree, and he too, though he may not have to shave off his beard—the sign of wisdom (though goats also have one)[5]—he certainly will have to swallow his pride; he will have to smooth out his frowns, put aside his iron clad principles, and indulge just a bit in childish and fantastic trifles. In short, I am the one that wise man must come to—I repeat, he must come to me—if he ever wants to be a father.

But let me take you into my confidence even more candidly, as is my fashion. I ask you, is it the head, or the face, or the chest, or the hand, or the ear—all considered respectable parts of the body —is it any of these which generates gods and men? No, I think not. Rather, the human race is propagated by the part which is so foolish and funny that it cannot even be mentioned without a snicker. That is the sacred fount from which all things draw life, not the Pythagorean tetrad.[6] Come now, would any man ever submit to the

---

1: 8 is not the source of the equation between the first letter and the highest position and is not Erasmus' primary allusion here.

1. The two Greek epithets are Homeric formulae.

2. See Virgil (*aen.* 1.65, 2.648, 10.2, 10.743) and p. 15, footnote 5, above.

3. Cf. Virgil (*aen.* 9.106, 10.115).

4. The Greek word, though Lucian used it in a comic context (*dial. deorum* 22.1), can also be used seriously (e.g., Euripides *Heracl.* 524).

5. In *Adag.* 195, Erasmus cites the same idea from Horace (*serm.* 2.3.35) and Lucian (*eun.* 9).

6. Pythagoras (*Golden Verses* 47–48) believed that the intervals found in the first four numbers were basic to the whole universe.

halter of matrimony[7] if he followed the usual method of these wisemen and first considered the drawbacks of that state of life? Or what woman would ever yield to a man's advances if she either knew about or at least called to mind the perilous labor of childbirth, the trials and tribulations of raising children? So, if you owe your life to matrimony, and you owe matrimony to my handmaid *Anoia*, you can easily see how much you owe to me. Then again, what woman who has once had this experience would ever consent to go through it again if it were not for the divine influence of *Lethe*? Even Venus herself (in spite of what Lucretius says)[8] would never deny that her power is crippled and useless without the infusion of our divine influence. Thus, this game of ours, giddy and ridiculous as it is, is the source of supercilious philosophers (whose place has now been taken by so-called monks),[9] and kings in their scarlet robes, and pious priests, and pope-holy pontiffs and, finally, even that assembly of poetic gods, so numerous that Olympus, large as it is, can hardly accommodate the crowd.

But it would be little enough for me to assert my role as the fountain and nursery of life, if I did not also show that all the benefits of life depend completely on my good offices. After all, what is this life itself—can you even call it life if you take away pleasure? . . . Your applause has answered for you. I was certain that none of you is so wise, or rather foolish—no, I mean wise—as to be of that opinion. In fact, even these Stoics do not scorn pleasure, however diligently they pretend to—ripping it to shreds in their public pronouncements for the very good reason that when they have driven others away from it they can enjoy it all the better by themselves.[1] But for god's sake, I wish they would tell me, is there any part of life that is not sad, cheerless, dull, insipid, and wearisome unless you season it with pleasure, that is, with the spice of folly? To this fact Sophocles, a poet beyond all praise, offered ample

7. Cf. Juvenal 6.43.

8. *de rer. nat.* 1.17-23.

9. Like monks, some ancient philosophers (such as Pythagoras) professed a strict, secluded, common life.

1. Philoxenos used to blow his nose into the sauce to drive away others and have it all to himself (Plutarch *mor.* 1128b).

testimony when he paid us that most elegant compliment: "*Never to think, that is the good life.*"[2] Nevertheless, let us examine (if you please) everything point by point.

First of all, who can deny that everyone finds the first age of man most charming and delightful? What is it about babies that makes us hug and kiss and coddle them, so that even an enemy would assist them at that age? Nothing but the allurement of folly, which Nature in her wisdom purposely provided to newborn babes so that by giving a recompense (as it were) of pleasure they might lighten the burden of rearing them and wheedle their way into the good graces of their guardians. Then the next age, adolescence, how charming everyone finds it, how generously they take care of teenagers, how eagerly they further their careers, how solicitously they extend a helping hand! Now I ask you, where do adolescents get this youthful charm? Where but from me? By my favor they know very little and hence are very easy to get along with: naiveté is not snappish.[3] Before long, when they have grown up a bit and through experience and study have begun to think more maturely, call me a downright liar if the fine flower of their beauty does not suddenly wilt. Their energy slackens, their gracefulness stiffens, their vigor withers away. The further they are withdrawn from me, the less they are alive, until they finally reach τὸ χαλεπὸν γῆρας,[4] that is, burdensome old age, hateful not only to others but even to itself.[5] Clearly, no mortal could tolerate the pains of age if I did not take pity on them and offer my help: just as the gods of mythology help the dying by some metamorphosis, so I too bring those who already have one foot in the grave, back once more as close as possible to childhood. Thus, the widespread notion of *second childhood*[6] is quite accurate. Now, if someone wants to know how I change them, I will not withhold that either: I bring them to the spring of our handmaid Lethe, which has its origin in the Isles of

2. *Ajax* 554.
3. Horace *epist.* 2.2.128.
4. Homer *il.* 8.103.
5. Seneca *Oed.* 594.
6. *Adag.* 436, where Erasmus quotes Lucian (*saturn.* 9).

the Blest (the Lethe in the underworld is only a rivulet flowing from the main spring),[7] so that they may drink large drafts of oblivion[8] and thus by gradually dissipating their cares grow young once again.

But then they have lost their grip on reality, someone may say; their minds are wandering. True enough, but that's what it means to return to childhood. Isn't childhood distinguished by a weak grasp of reality and a wandering mind? Isn't the principal charm of childhood the fact that it knows nothing? Aren't we put off by the child who has the knowledge of a grown man? Don't we avoid such precocious prodigies like the plague? That we do so is confirmed by the widespread proverb: a child wise beyond his years is a pest.[9] On the other hand, who would want any contact or association with an old man who added to his wealth of experience a corresponding vigor of mind and sharpness of judgment?

And so through my favor an old man loses contact with reality. But at the same time he is relieved of all those wretched worries that torment the wise man. He is also an entertaining drinking companion. He never feels that 'taedium vitae'[1] which even younger, stronger men can hardly bear. Sometimes, like the old man in Plautus, he regresses to those three letters (a m o)[2]—then, if he had any wisdom at all, he would be miserable beyond belief. But now, through my favor, he is happy, well-liked by his friends, a hale fellow well met. That is why, in Homer, Nestor's speech flowed from his mouth sweeter than honey, whereas Achilles' speech was bitter;[3] and Homer also says that the old men sitting on the wall spoke with voices *as soft and lovely as a lily*.[4] In this respect old age

7. The Lethon, derived from the river Lethe in the underworld, flowed near the gardens of the Hesperides in North Africa (Pliny *HN* 4.4.31, and Lucan 9.355–68). The Hesperides, like the Fortunate Isles, were sometimes said to be in the Atlantic (Pliny *HN* 5.36–37).

8. Virgil *aen.* 6.715.

9. *Adag.* 3100, which cites Apuleius (*apol.* 535).

1. This phrase ("weariness of life"), repeated five more times, becomes a sort of leitmotiv. See below, pp. 22, 30, 48, 109. Cf. Gellius *NA* 6(7).18.11.

2. Meaning "I love." Cf. Plautus *merc.* 304.

3. Homer *il.* 1.249 and 1.223.

4. Homer *il.* 3.149–52. The Listrius commentary points out that the Homeric epithet is a pun on another Greek word meaning "trifles, nonsense."

even surpasses childhood: infants are sweet indeed, but speechless,[5] deprived of one of the chief blessings of this life, namely gossiping. Also keep in mind that old men are immoderately fond of children, and, conversely, children are delighted by old men—'*so birds of a feather flock together.*'[6] After all, what difference is there between them, except that an old man has more wrinkles and has had more birthdays? Otherwise they agree exactly: both have whitish hair, toothless gums, a small bodily frame, and a liking for milk; both stutter and babble and engage in tomfoolery; both are forgetful and thoughtless; in short, they resemble each other in every respect.[7] And the older they get the nearer they come to childhood, until like children, without being bored by life or afraid of death, they depart from this life.

Now anyone who likes can go and compare this benefit of mine with the sort of metamorphosis bestowed by the other gods. No need to mention what they do when they are angry: those whom they favor most, they have a habit of turning into a tree, a bird, a locust, or even a snake[8]—as if to become something else were not in itself a kind of death. But I, on the other hand, restore the same man to the happiest part of his life. In fact, if mortals would refrain completely from any contact with wisdom and live their entire lives with me, there would not be any old age at all. Instead, they would enjoy perpetual youth and live happily ever after.

You see, don't you, how these grave and sober personages who devote themselves to philosophical studies or to serious and difficult tasks seem to enjoy hardly any youthful years at all; they grow old before their time because they are forever worrying and beating their brains out about knotty problems, so that their vital spirits

5. A pun on the root meaning of "infant" ("having no speech").

6. *Adag.* 122, which quotes Homer (*od.* 17.218).

7. Folly distorts the *topos* "puer-senex." See Curtius, pp. 98–101.

8. Daphne and Myrrha were changed into trees (Ovid *met.* 1.542–48, 10.488–500); Alcyone, Philomela, Procne, and Ciris, into birds (Ovid *met.* 11.731–42, 6.667–70, 8.148–51); Tithonus, into a locust (Servius' comments on Virgil's *georg.* 3.328 and *aen.* 4.585); Cadmus and Hermione, into snakes (Ovid *met.* 4.571–603).

gradually dry up,[9] leaving them exhausted and juiceless, as it were. My fools, on the other hand, are plump and rosy, with a very well-preserved complexion;[1] they are *as fit as a fiddle*,[2] as the saying goes. In fact, they would never feel the slightest discomfort of old age, except that they are occasionally infected with a bit of wisdom by contagion. So it is that nothing in man's life can be absolutely flawless.[3]

These arguments are also confirmed by the authority (not to be taken lightly) of the proverb which asserts that Folly is the only means of preserving youth, otherwise so evanescent, and of keeping harsh old age at a distance.[4] Not without reason do people bandy about the vernacular saying that, whereas other men usually grow wiser with age, the people of Brabant grow more and more foolish the older they get.[5] And yet no other nationality is more cheerful in the ordinary affairs of everyday living or less subject to the gloom of old age. Close to the Brabanters not only in geographical location but also in their way of life are those Dutchmen of mine—and why shouldn't I call them mine, since they promote my cult so eagerly that they are proverbially described by a well-deserved epithet taken from my name.[6] And so far are they from being ashamed of the label "foolish" that they boast of it as one of their chief claims to fame.

9. A serious medical opinion propounded by such authorities as Aristotle (*part. an.* 651b, 9-13), Galen (*san. tuend.* 1.2), and Marsilio Ficino (*de sanitate tuenda, Opera omnia*, Basel, 1576, repr. Turin, 1953, I, 496). The vital spirits, a fluid produced by the heart, were thought to be further refined into the animal spirits in the brain, which control the sense perception that underlies intellectual cognition. Excessive thinking depletes the supply of vital spirits.

1. Horace *epist.* 1.4.15.

2. Literally, "the Acarnanian pigs" (*Adag.* 1259).

3. Cf. Horace *carm.* 2.16.27-28.

4. The closest proverb I have found is the medieval Latin saying "A stupid head grows neither gray nor bald" (Walther 30436a).

5. A Dutch proverb says of the Brabanters that the older they get the dumber they are.

6. A Dutch proverb says about Dutchmen that the older they get the more foolish they are.

What fools these mortals are to look for eternal youth from Medeas,[7] or Circes,[8] or Venuses,[9] or Auroras,[1] or some fountain or other,[2] when I alone both can and do in fact bestow it! Only I can provide that miraculous potion which the daughter of Memnon employed to prolong the youth of her grandfather, Tithonus.[3] I am that Venus who restored the youth of Phaon so that Sappho fell madly in love with him.[4] Mine are those herbs (if any there be), mine are the magic formulas, mine is the fountain which not only recalls lost youth but also (what is even better) preserves it forever unimpaired. Now, if you all subscribe to the opinion that nothing is more desirable than youth, nothing more horrible than old age, you can easily see, I imagine, how much you owe to me, since I preserve the one and prevent the other.

But why am I still talking about mortals? Survey all of heaven, and anyone who likes may reproach me with my own name if you can find a single one of the gods who is not repulsive and contemptible unless he comes recommended by a share of my divine afflatus. Why, for example, does Bacchus always appear as a youth with flowing locks?[5] Simply because he is a rowdy roisterer, who spends all his time partying, singing and dancing, having a good time, and has absolutely nothing to do with Pallas. Moreover, he is so far from

7. Medea restored the youth of Jason's father, Aeson (Ovid *met.* 7. 262–93).

8. When Circe changed Odysseus' men from swine back to human form, they were younger and more handsome than before (Homer *od.* 10.229–399).

9. Venus gave Phaon youth and beauty (Servius' comment on Virgil *aen.* 3.279, and Lucian *dial. mort.* 9.2).

1. See above, p. 22, footnote 8. Aurora obtained immortality for her lover, Tithonus, but she failed to get eternal youth for him (*Homeric hymns* 5.218–38). Taking pity on him, she changed him into a locust. Locusts were thought to shed their skins in old age, thus renewing their youth (Tzetzes *schol. Lycrophron* 18).

2. There were many legends about the fountain of youth (E. Rohde, *Der Griechische Roman und seine Vorläufer*, Leipzig, 1914, p. 222).

3. Erasmus (or perhaps only Folly) errs here. Memnon, son of Tithonus and Aurora, had no daughter, and the youth of Tithonus was not prolonged. See above, p. 22, footnote 8, and p. 24, footnote 1.

4. See above, p. 24, footnote 9.

5. After Praxitiles (fourth century B.C.), Bacchus was regularly represented as a beautiful, beardless youth.

wanting to be considered wise that he is most pleased when his followers worship him with games and jokes. He is not even offended
by the proverb which labels him "foolish"—namely, *'more foolish
than Morychus.'* (They gave him the name "Morychus" because the
statue of him sitting before the doors of the temple used to be
smeared with new wine and green figs by the farmers during
country festivals.)[6] Then too, look at the insults hurled at him in
the old Greek comedy! "Oh, what a stupid God!" they say. "No
wonder he was born from the thigh!"[7] But who would not rather
be this witless dullard—always merry, always in the first bloom of
youth, always entertaining everyone with fun and games—than
Jupiter *of the crooked counsels,*[8] who terrifies everyone, or Pan, whose
sudden outbursts inspire fits of helpless terror,[9] or Vulcan, covered
with soot and always filthy from working in his forge, or even
Pallas herself, fearsome with her spear and Gorgon's head and
always scowling fierce glances.[1] Why is Cupid always a boy? Why?
Simply because he is a trifler who never does, or even considers,
'anything worthwhile.'[2] Why does the beauty of golden Venus
always remain as fresh as springtime? Simply because she is related
to me. That is the reason her face displays my father's color, and
that is why Homer calls her *"golden Aphrodite."*[3] Then too, she is

6. "Morychus" is derived from the Greek word for "smear." Because the
statue is sitting outside the temple instead of inside as usual, the proverb
applies to those who neglect their duties at home and concern themselves
with outside affairs (*Adag.* 181; Zenobius 5.13).

7. Bacchus is frequently insulted in Aristophanes' *Frogs*, but not in the exact
words Folly gives here. On Bacchus' second birth from Jupiter's thigh, see
Ovid *met.* 3. 310–12.

8. Homer applies this epithet only to Cronos (*il.* 2.205, *od.* 21.415), but in
both cases he is referring to Zeus, the "son of Cronos of the crooked counsels."
Hesiod applies it to Prometheus (*theog.* 546, *op.* 48), but only when the hero
is dealing with Zeus.

9. Pan was thought to inspire sudden, unreasonable fear (E. Harrison,
Classical Review, 40, 6–8; *Adag.* 263, *Op. 2,* 884C).

1. Cupid applies this phrase to Pallas' glances in Lucian's *dial. deorum* 19.1.

2. In *Adag.* 738, Erasmus quotes Aristophanes *Plut.* 37 and *thesm.* 394,
Euripides *Andr.* 448 and Cicero *Att.* 15.1.

3. This epithet is applied to her ten times by Homer (e.g., *od.* 8.337 and 342,
il. 5.427). Folly's father, Plutus, has a golden face because he is the god of riches.

always smiling, if we may believe the poets or their emulators, the sculptors.[4] What divinity did the Romans ever worship more religiously than Flora, the mother of all pleasures?[5] Though, in fact, if anyone examines more closely the lives of those sober gods in Homer and the other poets, he will find all of them full of folly. What good would it do to mention the deeds of other gods, since you are all quite familiar with the love-affairs and pranks of Jupiter himself, the master of the thunderbolt,[6] and since even grave Diana, forgetting the modesty proper to her sex, spends all her time hunting—that is, when she is not madly in love with Endymion.[7]

But I would rather they heard their transgressions from Momus,[8] who used to rebuke them rather frequently. But not long ago they became so angry that they hurled him, together with Ate,[9] headlong down to earth, because he was always rudely disturbing the happiness of the gods with his wisdom. And no mortal at all deigns to offer him hospitality in his exile,[1] much less is there any room for him in the courts of princes, where my handmaid *Kolakia* has the greatest influence (Momus and she can no more get along together than the lion and the lamb).[2] Now that Momus is gone, the gods

4. Homer applies the epithet "laughter-loving" to Venus six times (e.g., *od.* 8.362, *il.* 3.424). Some early Ionic statues represent her as smiling, but most later statues do not. Lucian mentions a well-known statue of Aphrodite smiling (*imag.* 6).

5. The spring rites of Flora were so lascivious that even Ovid found them a little shocking (*fast.* 5.331–54).

6. Apart from his seven wives (Hesiod *theog.* 886–922), Jupiter begot a large brood of bastards.

7. The "virginal" moon-goddess prolonged the sleep of Endymion so that she might enjoy him every night (Cicero *tusc.* 1.38; Ovid *her.* 18.49–74). Hunting was an almost exclusively masculine pursuit (Xenophon *de venatione*).

8. The god of reprehension (Lucian *deor. concil.* and *Hermotimos* 20). In post-classical times he was portrayed as a king's jester holding a fool's bauble, but he is portrayed as a sharp-toothed, decrepit old man in *anth. pal.* 16.265–66. It seems unlikely that Erasmus wished us to imagine Momus, Folly's enemy, as dressed in her livery.

9. Aesop *fab.* 125 (ed. A. Chambry, Paris, 1925); *il.* 19.126–31. On Ate, the goddess of discord, see *Adag.* 613.

1. Lucian *Iup. trag.* 22.

2. *Adag.* 310.

revel much more freely and pleasantly, *"living an easy life,"*[3] as Homer says, unchecked by any critic. What endless jokes are provided by Priapus, that worthless fig-wood puppet.[4] What fun is supplied by Mercury with his pocket-picking and magic tricks.[5] Indeed, even Vulcan himself often plays *the clown* at the banquets of the gods, enlivening their drinking bouts by limping around, or making smart remarks, or telling funny stories.[6] Then Silenus,[7] that white-haired wooer, dances *a frisky jig*,[8] Polyphemus stomps around to the *thrum-thrum of a guitar*,[9] and the nymphs jump about *dancing with bare feet*.[1] The satyrs, human above and goat below, flounce around doing bumps and grinds.[2] Pan makes everybody laugh by singing some silly song, which they would rather hear than a performance by the Muses themselves, especially when they are beginning to get soused on nectar. I suppose there is no need to mention what the gods do after the banquet, when they are quite drunk—such tomfoolery that sometimes it's all that I can do to keep from laughing out loud. But in such matters, it is better to remember Harpocrates[3] and keep still, lest some eavesdropping god[4] should hear us too, telling such things as even Momus could not speak out with impunity.

3. Homer *od.* 4.805, 5.122, *il.* 6.138.

4. An obscene wooden garden-god (Horace *serm.* 1.8.1; *Adag.* 685).

5. Horace *carm.* 1.10. Lucian *gallus* 28, *Prometh.* 5, *deor. dial.* 7.1–3.

6. Homer *il.* 1.584–600.

7. A deity portrayed as a drunken, potbellied old man, the tutor and companion of Bacchus.

8. Literally, "cordax," a comic dance (Aristophanes *nub.* 540), vulgar (Athenaeus 14.631d) or obscene (Theophrastus *char.* 6.3). Lucian *Icaromen.* 27, *salt.* 26.

9. The dance of the one-eyed giant, lover of Galatea, is imitated in Aristophanes *Plut.* 290.

1. Lucian *salt.* 12.

2. Literally, "doing Atellan skits," which were so obscene that they were suppressed (Tacitus *ann.* 4.14). St. Jerome condemns them (*ep.* 147.5).

3. The god of silence, portrayed as pressing his finger against his lips (Varro *ling.* 5.57; Augustine *City of God* 18.5; Ovid *met.* 6.692).

4. Literally, "Corycaean god." In *Adag.* 144, Erasmus quotes Strobaeus 14.1.32.644 and notes that such an eavesdropping god had been brought on the comic stage.

But now it is time for us to leave the heaven-dwellers behind (taking our cue from Homer) and come back down to earth to see how there, too, nothing is joyful or happy without my services. First of all, you see how carefully nature, the parent and provider of the human race,[5] saw to it that the spice of folly should nowhere be lacking. Thus, according to the Stoic definition, wisdom consists in nothing but being led by reason and, conversely, folly is defined as being swept along at the whim of emotion.[6] Now, in order to keep human life from being dreary and gloomy, what proportion did Jupiter establish between reason and emotion? A pound of feeling to an ounce of thought. Moreover, he limited reason to the narrow confines of the head, leaving all the rest of the body to passion. Then he set up against solitary reason two most fierce tyrants, as it were: anger, which occupies the citadel and very fountainhead of life, the heart; and passionate desire, which holds wide sway over the rest, all the way down to the genitals.[7] How much reason can do against the forces of these two is sufficiently clear from the everyday life of mankind: she does all she can, which amounts to no more than shouting herself hoarse and preaching moral rules, but the passions tell their ruler to go to the devil and shout her down all the more impudently, until she is so tired that she gives in and knuckles under.

But because it was necessary to add just a pinch more of reason to the male, who is naturally destined for the administration of affairs, Jupiter took me into his counsel on this occasion (as on others) so that he might provide for this extra bit of reason as well as he could; and I very quickly gave him advice worthy of myself, namely, that he join woman to man (for women are foolish and silly creatures, but nevertheless amusing and pleasant) so that by living with him she can season and sweeten the sourness of the masculine mind with her folly.[8] For where Plato is uncertain

5. Cicero *nat.* 1.8; Pliny *HN* 31.1.1.1.

6. Cicero *leg.* 1.7.22, *tusc.* 3.19 and 4.12.

7. This division of man's faculties is Platonic (*tim.* 69b–71a, *rep.* 435c–41c and 444b–e). It was popularized by Cicero (*tusc.* 1.10.20, 4.5.10).

8. Gellius *NA* 15.25.2.

whether to place women among rational or irrational creatures,[9] he intended no more than to point out the extraordinary folly of that sex. And if by chance a woman should wish to be considered wise, she simply shows that she is twice foolish,[1] since she is attempting something 'completely against the grain,'[2] as they say, like someone bringing 'a bull to a chinashop.'[3] For a fault is redoubled if someone tries to gloss it over with unnatural disguises and to work against the inborn bias of the mind. The Greek proverb says "An ape is still an ape, even if it is dressed up in royal purple";[4] just so, a woman is still a woman—that is, a fool—no matter what role she may try to play.

Still, I don't think women are so foolish as to be angry at me because I, who am both a woman and Folly herself, attribute folly to them. For if they see the matter in the right light, they will recognize that they owe it to folly that they are better off than men in so many ways. First, because of their beauty, which they quite rightly value above everything else and which protects them so well that they can tyrannize even over tyrants. Where do men get their rough features, coarse skin, bushy beards—all of them clearly signs of old age? Where but from the vice of prudence? Women, on the other hand, have soft cheeks, a high voice, a delicate and smooth complexion, so that they seem to preserve forever unchanged the marks of adolescence. Then again, what do women want more than anything else in the world? Isn't it to be most attractive to men? Isn't that the reason for so many toiletries, cosmetics, baths, coiffures, lotions, perfumes, so many clever ways of highlighting, painting, disguising their faces, eyes, and skin? Now, is there anything which makes them more attractive to men than folly? What is there that men will not grant to women? But what recompense

9. *Tim.* 76e, 42a–c, 91a. Folly conveniently overlooks Plato's insistence on the essential equality of the sexes (*rep.* 452e–56a).

1. In Erasmus' *Coll.* (p. 222) Antronius remarks "I've often heard the common saying, *A wise woman is twice foolish.*"

2. Literally, "against the wishes of Minerva" (*Adag.* 42).

3. Literally, "like bringing a bull to the wrestling ring" (*Adag.* 362).

4. *Adag.* 611.

do men expect but pleasure? Now, women have no way of giving pleasure except through folly. No one will deny this if he takes the trouble to consider how childishly men talk, how frivolously they act when they have decided to indulge in the pleasure to be found in women. There you have it: the source from which springs the first and foremost pleasure in life.

But there are some people—especially old men—who are boozers rather than woman-chasers and who find the greatest pleasure in drinking bouts. Whether there can be a really fine party with no women present is a question I leave to others. But this much is certain: without the spice of folly there is no such thing as an enjoyable party. So much so that if there is no one who can make people laugh, either by genuine or simulated folly, they get some *comedian*—and pay him a good fee too—or find some ridiculous hanger-on to dispel the silence and boredom of the party with his laughable (that is, foolish) quips. What good would it do to stuff the belly with so many hors d'oeuvres, so many tidbits and delicacies, unless the eyes and ears too, indeed, unless the whole mind be replenished with laughter, jokes, and witticisms? But I am the one and only deviser of such delicacies. Of course, those customary amusements at parties—such as choosing a master of the revels,[5] playing dice, drinking each other's health, *passing the bottle around the table*, having everybody (one after the other) sing a song,[6] dancing around and cutting up—all these pastimes were hardly invented by the seven sages of Greece but rather were thought up by us for the well-being of the human race. But the nature of all such amusements is that the more foolish they are, the more they contribute to the life of mortals. Indeed, a sad life can hardly be called life at all. But sad it must be unless you employ such entertainments to dispel the inherent tedium of living.

But perhaps there will be some who do not care for this kind of pleasure either, who find their satisfaction in the mutual affection and companionship of friends. Friendship, they keep insisting,

5. The "king" of the banquet prescribed who, when, how much each must drink or sing (Horace *carm.* 1.4.18, 2.7.25; Tacitus *ann.* 13.15).
6. Literally, "singing to the myrtle" (*Adag.* 1521).

takes precedence over everything else.[7] It is just as essential as air or fire or water,[8] so pleasurable that we can no more do without it than we can do without the sun,[9] and (finally) so honorable (as if that had anything to do with it) that philosophers have not hesitated to place it among the chief goods of life.[1] But what if I can show that I constitute this great blessing 'from stem to stern'?[2] I will not demonstrate it through the crocodile's dilemma,[3] or the argument of the growing heap,[4] or the argument of the horns,[5] or any other dialectical subtlety of that sort. Rather I will use simple evidence to make it 'as plain as the nose on your face,'[6] as they say. Tell me now, to wink at a friend's faults, to be deceived, to be blind to his vices, to imagine them away, even to love and admire certain notorious vices as if they were virtues—surely this is not far from folly? What about the man who kisses the mole on his mistress or the one who is delighted with his sweetheart's polyp, or the doting father who insists his cross-eyed boy merely has a slight squint—what is all this, I say, but sheer folly? They can call it as foolish as they like— they can say it over and over again—but it is this very same foolishness that brings friends together and keeps them together. I am

7. Cicero *amic.* 4.17.

8. *Adag.* 1175.

9. Cicero *amic.* 13.47.

1. Cicero *fin.* 1.20.65, 3.21.70.

2. *Adag.* 8, and Cicero *fam.* 16.24.1.

3 A crocodile tells a woman that he will return her child if she correctly foretells what he will do. If she says he will, he has only to eat the child to make her wrong. If she says he will not, she will be wrong unless he eats it. Lucian *vit. auct.* 22; Quintilian *inst.* 1.10.5.

4. Lister explains this argument (called Sorites) thus: If ten coins are not enough to make a man rich, what if you add one coin? What if you add another? Finally, you will have to say that no one can be rich unless one coin can make him so. Cicero *div.* 2.4.11, *acad.* 2.16.49. Lucian *symp.* 23. Horace *epist.* 2.1.45–47.

5. A kind of sophistical argument mentioned by Quintilian (*inst.* 1.10.5) and Lucian (*symp.* 23). Gellius (*NA* 18.2.9) gives the following example: What you have not lost, you still have. But you have not lost horns. Therefore you have horns.

6. Literally, "with a doltish Minerva" (*Adag.* 37).

talking about mortal men, none of whom is born without faults (indeed, he is best who is afflicted with the fewest);[7] as for these gods of wisdom, either they never strike up any friendship at all, or they occasionally fall into a gloomy and unpleasant sort of friendship, and even that with very few men (I hesitate to say with none at all) because most men are foolish—indeed, there is no one who does not have many foolish delusions—and, of course, friendship cannot spring up except between those who are alike.[8] But if it should happen that some of these severe wisemen should become friendly with each other, their friendship is hardly stable or longlasting, because they are so sour and sharp-sighted that they detect their friends' faults with an eagle eye and 'a bloodhound's nostril,'[9] so to speak. Nevertheless, they are completely blind to their own faults and utterly ignore the wallet hanging on their own backs.[1] Therefore, since man's nature is such that no personality can be discovered which is not subject to many faults, and when you add to this the great variety of temperaments and interests, the many mistakes and errors and accidents to which the lives of mortals are subject, how could the joy of friendship possibly last even for a single hour among these 'critics who ferret out every fault'[2] if it were not for that quality which the Greeks designate by the remarkable word εὐήθεια, which may be translated either "folly" or "an easy-going temperament"?[3] And what about this: isn't Cupid, the author and father of all friendship, completely blind?[4] Just as *things not beautiful seem beautiful to him*,[5] so too he is responsible for a

7. Horace *serm.* 1.3.40–69.

8. *Adag.* 120–21.

9. Literally, "as vigilant as the Epidaurian serpent." Horace *serm.* 1.3.27; *Adag.* 896. Asclepius, the god of medicine, sometimes assumed the form of a snake. His principal place of worship was the city of Epidaurus.

1. Phaedrus 4.10; *Adag.* 690.

2. Literally, "Argus's." He had one hundred eyes (Ovid *met.* 1.625).

3. Plato *rep.* 400e.

4. Cupid's blindness, which is almost never found in ancient art and literature, is a medieval invention with moral overtones (E. Panofsky, "Blind Cupid" in *Studies in Iconology*, New York, 1962, pp. 95–128).

5. Theocritus 6.18–19.

similar phenomenon among you: to each his own seems fair,[6] 'Punch dotes on Judy, Jack must have his Jill.'[7] Such things happen everywhere and are laughed at everywhere, but still it is just such laughable absurdities that fit and join together the whole framework of society and make the wheels of life run smoothly.

Now, what has been said about friendship is even more applicable to marriage, which is, after all, no more than an inseparable joining of two lives into one.[8] Good lord! how many divorces (or things worse than divorces) would be happening everywhere if it were not that the everyday life of married couples is supported and sustained by flattery, laughing things off, taking it easy, being deceived, pretending things are not as they are—all of which belong to my retinue. Good grief! how few marriages would take place if the bridegroom prudently investigated the pranks played long before the wedding by that refined and (to all appearances) modest maiden. And then, of the marriages actually entered into, how very few would last if many of the wife's carryings on did not remain secret from her husband, either through his negligence or his stupidity. Such blindness is quite rightly attributed to folly, but it is this same folly which makes it possible for the wife to remain in her husband's good graces and he in hers, for the home to remain peaceful and their relatives to remain on good terms. The deceived husband is a standing joke. People call him cuckold. They make fun of his horns and whatnot when he kisses away the tears of his whorish wife.[9] But how much happier it is to be thus deceived than to eat out your own heart with jealous suspicion and to turn everything into a tragic uproar![1]

In short, without me no companionship among friends, no blending of lives in marriage can be either pleasant or stable. The people would no longer tolerate their prince, nor the master his

6. See *Adag.* 115, and *CW 4*, 56/32–33n.

7. *Adag.* 162.

8. A condensation of the definition of marriage in civil (Justinian *inst.* 1.9.1) and canon (*Decretum Gratiani*, II, causa 27, q. 2) law.

9. Juvenal 6.276.

1. Cf. *Adag.* 281, 285, 1791, and 2154.

servant, nor the maidservant her mistress, nor the teacher his pupil, nor one friend another, nor the wife her husband, nor the landlord his tenant, nor a soldier his barracks-buddy, nor one messmate another, if in their relations with one another they did not sometimes err, sometimes flatter, sometimes wisely overlook things, sometimes soothe themselves with the sweet salve of folly. These achievements, I know, seem to be the greatest possible, but you shall hear even greater ones.

I ask you, can someone who hates himself love anyone else? Can he get along with anyone else if he is always at odds with himself? Can he bring pleasure to others if he is demanding and displeased with himself? No one would say so, I think, unless he were more foolish than folly herself. But if you exclude me, everyone would not only be utterly unable to put up with others, he would also be disgusted with himself, dissatisfied with everything he has, filled with self-hatred. The reason is that Nature, in many ways more of a stepmother than a loving parent,[2] has implanted a defect in the minds of mortals—especially those who have a little more intelligence—namely, the tendency to be dissatisfied with what they have and to admire what belongs to others. Hence it is that all the endowments, all the charm and beauty of life, are undermined and destroyed. For what good is beauty, the foremost gift of the immortal gods, if it is infected with the blight of disgust? What good is youth if it is spoiled and rotted away by the sadness of old age? Finally, in all of life, what task can you perform alone, what job can you do for others, with decorum[3] (for decorum is the guiding principle not only in art but also in all the actions of life) if you do not have the help of Philautia, who is like a sister to me—and rightly so, since she everywhere takes my part with all her strength. For what is so foolish as to be pleased with yourself? to admire yourself? On the other hand, if you have a low opinion of yourself, what can you do that is charming or graceful, what can you do that will not be indecorous and awkward? Take away Selflove, the very

2. Quintilian *inst.* 12.1.2; Pliny *HN* 7.1; *Adag.* 1195.
3. See above, pp. 11, 5, and below, p. 160. *Adag.* 3402. Quintilian *inst.* 11.3. 177. Cicero *de or.* 1.29.132, *or.* 21.70–71, *off.* 1.4.14 and 1.27–28, 1.93–99.

spice of life, and immediately the orator with all his gestures will seem stale, the musician with all his harmonies will please no one, the actor with all his poses will be hissed off the stage, the poet with his muses will be ridiculed, the painter with all his skill will seem insipid, the doctor with his medicines will starve to death. In short, you will immediately seem transformed from a handsome youth to an ugly old man,[4] from a minion of Minerva to a dumb-ox,[5] from an eloquent speaker to a babbling idiot, from a well-bred man about town to a country bumpkin. So needful is it that everyone should first be kind to himself, should flatter himself just a bit, should be a little pleased with himself, before he can be pleasing to others.

Finally, since the chief point of happiness is to wish to be what you actually are,[6] certainly my Philautia accomplishes this in each and every way: no one is displeased by his own looks, his intelligence, his lineage, his place of residence, his education, his country—so much so that an Irishman would not change places with an Italian, nor a Thracian with an Athenian, nor someone from Scythia with an inhabitant of the Isles of the Blest.[7] Oh, the extraordinary solicitude of Nature! How marvelously she manages to equalize everything, even in the midst of such teeming variety! Wherever she withholds some of her gifts, just there she will add a little more selflove—but here I have made a mistake that is foolish indeed, since selflove is the greatest gift of all.

I need hardly add that no glorious deed was ever performed except at my instigation, no branch of learning was ever discovered except at my inspiration. Is not war the very seedbed and fountainhead of all praiseworthy deeds? Now then, what could be more foolish than to undertake, for some reason or other, a struggle from which both sides emerge more harmed than helped? As for those

---

4. Literally, "from a Nireus to a Thersites, from a Phaon to a Nestor." Nireus was the handsomest of all who came to Troy; Thersites, the ugliest (Homer *il.* 2.216 and 2. 673). On Phaon, see above, p. 24. Nestor lived through three generations (Homer *il.* 1. 250–52).

5. *Adag.* 40.

6. Martial 10.47.12.

7. See above, p. 21, footnote 7.

who fall in battle, mum's the word—'like the Megarensians, they are of no account.'[8] Then, when the iron-clad battlelines are drawn up on both sides and the shrill song of the trumpets has signaled the advance,[9] I ask you, what use are these wisemen? Worn out by their studies, they have such thin, cold blood in their veins it is hardly enough to keep them alive. No, you need thick-skulled, lumbering louts, whose boldness is in direct proportion to their lack of intelligence. Unless someone thinks Demosthenes made a good soldier: following the advice of Archilochus, he had no sooner caught sight of the enemy than he threw down his shield and ran away—as cowardly in a battle as he was wise in a speech.[1]

But good judgment, they say, is very important in warfare. I grant you, it is, at least for the general, but even that judgment must be of a military sort, not philosophical. Otherwise it is parasites, pimps, thieves, assassins, peasants, dolts, bankrupts, the very dregs of humanity, who perform this noble feat, not ivory-tower philosophers. In fact, you can see how useless they are in the ordinary affairs of life from the example of Socrates, the wisest man in the world according to the judgment of Apollo's oracle[2] (hardly a very wise judgment): once when he was attempting something or other in public, he was driven away by gales of laughter.[3] But I will say this, the man was not absolutely stupid, since he refused to accept the title of wiseman, reserving wisdom for god alone,[4] and since he thought that a wiseman should refrain from political activity[5]— though it would have made better sense if he had taught that anyone

8. *Adag.* 1079.

9. Virgil *aen.* 8.2.

1. Plutarch *vit.* 855a, *mor.* 239b.

2. Plato *apol.* 20d–21d; Diogenes Laertius 2.37.

3. No such incident is recorded about Socrates. Folly seems to be indulging in vague sophistry ("something or other"). In fact, Socrates was successful in public office (Plato *apol.* 32a–d). Erasmus praises his eloquence (*Op. 5*, 138D–E).

4. Plato *apol.* 23a; Erasmus *Op. 4*, 159A.

5. Plato *rep.* 496c–97a, *apol.* 31c–32a, *Gorg.* 521d–22a. Xenophon *mem.* 1.6.15. But Socrates' view is much more complex than Folly admits: Plato *Hipp. mai* 281a–82d, *Euthyd.* 306b–c, *epist.* 7.328–31, *rep.* 473d–74b (cited by Folly herself at the beginning of the next paragraph), and Xenophon *mem.* 3.7.1–9.

who wants to be considered part of the human race should abstain from wisdom. Then again, what but wisdom caused him to be sentenced to drink hemlock? For while he was philosophizing about clouds and ideas, while he was measuring a flea's foot, while he was struck with admiration by the gnat's voice,[6] he neglected to learn what pertains to everyday life. But look, here comes his disciple, Plato, to help his teacher in his hour of mortal danger—a great help, indeed: he was so disconcerted by the noise of the crowd that he left off before he had spoken half a sentence.[7] What should I say about Theophrastus? When he had gone out to make a speech, he suddenly fell silent, 'as if the cat had got his tongue.'[8] How then could he ever shout encouragement to the soldiers in battle? Isocrates, because of his temperamental timidity, never once dared to open his mouth.[9] Cicero, the father of Roman eloquence, always used to begin his speech with unseemly trepidation, just as if he were a sobbing little boy.[1] And Quintilian interprets this fear as the sign of a wise orator well aware of the dangers of his task.[2] But when he says this, doesn't he clearly admit that wisdom is a hindrance to doing a job properly? What can we expect such people to do when the battle is fought with steel,[3] since they are utterly disabled by fear when they have to fight with bare words only?

And after all this (by all that's holy!) people still make much of that celebrated saying of Plato, that the state will be happy when philosophers become kings or kings become philosophers.[4] In fact, if you consult the historians, you will find that no prince ever

6. Aristophanes *nub.* 144–52, 156–64, 252. Xenophon *symp.* 6.8. On "ideas", see Plato *rep.* 476–80, 497–98, *Parm.* 131–32.

7. Diogenes Laertius 2.41.

8. Gellius *NA* 8.9. The original proverb is "as if he had seen a wolf" (*Adag.* 3450, 2756).

9. Isocrates *Phil.* 81, *Panathen.* 9-10, *ep.* 8.7. Cicero *de or.* 2.3.10.

1. Cicero *S. Rosc. Am.* 4.9, *Mil.* 1.1.

2. Quintilian *inst.* 12.5.4.

3. Socrates, Cicero, and perhaps Isocrates served creditably as soldiers.

4. Plato *rep.* 473c–d, *epist.* 7. 326a–b and 328a. Erasmus himself frequently praised Plato's saying (*Educ. Chr. Pr.*, pp. 133, 150, *Adag.* 201, *Op. 4*, 559 and 566, *5*, 228 and 730), which is also a crux in the argument of *Utopia* (*CW 4*, 86/11–12n).

plagued a state more than when the scepter fell into the hands of some pseudo-philosopher or devotee of literature. The two Cato's give ample evidence of this: one of them disturbed the quiet of the republic with his wild reproaches;[5] the other, attempting to defend the liberty of the Roman people through misplaced wisdom, utterly destroyed it.[6] Add to these your Brutus's, Cassius's,[7] Gracchus's,[8] and even Cicero himself, who was as much of a plague to the Roman republic as Demosthenes was to the Athenian.[9] As for Marcus Aurelius, even if we grant that he was a good emperor—for I could wrench that distinction from him too, since he was burdensome to the citizens and despised by them precisely because he was such a philosopher[1]—but nevertheless, even granting that he was good, there can be no doubt that he did more damage to the state by leaving such a son[2] behind him than he ever benefited it by his own rule. Notice how the type of person who devotes himself to the pursuit of wisdom is most unlucky in everything, but above all in begetting children—as if Nature had taken pains, I suspect, to keep the disease of wisdom from spreading too widely among mortals. ⟨Thus, it is quite clear that Cicero's son was quite un-

5. Cato the Censor (234–149 B.C.) was litigious and disruptively severe (Plutarch *vit.* 338a–b, 342b–c, 344d–f, 345a–47e, 349a).

6. Cato of Utica (95–46 B.C.), a Stoic philosopher and ally of Pompey, lost the civil war to Caesar, who put an end to the liberty of the Roman republic by establishing the empire.

7. Brutus and Cassius assassinated Julius Caesar. Defeated by Octavian at Phillipi, they committed suicide.

8. Gaius and Tiberius Gracchus (second century B.C.) attempted to unite the middle and lower classes against the senate. Praised by Plutarch (*vit.* 19), they were frequently condemned as rebellious demagogues (Valerius Maximus 8.10.1; Tacitus *ann.* 3.27). But even Cicero, who normally vilified them, occasionally found it necessary to praise their virtues (*leg. agr.* 2.5.10).

9. Cicero provoked Anthony to destroy the Roman republic; Demosthenes urged the Athenians into waging a disastrous war with Phillip. The two were often compared as writers (*Ep. 10*, 74) and as statesmen (Plutarch *vit.* 20).

1. An empty boast. Apart from a few facts which Folly might have twisted against him, Marcus Aurelius actively promoted the welfare of the people and was beloved by them (Julius Capitolinus *script. hist. Aug.* 8.3, 12.1, 18.1–3). See *Educ. Chr. Pr.*, p. 223.

2. Commodus, privately vicious and publicly ruinous, was detested (*Op. 4*, 281E, 282B).

worthy of his ancestry,[3] and that wiseman Socrates had children "more like their mother than their father" (as some writer cleverly put it),[4] that is, foolish.⟩

But somehow or other we could put up with them if it were only in public affairs that they were such '*square pegs in round holes.*'[5] But they are just as inept in absolutely all the activities of human life. Bring a wiseman to a party: he will disrupt it either by his gloomy silence or his tedious cavils. Invite him to a dance: you would think it was 'a camel dancing.'[6] Drag him along to a public festival: his face alone will be enough to put a damper on people's gaiety—wise Cato will be forced to leave the theater because he cannot put off his supercilious airs.[7] If he joins a conversation, everyone suddenly 'clams up.'[8] If something has to be bought, if some contract has to be negotiated, in short, if any of those things must be done without which everyday life cannot be carried on, you would say this wiseman is more of a blockhead than a man. So useless is he to himself, to his country, to his dependents—and all because he is unskilled in ordinary affairs and flies in the face of public opinion and popular morals. Such a stance could not but earn him the hatred of the people, simply because of this marked difference in mental outlook and style of life. Is anything at all done among mortals that is not full of folly? Isn't everything done by fools, among fools? But if some one person wants to swim against the stream, my advice to him is to imitate Timon[9] by going away to some deserted spot where he can enjoy his wisdom all by himself.

But to return to my original point, what force but flattery drove

3. On Cicero's ne'er-do-well son, see Seneca the elder (*suas.* 8) and Pliny (*HN* 14.22(28).147). For the meaning of the pointed brackets, see above, p. xxxiv.

4. Seneca *epist.* 104.27. On Socrates' shrewish wife, see Gellius (*NA* 1.17. 1–3); on his stupid sons, see Aristotle (*rhet.* 1390b) and Plutarch (*vit.* 347f).

5. Literally, "an ass playing a harp" (*Adag.* 335).

6. *Adag.* 1666.

7. The spectacle he was forced to leave was the Floralia (Martial 1. *praef*). See above, p. 26, footnote 5.

8. See above, p. 37, footnote 8.

9. In 1506 Erasmus translated Lucian's *Timon or the Misanthrope* (Amsterdam ed. *1*, part 1, 488–505).

together those primitive men, hard and rough as stone or oak, and joined them into a community? For such flattery is all that is signified by the harp of Amphion or Orpheus.[1] When the people of Rome were ready to rebel, what recalled them to a sense of civic duty? A philosophical oration? Hardly. Rather, a childish cock-and-bull story about the belly and the other parts of the body.[2] A similar fable of Themistocles about the fox and the hedgehog had the same effect.[3] What wiseman's oration could ever accomplish as much as that imaginary hind of Sertorius,[4] or that silly trick of the Spartan and his two dogs,[5] or that absurd device of the same Sertorius about plucking the hairs from a horse's tail?[6] To say nothing of Minos or Numa,[7] both of whom controlled the foolish crowd by making up fables. Such trifles as these have an effect on that enormous and powerful monster, the mob. On the other hand, what state has ever accepted the laws of Plato or Aristotle or the teachings of Socrates?[8]

1. Amphion's music built the stone walls of Thebes; that of Orpheus drew to him animals and trees (Horace *ars* 391–96; Ovid *met.* 10.86–91).

2. With this fable Menenius Agrippa calmed the Roman mob (Livy 2.32.8–12).

3. A fox covered with blood-sucking flies, forbids a hedgehog to drive them away because they would only be replaced by less satiated successors; so too, the Athenians were urged not to throw off their greedy magistrates. Both Lister and Erasmus (*Op. 1*, 98E) mistakenly attribute the story to Themistocles. Aristotle (*rhet.* 1393b) and Plutarch (*mor.* 790d) attribute it to Aesop.

4. Sertorius convinced his Spanish followers that he received divine guidance by means of a white hind (Plutarch *vit.* 573b–d, 578d–f; Gellius *NA* 15.22.1–9).

5. The Spartan lawgiver Lycurgus showed the importance of education by placing a bowl of food and a rabbit between two dogs, one trained for the hunt, the other untrained (Plutarch *mor.* 3a–b, 225f–226b).

6. To show his troops that they should not risk all on one large-scale attack on the Romans, Sertorius instructed a strong man to pull the hairs from a scraggly horse's tail all at once while a weak man was to pull the hairs from a full tail one by one (Plutarch *vit.* 576a–b; Valerius Maximus 7.3.6).

7. Minos pretended that he was allowed to consult Jove every nine years (Homer *od.* 19.178; Plato *Min.* 320d). Numa said he received divine guidance from the nymph Egeria (Livy 1.19.5; Plutarch *vit.* 62a, 65ab).

8. Erasmus himself implies that Plato's laws are unworkable (*Adag.* 2036), but he also praises the political works of Aristotle and (especially) Plato as very valuable to a Christian prince (*Educ. Chr. Pr.,* pp. 200–201).

Then again, what persuaded the Decii to sacrifice their lives?[9] What drew Quintus Curtius into the pit, if not vainglory,[1] the sweetest of Sirens,[2] but how roundly condemned by these wisemen![3] For what could be more foolish, they say, than for a candidate to flatter and plead with the people, to buy their favor by scattering money here and there, to hunt for the applause of fools, to take pleasure in the cheers of the crowd, to be carried around in triumph as if you were some banner or placard to be viewed by the people, to overlook the forum in the form of a bronze statue?[4] Add to these absurdities the conferral of titles and surnames, add the divine honors paid to some puny mortal, add the public ceremonies elevating the most wicked tyrants to the rank of the gods: these things are foolish indeed—one Democritus[5] would not be enough to make fun of them. Who denies it? Nevertheless, from this source flow all those exploits of brave heroes which have been praised to the skies in the writings of so many eloquent men. Such foolishness as this creates states, it constitutes empires, civil offices, religion, counsels, judgments—in fact, human life is nothing more than an entertainment staged by Folly.

To say a few words now about arts and sciences: what motivated the minds of mortals to think out and hand down to posterity so many extraordinary (or so they imagine at least) branches of learning? What was it but a thirst for glory? Men who believed that anything as vague and empty as fame was worth so many sleepless

---

9. P. Decius Mus and his son died to save the Roman republic (Livy 8.6.8–13 and 8.9.1–12). (Psuedo) Cicero mentions glory as the motive of the younger Decius (*rhet. ad. Her.* 4.44).

1. Quintus (an error for Marcus) Curtius rode his horse into a great abyss in the forum because it was foretold that it could not be closed unless Rome's best jewel was thrown into it. Livy (7.6.1–6) and (especially) St. Augustine (*City of God* 5.18) stress glory as the cause and effect of Curtius' deed.

2. Folly adapts to her purpose a fallacious premise exposed by Cicero (*inv.* 1.49.91). "Siren" was traditionally derived from the Greek "to draw" or "chain."

3. For example, St. Augustine (*City of God* 5.18) and Erasmus himself (*Enchiridion*, pp. 76, 135, 141–42, 189–90).

4. Horace *serm.* 2.3.1ᵖ3.

5. See above, p. 2, footnote 5.

nights, so much sweat, must be the greatest fools of all. Meanwhile, you owe to such folly very many remarkable conveniences, and (what is most delicious of all) you profit from the madness of others.[6]

Well, now that I have laid claim to the praise owing to fortitude and industry, what if I should also claim the praise belonging to prudence? But someone will say, you can no more do that than you can mix fire with water.[7] But I think I can carry this off also, if only you will lend me your ears and give me your attention, as you have heretofore.

First, if prudence consists in wide experience, which of the two deserves ⟪the honor of this title⟫ : the wise man, who undertakes nothing (partly because he is overcome by modesty, partly because his spirit is too timid), or the fool, who is never restrained from any undertaking whatsoever—neither by modesty (because he has none), nor by danger (to which he pays no attention)? The wise man retreats to the books of the ancients, and there learns mere verbal trifles. The fool plunges into the thick of things, staring danger in the face, and in this way (unless I am badly mistaken) he acquires true prudence.[8] Homer seems to have seen this (in spite of his blindness) when he said "*a fool is wise after the event.*"[9] For there are two main obstacles to gaining a knowledge of affairs: modesty, which throws the mind into confusion; and fear, which keeps people from undertaking noble exploits once the danger becomes apparent. But folly removes these hindrances in fine fashion. Few mortals understand how very advantageous it is in other ways as well, never to feel modest and to be so bold as to stick at nothing.

But if they prefer to take prudence as consisting in good judgment, listen (I beg you) and hear how far the men who boast of this quality actually are from possessing it. First, it is clear that all

6. Pliny *HN* 18.6.31.

7. *Adag.* 3294.

8. Folly adapts to her own purposes Gellius' attack (*NA* 10.22) on ivory-tower philosophers.

9. *il.* 17.32; *Adag.* 30–31.

human affairs, like the Sileni of Alcibiades,[1] have two aspects quite different from each other. Hence, what appears 'at first blush' (as they say) to be death, will, if you examine it more closely, turn out to be life; conversely, life will turn out to be death; beauty will become ugliness; riches will turn to poverty; notoriety will become fame; learning will be ignorance; strength, weakness; noble birth will be ignoble; joy will become sadness; success, failure; friendship, enmity; what is helpful will seem harmful; in brief, you will find everything suddenly reversed if you open the Silenus. Now, if anyone thinks this argument is too abstract and philosophical, well then, I'll make it all clear 'in words of one syllable,'[2] as they say. Doesn't everyone admit that a king is both rich and powerful? But suppose he possesses none of the goods of the mind; suppose nothing is ever enough for him: then clearly he is the poorest of the poor. Then, say that his mind is subject to many vices: then he is the basest sort of slave. One can philosophize in the same way about the other qualities, but this single example should suffice. But someone will say, so what? What is all this leading up to? Listen, then, to how I will develop the argument. If someone should try to strip away the costumes and makeup from the actors performing a play on the stage and to display them to the spectators in their own natural appearance, wouldn't he ruin the whole play? Wouldn't all the spectators be right to throw rocks at such a madman and drive him out of the theater? Everything would suddenly look different: the actor just now playing a woman would be seen to be a man; the one who had just now been playing a young man would look old; the man who played the king only a moment ago would become a pauper; the actor who played god would be revealed as a wretched human being. But to destroy the illusions in this fashion would spoil the whole play. This deception, this disguise, is the very thing that holds the attention of the spectators. Now the whole life of mortal

1. Cases carved like an ugly Silenus (see above, p. 27, footnote 7) could be opened to reveal beautiful, precious objects (*Adag.* 2201; tr. Margaret Mann Phillips, *Erasmus on his Times*, pp. 77–97). See below, p. 159, footnote 8.
2. See above, p. 31, footnote 6.

men, what is it but a sort of play,[3] in which various persons make their entrances in various costumes, and each one plays his own part until the director gives him his cue to leave the stage? Often he also orders one and the same actor to come on in different costumes, so that the actor who just now played the king in royal scarlet now comes on in rags to play a miserable servant. True, all these images are unreal, but this play cannot be performed in any other way.

If at this point some wiseman, dropped down direct from heaven,[4] should suddenly jump up and begin shouting that this figure whom everyone reverences as if he were the lord god is not even a man because he is controlled by his passions like an animal, that he is a servant of the lowest rank because he willingly serves so many filthy masters; or if he should turn to another man who is mourning the death of his parent and tell him to laugh instead because the dead man has at last really begun to live, whereas this life is really nothing but a sort of death; if he should see another man glorying in his noble lineage and call him a low-born bastard because he is so far removed from virtue, which is the only true source of nobility; and if he addressed everyone else in the same way, I ask you, what would he accomplish except to make everyone take him for a raving lunatic? Just as nothing is more foolish than misplaced wisdom, so too, nothing is more imprudent than perverse prudence. And surely it is perverse not to adapt yourself to the prevailing circumstances, to refuse 'to do as the Romans do,' to ignore the party-goer's maxim 'take a drink or take your leave,'[5] to insist that the play should not be a play. True prudence, on the other hand, recognizes human limitations and does not strive to leap beyond them;[6] it is willing to run with the herd, to overlook faults tolerantly or to share them in a friendly spirit. But, they say, that is exactly what we mean by folly. ⟨I will hardly deny it—as long as they will reciprocate by admitting that this is exactly what it means to perform the play of life.⟩

3. Lucian *nigr.* 20, *Men.* 16. Erasmus *Ep. 9,* 167, 319. On the topos of life as a play, see Curtius (pp. 138–44) and More (*CW 2,* 258; *CW 4,* 372).
4. *Adag.* 786.
5. *Adag.* 92 and 947.
6. Cato *disticha* 2.2.3; *Adag.* 569.

Another point—by all the gods in heaven! Should I say it or keep still? But why keep still, since it is 'truer than truth itself.'[7] But perhaps in such a weighty matter it would be well to summon the Muses from Helicon[8]—the poets often enough invoke them for the merest trifles. Be present, then, you daughters of Jove, for a bit, while I show that no one can reach the heights of wisdom and the very 'inner sanctum,' as they themselves say, 'of happiness'[9] except with the guidance of Folly.

First of all, everyone admits that the emotions all belong to Folly. Thus, the usual distinction between a wiseman and a fool is that the fool is governed by emotion, the wiseman by reason. That is why the Stoics eliminate from their wiseman all emotional perturbations, as if they were diseases.[1] But actually the emotions not only function as guides to those who are hastening to the haven of wisdom, but also, in the whole range of virtuous action, they operate like spurs or goads, as it were, encouraging the performance of good deeds.[2] I know that died-in-the-wool Stoic, Seneca, strenuously denies this, removing all emotion whatsoever from his wiseman.[3] But by doing this he is left with something that cannot even be called human; he *fabricates*[4] some new sort of divinity that has never existed and never will. Frankly, he sets up a marble statue of a man, utterly unfeeling and quite impervious to all human emotion. They can enjoy their wiseman all they like and have him all to themselves, or (if they prefer) they can live with him in Plato's republic, or in the realm of Platonic ideas,[5] or in 'the gardens of Tantalus.'[6] Who would not

---

7. *Adag.* 3802.

8. Virgil *aen.* 7.641, 10.163.

9. Augustine *City of God* 12.21, Sidonius Apollinarius *epist.* 2.4.1.

1. Seneca *epist.* 75.8–14.

2. A Peripatetic doctrine (Aristotle *mag. mor.* 1.5.1–2, 1.7.1–4, *eth. Nic.* 2.2.7). Cf. *Enchiridion*, p. 68.

3. Seneca *epist.* 71.27, 85.2–12.

4. Plato *tim.* 29a, 31a; Xenophon *mem.* 1.4.7.

5. Lucian (*ver. hist.* 2.17.115) says Plato was the only person fit to live in his republic. Aristotle makes fun of Plato's separate forms or ideas (*metaph.* 990a–92b).

6. Proverbial for what exists nowhere (*Adag.* 1046).

flee in horror from such a man, as he would from a monster or a ghost—a man who is completely deaf to all human sentiment, who is untouched by emotion, no more moved by love or pity than 'a chunk of flint or a mountain crag,'[7] who never misses anything, who never makes a mistake, who sees through everything as if he had 'x-ray vision,'[8] measures everything 'with plumb line and T square,'[9] never forgives anything, who is uniquely self-satisfied, who thinks he alone is rich, he alone is healthy, regal, free,[1] in brief, he thinks that he alone is all things (but he is also alone in thinking so), who cares nothing about friendship, who makes friends with no one, who would not hesitate to tell the gods themselves to go hang, who can find nothing in all human life that he does not condemn and ridicule as madness? Yet just such a creature as this is that perfect wiseman of theirs. I ask you, if an office were to be awarded by election, what state would choose such a man for civic office, what army would select him for their general? Indeed, what woman would consent to marry him or put up with him as a husband? What host would want him (or tolerate him) as a guest? What servant would ever enter his service or continue in it? Who would not prefer someone chosen at random from the mob of out-and-out fools? Being a fool himself, he could either command fools or obey them, please his peers (who are clearly in the majority), be companionable with his wife, cheerful with his friends, a fine table companion, an easy-going messmate. In short, he considers nothing human foreign to him.[2] But for some time now I have been sick and tired of this wiseman. Therefore I shall proceed in my speech by returning to the remaining benefits.

Just think, if a person could look down from a watchtower,[3] as

7. Virgil *aen.* 6.471.

8. Literally, "as sharp-sighted as Lynceus," one of the Argonauts who could see through walls (*Adag.* 1054; Horace *epist.* 1.1.28–29).

9. *Adag.* 490.

1. On these Stoic paradoxes, see Plutarch (*mor.* 101d–e) and Horace (*epist.* 1.1.106–8, *serm.* 1.3.124–25).

2. Terence *heaut.* 77.

3. *Adag.* 3395.

46

Jupiter sometimes does according to the poets,[4] and could see how many disasters human life is exposed to, how miserable and messy childbirth is, how toilsome it is to bring children up, how defenseless they are against injuries, how young men must make their way by the sweat of their brow, how burdensome old age is, how death comes cruel and ineluctable; and then too, if he could see during the course of life itself how man is besieged by a whole army of diseases, threatened by accidents, assailed by misfortunes, how everything everywhere is tinged with bitterness—to say nothing of the evils men inflict on each other, such as poverty, prison, disgrace, shame, torture, entrapment, betrayal, insults, quarrels, deception, but I might as well try 'to number the sands of the seashore'[5]—now, as for what crimes man committed to deserve all this or which god in his anger caused men to be born to all these miseries, those are things it is not proper for me to declare at the present time,[6] but whoever gives these things serious consideration cannot but approve the example of the Milesian virgins, however pitiable their case was.[7] But in fact, who have been the most likely to commit suicide out of weariness with life? Isn't it those who have come closest to wisdom? Among these (to say nothing of such people as Diogenes, Xenocrates, Cato, Cassius, and Brutus)[8] was Chiron,[9] who had an opportunity to be immortal but freely chose death instead. You can see, I imagine, what would happen if men everywhere were

4. Homer *il.* 8.51–52.

5. *Adag.* 344.

6. The Lister commentary remarks that Folly carefully suspends judgment to avoid touching on original sin (which would hardly be appropriate), or perhaps because she agrees with the opinion of Plato and Origen, who teach that souls sinned before they came into human bodies.

7. A large number of virgins in the city of Miletus hanged themselves for no apparent reason (Gellius *NA* 15.10).

8. Of the philosophers Diogenes and Xenocrates, the first killed himself, but the second died by accident (Diogenes Laertius 6.77–78, 4.14–15). Cato of Utica, Brutus, and Cassius committed suicide after being defeated in battle (Plutarch *vit.* 794, 1004, 1009). See above, p. 38, footnotes 6 and 7.

9. This wise centaur, wounded by a poisoned arrow of Hercules, chose death over immortality (Lucian *dial. mort.* 26; Ovid *met.* 2.649–54).

wise: we would need another batch of clay, another potter like Prometheus.[1] But I, partly through ignorance, partly through thoughtlessness, sometimes through forgetfulness of past misfortunes, sometimes through hope of good things to come, now and then mixing some honey with their pleasures, I rescue men from such terrible sufferings—so effectively that they are even unwilling to leave this life behind when the thread is all unwound[2] and life leaves them behind. The less cause they have to remain in this life, the more they want to stay alive—so little are they touched by the tedium of life.

It is my doing that you see everywhere men as old as Nestor,[3] who no longer even look like men: driveling, doting, toothless, whitehaired, bald, or (in the words of Aristophanes) *"filthy, crookbacked, wretched, shriveled, bald, toothless, and lame of their best limb"*[4]; but yet they are so in love with life and *'have such young ideas'*[5] that one of them will dye his hair, another will hide his baldness with a toupee, another will wear false teeth (borrowed perhaps from some hog),[6] another will fall head over heels in love with some young girl and outdo any beardless youth in amorous idiocy.[7] In fact, to see old codgers with one foot in the grave marry some sweet young thing—with no dowry at that, and of far more use to other men than to him—this sort of thing happens so often that people almost consider it praiseworthy.

But it is even more amusing to see these old women, so ancient they might as well be dead and so cadaverous they look as if they had returned from the grave, yet they are always mouthing the proverb *"life is sweet."*[8] They are as hot as bitches in heat, or (as the

1. According to some legends, Prometheus molded men and animals of clay and animated them with fire (Lucian *Prometh.* 2.11–13).
2. *Adag.* 567.
3. See above, p. 35, footnote 4.
4. Aristophanes *Plut.* 266–67.
5. *Adag.* 3083.
6. In Erasmus' time false teeth (often merely cosmetic) were made out of various substances, including animals' teeth.
7. Ovid *am.* 1.9.4.
8. Literally, "light is good." An old woman who wished to make love with-

Greeks say) they *rut like goats.*[9] They pay a good price for the services of some handsome young Adonis.[1] They never cease smearing their faces with makeup. They can't tear themselves away from the mirror. They pluck and thin their pubic bush.[2] They show off their withered and flabby breasts. They whip up their languid lust with quavering whines and whimpers.[3] They drink a lot. They mingle with the young girls on the dance floor. They write billets-doux. Everyone laughs at these things as utterly foolish (and indeed they are), but the old bags themselves are perfectly self-satisfied. They lead a life of the utmost pleasure. They swim in honey up to their ears. Through my blessing, they live in bliss. Now if anyone thinks such goings-on are absurd, I wish he would take the trouble to decide whether he thinks it better to live a life of perfect bliss by means of such folly or to look for a way to 'end it all,'[4] as they say.

Now, the fact that such absurdities are generally considered disgraceful, that doesn't bother my fools at all: they are either unaware of their notoriety, or, if they are aware, they find it easy to ignore it. If a rock falls on your head, that is certainly bad for you. But shame, disgrace, reproaches, curses do harm only insofar as they are perceived. If they are not noticed, they are not harmful. "What harm if all the crowd should hiss and boo; you're safe as long as you can clap for you."[5] But that is made possible only by Folly.

Even so, I can imagine the philosophers' objections: "But to be caught in the toils of such folly, to err, to be deceived, to be ignorant—such an existence is itself miserable." One thing is sure: such it is to be a man. But I don't see why they should call him miserable,

---

out being embarrassed by the wrinkles on her body put out the lamp, saying "*Chaire philon phos,*" which is wittily ambiguous: (1) Farewell, dear light or (2) Welcome, dear life. See *Paroemiographi Graeci,* ed. E. L. Leutsch and F. G. Schneidewin, Göttingen, 1839, pp. 173, 319; and the *Supplementum,* repr. Olms, Hildesheim, 1961, Crusius' *Analecta,* pp. 73–74

9. Aristophanes *Plut.* 1024; *Adag.* 809.

1. Literally, "Phaon" (see above, p. 24).

2. Martial 10.90.

3. Horace *epod.* 8.7–8, *carm.* 4.13.5–6.

4. *Adag.* 921.

5. Horace *serm.* 1.1.66–67.

since this is the way you are born, this is the way you are formed and fashioned, this is the common lot of everyone. But nothing is miserable merely because it follows its own nature, unless perhaps someone thinks man's lot is deplorable because he cannot fly like the birds, or run on all fours like other animals, and is not armed with horns like a bull. But by the same token, he should argue that even a fine, thoroughbred horse is unhappy because he has never learned grammar and doesn't eat pancakes, or that a bull is miserable because he cannot work out in the gym.[6] Therefore, just as a horse who is ignorant of grammar is not miserable, so too, a man who is a fool is not unhappy, because these things are inherent in their natures.

But these word-jugglers are back at it again: "The knowledge of various branches of learning," they say, "was especially added to human nature so that with their help he could use his mental skill to compensate for what Nature left out." As if it were the least bit likely that Nature, who was so alert in providing for gnats (and even for tiny flowers and blades of grass), should have nodded only in equipping mankind, so that there should be a need for the different branches of learning—which were actually thought up by Theutus, a spirit quite hostile to mankind, as instruments of man's utter ruination. So little do they contribute to man's happiness, that they defeat the very purpose for which they were supposedly invented—as that most wise king in Plato cleverly argues concerning the invention of writing.[7] Thus, the branches of learning crept in along with the other plagues of man's life, and from the very same source from which all shameful crimes arise, namely, the demons—who also derive their name from this fact, since "demon" comes from δαήμονες ("scientes," knowing ones).[8] Now

6. See above, p. 29, footnote 3.

7. In Plato the Theban king, Thamus, argues that the invention of the alphabet by the Egyptian god Theutus impaired man's knowledge because it made it unnecessary for him to remember as much as before (Plato *Phaedr.* 274c–75a).

8. Plato *Cratyl.* 398b; Lactantius *div. inst.* 2.14.6 (*CSEL 19*, 163).

the simple people of the golden age,[9] who were not armed with any formal learning, lived their lives completely under the guidance of natural impulses. What need was there for grammar when everyone spoke the same language and when speech served no other purpose than to let one person understand another? What use was there for dialectic, when there was no disagreement among conflicting opinions? What room was there for rhetoric when there were no litigious troublemakers? What demand was there for legal learning when there was no such thing as bad morals—for good laws undoubtedly sprang from bad conduct.[1] Then too, they had more reverence than to pry into the secrets of Nature with irreligious curiosity—to measure the stars, their motions and effects, to seek the causes of mysterious phenomena—for they considered it unlawful for mortals to seek knowledge beyond the limits of their lot.[2] As for what is beyond the range of the furthest stars, the madness of exploring such things never even entered their minds. But when the purity of the golden age had gradually declined, then evil spirits, as I said, first began to invent the learned disciplines, but only a few at first and even those taken up only by a few. Afterwards, the superstition of the Chaldeans[3] and the idle frivolity of the Greeks added hundreds more, all of them nothing but forms of mental torture, so painful that the grammar of even one language is more than enough to make life a perpetual agony.[4]

Still, even among these disciplines, the ones held in highest esteem are those which come closest to the ordinary understanding—that is, the folly—of mankind. Theologians starve, physicists freeze, astronomers are ridiculed, logicians are ignored. *"One physician alone is worth whole hosts of other men."*[5] And even among physicians, the

9. See Harry Levin, *The Myth of the Golden Age in the Renaissance* (Oxford, 1969).
1. *Adag.* 961; Macrobius *sat.* 3.17.10.
2. See above, p. 44, footnote 6.
3. Gellius *NA* 14.1.1–10.
4. See below, pp. 80–81.
5. Homer *il.* 11.514.

more ignorant, bold, and thoughtless one of them is, the more he is valued by these high and mighty princes. Besides, medicine ⟨(certainly as it is now practiced by most doctors)⟩ is nothing but a subdivision of flattery, ⟨just like rhetoric⟩.[6] The next rank beneath the doctors belongs to pettifogging lawyers; in fact, I wonder if they don't hold the highest rank of all, since their profession—not to speak of it myself—is universally ridiculed as asinine by the philosophers. Still, all business transactions, from the smallest to the greatest, are absolutely controlled by these asses. They acquire large estates, while a theologian who has carefully read through whole bookcases of divinity nibbles on dried peas, waging continual warfare with bedbugs and lice.

Moreover, just as those disciplines which are most closely related to Folly contribute most to happiness, so too, those men who have nothing whatever to do with any branch of learning and follow Nature as their only guide[7] are by far the happiest of all. For she is completely adequate in every way, unless perhaps someone wants to leap over the bounds of human destiny. Nature hates disguises, and whatever has not been spoiled by artifice always produces the happiest results. After all, don't you see that, among all the other kinds of living creatures, those which remain at the furthest remove from any formal learning and take Nature for their only teacher lead the happiest lives? What could be happier or more marvelous than the bees?[8] And yet they do not even have all the bodily senses.[9] What architect has ever produced buildings like theirs? What philosopher has ever established a comparable republic? The horse, on the other hand, because his senses resemble those of man and because he left his original abode to dwell with men, has also become a sharer in the sufferings of men. Thus, often enough a horse that is ashamed to be defeated in a race becomes broken-winded,[1]

6. Plato *Gorg.* 463a–65c.

7. Cicero *amic.* 5.19, *sen.* 2.5.

8. The orderly politics of the beehive was widely admired, especially because of Virgil (*georg.* 4.149–227).

9. Contrary to Aristotle (*hist. an.* 4.8.15), Pliny says that very few insects have all five senses (*HN* 11.3.10).

1. Horace *epist.* 1.1.9–10.

and a horse that strives for victory in warfare is stabbed and bites the dust[2] with his rider. To say nothing of the sharp-toothed curb bits, the points of the spurs, the imprisonment of the stable, the whips, cudgels, fetters, the rider—in short, that whole miserable panorama of servitude that he willingly accepted when (like brave men of honor) he was overcome by a burning desire for revenge on his enemy.[3] How much more attractive is the life of flies and little birds, who live for the moment purely by natural instinct, as long as they can avoid the snares of men. But if they should be put into cages and learn to speak human sounds, it is quite remarkable how they decline from their native sleekness and elegance. So certain is it that the creations of Nature are in every way more joyous than the fabrications of artifice.

Accordingly, I could never bestow sufficient praise on that cock embodying Pythagoras,[4] who had been, in his single person, a philosopher, a man, a woman, a king, a private citizen, a fish, a horse, a frog, even a sponge (I think),[5] but who decided that no creature was more miserable than man because all the others were content to remain within the limits of Nature, while man alone tried to go beyond the bounds of his lot. Moreover, among men he places natural-born fools far above great and learned men; ⟨and Gryllus[6] was not a little wiser than *wily* Odysseus,[7] since he preferred to grunt in the pigsty instead of being exposed with Odysseus to so many unexpected calamities⟩. With Gryllus and the cock, Homer himself, the father of foolish fables, seems to be in agreement, since he repeatedly calls all mortals *"miserable and wretched"*[8] and fre-

2. Virgil *aen.* 10.482, 11.418. Homer *il.* 22.17.

3. The horse submitted to man in order to drive the stag from his pasture (Horace *epist.* 1.10.34–38; Aristotle *rhet.* 1393b).

4. Lucian *Somnium siue Gallus,* tr. by Erasmus (Amsterdam ed. *1*, part 1, 471–85).

5. Aristotle (*hist. an.* 5.16) and Pliny (*HN* 9.69.148) classify the sponge as an animal.

6. See above, p. 3, footnote 9.

7. In the *Odyssey* Homer applies this epithet to Odysseus over eighty times (e.g., 7.207 and 302).

8. Homer applies the first epithet to mortals five times (e.g., *il.* 24.525) but does not use the second at all.

quently applies the epithet *"unhappy"* to Ulysses, his model of wisdom, but never to Paris or Ajax or Achilles.[9] And why this distinction? Wasn't it because the clever and cunning Ulysses never did anything without consulting Pallas Athene and was too smart for his own good, departing as far as possible from the guidance of Nature?

Therefore, just as among mortals those men who seek wisdom are furthest from happiness—indeed, they are fools twice over because, forgetting the human condition to which they were born, they aspire to the life of the immortal gods and (like the giants)[1] wage war against Nature with the engines of learning—so too, the least miserable among men are those who come closest to the level of intelligence (that is, the folly) of brute animals and never undertake anything beyond human nature. Come on, then, let us see if we can't show this, not with the fine-spun arguments of the Stoics, but with some plain, ordinary example. But by all the gods above! is anyone happier than the sort of men who are usually called fools, dolts, simpletons, nincompoops—actually very fine titles, as I see it? At first glance, what I am saying may perhaps seem foolish and absurd, but it is nevertheless true as can be.

First, they are spared all fear of death, a burden hardly to be taken lightly. They are not tortured by pangs of conscience. They are not frightened by silly tales about the underworld. They are not terrified by apparitions and ghosts. They are not tormented by the fear of impending evils, nor kept on tenterhooks by the hope of coming good. In brief, they are not harried by the thousands of cares to which this life is subject. They feel no shame, no fear, no ambition, no envy, no love. Finally, if they come close to the ignorance of brute animals, they do not even commit sins, according to the theologians.[2] Now at this point, most foolish wiseman, do me a favor:

9. Homer applies the epithet to Odysseus fifteen times (e.g., *od.* 17.10 and 483) but never to the other three.

1. Cicero *sen.* 2.5; *Adag.* 2993.

2. E.g., Aquinas teaches that "folly" is not sinful if it results from congenital indisposition, but only if it springs from immersion in worldly things (*S.T.* 2a–2ae, q. 46, a. 2).

just consider how many ways your mind is tortured day and night—pile up all the troubles of your life into a single heap, and then you will finally understand how many evils I have spared my fools. On top of that, note that they not only rejoice continually themselves—playing, laughing, and singing little tunes—but also, wherever they turn, they provide everyone else with entertainment, jokes, fun and laughter, as if the gods in their goodness had granted them to men for the specific purpose of brightening up the gloominess of man's life. Hence, whereas various people react variously to other people, everyone agrees unanimously in claiming these fools as their own—they seek them out, maintain them, pamper them, coddle them, help them in time of need, freely allow them to do or say anything they like. So far is anyone from wishing to harm them that even savage beasts refrain from hurting them, out of a certain natural awareness of their innocence. As a matter of fact, they are sacred to the gods, especially to me, and therefore it is not without reason that everyone treats them with such respect.

In fact, even the mightiest monarchs are so delighted with them that without these fools some of them can neither eat breakfast, nor make their entry, nor even so much as survive for a single hour. And they value these simpletons far more than those sour wisemen, though it is true that they usually maintain some of them too, for the sake of appearances. The reason why they value them more is not far to seek, I think, and ought not to surprise anyone, since those wisemen normally offer princes nothing but melancholy—indeed, relying on their learning, they sometimes do not hesitate to make harsh truth grate upon their tender ears[3]—whereas fools provide the very thing for which princes are always on the lookout: jokes, laughs, guffaws, fun. And don't forget another talent, by no means contemptible, that is peculiar to fools: they alone speak the plain, unvarnished truth. And what is more worthy of praise than truthfulness? True, Alcibiades' proverb in Plato attributes truthfulness to wine and children,[4] but actually the praise for that virtue is all

3. Persius 1.107–08; *Adag.* 1853.
4. The proverb is implied in Plato *symp.* 217e.

mine and mine alone, as Euripides himself testifies in that famous saying about us which has come down from him: "*a fool speaks like a fool.*"[5] Whatever a fool has in his heart, he reveals in his face and expresses in his speech. But wisemen have those two tongues, also mentioned by Euripides:[6] with one they speak the truth, with the other whatever they think convenient for the moment. They are the ones who turn black into white,[7] who blow hot and cold in one breath,[8] who profess to believe one thing in their speech but conceal quite another in their hearts. Princes, then, for all their great happiness, still seem to me most unhappy in one respect: there is no one from whom they can hear the truth, and they are forced to take flatterers for their friends.[9]

But "a prince's ears tingle at the truth," someone will say, "and for that very reason they shun those wisemen: they are afraid that perhaps one of them might be so frank as to say what is true rather than pleasant." Quite right—kings do hate the truth. But my fools, on the other hand, have a marvelous faculty of giving pleasure not only when they speak the truth but even when they utter open reproaches, so that the very same statement which would have cost a wiseman his life causes unbelievable pleasure if spoken by a fool. For truthfulness has a certain inherent power of giving pleasure, if it contains nothing that gives offense. But the skill to manage this the gods have granted only to fools.

For almost the same reasons women, who naturally tend to be more inclined to pleasures and trifles, are extraordinarily fond of this kind of men. Accordingly, whatever they do with this sort of person (even though it is sometimes sufficiently serious),[1] they explain away as mere entertainment and amusement—as indeed the fair sex is quite clever, especially in covering up their faux pas.

5. Euripides *Bacch.* 369.
6. Cf. Euripides *Rhes.* 394–95, *Andr.* 451–52.
7. Juvenal 3.30.
8. In fables of Avianus (Hervieux 29) and Aesop (Chambry 60, Perry 35).
9. See Erasmus, *Educ. Chr. Pr.*, pp. 195–97.
1. Folly coyly refers to sexual liaisons. See Willeford, pp. 11–12 and Ariosto *Orlando Furioso* 28.34–36.

Therefore, to return to the happiness of simpletons, having lived their lives with great joy, with no fear or even awareness of death, they depart directly to the Elysian fields, where their antics continue to delight the leisurely souls of the blessed.

And now let us compare the lot of this fool with any wiseman whatsoever. Imagine, if you please, a model of wisdom to set over against the fool: a man who has wasted his whole childhood and youth in mastering the branches of learning and has lost the sweetest part of life in sleepless nights and endless painstaking labors, a man who even in the rest of his life has not tasted the tiniest crumb of pleasure, always frugal, poor, gloomy, surly, unfair and harsh to himself, severe and hateful to others, wasted away into a pale, thin, sickly, blear-eyed figure, old and gray long before his time, hastening to a premature grave—though what does it matter when such a person dies, since he never really lived at all? And there you have a fine picture of your wiseman.[2]

But here *the frogs of the Stoic ilk*[3] croak at me once again. "Nothing," they say, "is more miserable than madness. But extraordinary folly is either very close to madness or is actually identical with it. For what does it mean to be mad but to be of unsound mind?"[4] But these cavilers are completely 'on the wrong track.'[5] Come, let us demolish this syllogism also, with the help of the Muses.[6] The argument is clever indeed, but just as Plato's Socrates taught when he divided one Venus into two and split one Cupid into two,[7] so

2. Folly congratulates herself on her use of the rhetorical figure *effictio* (*Op.* 5, 1010E).

3. As Lister notes, frogs were traditionally associated in biblical exegesis with sophistical and garrulous argumentation.

4. Horace *serm.* 2.3.221; Seneca *epist.* 94.17; Cicero *tusc.* 3.4.8–3.5.10.

5. *Adag.* 48; Terence *eun.* 245.

6. In *Adag.* 2589, Erasmus notes that this phrase is sometimes applied to an ignorant person who pretends to learning. Doubtless Folly is aware that the Muses can be expected to provide little help in refuting a syllogism by making a distinction.

7. In Plato *symp.* 180d–81e, Pausanias divides Venus and Cupid into earthly and heavenly forms by distinguishing bodily love (including sexual love) from the love by which the soul ascends to the divine.

these dialecticians should have distinguished[8] one kind of madness from the other if they ever intended to pass for sane themselves. For every sort of madness is not necessarily disastrous, in and of itself. Otherwise Horace would not have said "Or am I beguiled by a lovely madness";[9] nor would Plato have placed the frenzy of poets, prophets, and lovers among the chief goods of life;[1] nor would the prophetess have called the labor of Aeneas mad.[2]

For there are two kinds of madness: one which is sent up from the underworld by the avenging Furies whenever they dart forth their serpents and inspire in the breasts of mortals a burning desire for war, or unquenchable thirst for gold, or disgraceful and wicked lust, or parricide, incest, sacrilege, or some other such plague, or when they afflict the guilty thoughts of some criminal with the maddening firebrands of terror.[3] There is another kind far different from the first, namely the kind which takes its origin from me and is most desirable.[4] It occurs whenever a certain pleasant mental distraction relieves the heart from its anxieties and cares and at the same time soothes it with the balm of manifold pleasures. Indeed, in a letter to Atticus, Cicero wishes for this mental distraction as a great gift from the gods, because it would have deprived him of all awareness of the great evils around him.[5] Nor was there anything wrong with the judgment of the Greek who was so mad that he sat alone in the theater for whole days on end, laughing, applauding, enjoying himself, because he thought that wonderful tragedies were being

8. See below, p. 88.

9. Horace *carm.* 3.4.5–6.

1. In Plato *Phaedr.* 244a–45a, 265a–b, Socrates explains how the four forms of frenzy or furor (poetic, Bacchic, prophetic, and erotic) move the soul in its ascent to the divine.

2. Virgil *aen.* 6.135.

3. The fullest portrayal of the Furies or Erinyes is Aeschylus' *Eumenides,* but Folly is thinking especially of the madness inspired by Allecto in Virgil *aen.* 7, *passim* (see also, 4.469–73).

4. Cf. Cicero *tusc.* 3.4.9–3.5.11.

5. Hudson (p. 149) points out that Cicero (*Att.* 3.13) does not say what Folly here attributes to him. Erasmus probably intended to show Folly deliberately twisting Cicero's words. (Lister was apparently taken in by the sophistry.)

acted there, whereas nothing at all was being performed. But in the other duties of life he conducted himself very well: he was cheerful with his friends, agreeable with his wife; he could overlook the faults of his servants and not fly into a mad rage when he found a winejar had been secretly tapped. Through the efforts of his friends he took some medicine which cured him of his disease, but when he was completely himself again, he took issue with his friends in this fashion: "Damn it all!" he said, "you have killed me, my friends, not cured me, by thus wresting my enjoyment from me and forcibly depriving me of a most pleasant delusion."[6] And rightly enough. For they were the ones who were deluded, and they had more need of hellebore[7] than he did, since they thought such a felicitous and gratifying madness was some kind of evil that needed to be expelled by means of potions.

But in fact I haven't yet decided whether just any error of the senses or the mind ought to be designated by the name madness. Certainly, if a man with poor eyesight thinks a mule is an ass,[8] or if someone takes a piece of doggerel for a very skillful poetic composition, he does not immediately strike everyone as mad. But if a person is deceived not only in the perceptions of his senses but also in the judgments of his mind, and if his deception is continual and beyond the usual share, only then will he be thought to verge on madness[9]—as, for instance, if a person who hears an ass braying thinks he is listening to a marvelous choir, or if some poor beggar, born into the very lowest level of society, believes he is Croesus, king of Lydia.[1] But this kind of madness, if it errs in the direction of pleasure (as it usually does), brings no small share of delight both to those who experience it and to those who observe it without being mad

6. Horace *epist.* 2.2.128–40.

7. Used to cure madness. *Adag.* 751; Dioscorides 4.148.1; Horace *serm.* 2.3.82 and *ars* 300.

8. One proverbial expression (Tertulian *adv. Val.* 1912) equates the two animals as symbols of stupidity; another (Theognis 996; *Adag.* 2055) stresses the great superiority of the mule.

9. Socrates makes a similar distinction in Xenophon *mem.* 3.9.6–7.

1. Proverbial for his wealth (*Adag.* 574).

to the same degree themselves. For this species of madness is far more widespread than most people realize. But one madman mocks another, and they maintain between them a mutual interchange of merriment. And not infrequently you see the greater madman laugh louder at the less.[2] Still, everyone is all the happier the more ways he is deluded, as far as Folly can judge, as long as he remains within the category of madness that belongs peculiarly to us—a category which is in fact so widespread that I hardly know whether anyone at all can be found from the whole sum of mortals who is always impeccably wise[3] and who is not subject to some kind of madness. The real difference is only this: the man who sees a cucumber[4] and thinks it is a woman is labeled mad[5] because this happens very rarely. But if a man who shares his wife in common with many other men nevertheless swears that she is more faithful than Penelope[6] and warmly congratulates himself in his ignorant bliss, no one calls him mad because they see that this sort of thing happens to husbands everywhere.

This class of madness also includes those who look down on everything except hunting wild animals[7] and whose spirits are incredibly exhilarated whenever they hear the nerve-shattering blasts on the horns or the baying of the hounds. I imagine that even the dung of the dogs smells like cinnamon to them. And then what exquisite pleasure they feel when the quarry is to be butchered! Lowly peasants may butcher bulls and rams, but only a nobleman may cut up wild animals. Baring his head and kneeling down, he takes a special blade set aside for that purpose (for it would hardly do to use just any knife) and exercises the most devout precision in

2. Horace *serm.* 2.3.326.

3. *Adag.* 1329; Pliny *HN* 7.41.136.

4. Lister, a physician, points out that such an hallucination is caused by a disease of the imaginative faculty. The Latin word for "cucumber" ("cucurbita") could also mean "cupping-glass" (Pliny *HN* 32.42.123; Celsus 2.10.1–2), which was used to treat madmen (Juvenal 14.57–58) and was proverbial for "blockhead" (Otto No. 472).

5. Horace *serm.* 2.3.46–47.

6. The faithful wife of Odysseus in Homer's *Odyssey*.

7. Cf. More's strictures against hunters in *Utopia* (*CW* 4, 170/5–28n).

cutting up just these parts, with just these movements, in just this order.[8] Meanwhile, the surrounding crowd stands in silent wonder, as if they were seeing some new religious ceremony, although they have beheld the same spectacle a thousand times before. Then, whoever gets a chance to taste some of the beast is quite convinced that he has gained no small share of added nobility.[9] Thus, though these men have accomplished nothing more by constantly chasing and eating wild animals than to lower themselves almost to the level of the animals they hunt, still in the meantime they think they are living like kings.

Very like them is the sort of men who burn with an insatiable desire to build, replacing round structures with square and square with round.[1] Nor is there an end to it, nor any limit, until they are reduced to such utter poverty that nothing at all is left—neither place to live nor food to eat. What of it? In the meantime they have passed several years with the greatest pleasure.

The group that comes closest to these builders, I think, consists of those who strive to change one substance into another by means of novel, occult arts, and move heaven and earth to track down a certain fifth element or "quintessence."[2] This honied hope entices them so powerfully that they spare no effort or expense. They are wonderfully clever in thinking up some new way to deceive themselves. They cheat themselves with a pleasing sort of fraud, until they have spent everything and don't even have enough left to fire their furnaces. But still they never stop dreaming sweet dreams, and they also do everything they can to encourage others to pursue the

8. Lister remarks that such punctilios were common in England. On the elaborate process of cutting up a deer, see J. D. Bruce in *Englische Studien*, *32* (1903), 23–36.

9. Parts of the deer were distributed to the hunters according to a precise order of precedence (Julian Barnes, *Boke of Huntyng*, ed. G. Tilander, Cynegetica XI, Karlshamn, 1964, p. 74).

1. Horace *epist.* 1.1.100; Martial 9.46.

2. The purest extract of all corporeal things (which consist of mixtures of the other four elements). This quintessence (or elixir, or philosopher's stone), the goal of the alchemists, could change base metals to gold and cure all diseases. Erasmus wrote two colloquies against alchemy (*Coll.*, pp. 238–45, 248–54).

same happiness. Even when they have been completely deprived of all hope whatsoever, there is still one saying left—a great comfort indeed: "in great affairs the intent alone's enough."[3] And then they rail against the shortness of life, because it is inadequate for an enterprise of such great moment.[4]

As to gamblers, I am in some doubt whether they should be admitted to our fellowship. But still it is a foolish and altogether absurd spectacle to see some of them so addicted to it that their hearts leap up and throb as soon as they hear the clatter of the dice. Finally, when the hope of winning has kept luring them onward until they suffer the shipwreck of all their resources, ⟨splitting the ship of their fortune against the dice-reef (hardly less fearful than the coast of Malea),[5]⟩ and when they have barely escaped from the sea with the shirts on their backs, they will cheat anyone rather than the winner of their money, lest anyone should think they are not men of honor. What shall we say when even old men[6] who are already half-blind go on playing with the aid of eye-glasses? Or when they pay good money to hire a stand-in to roll the dice for them because their own finger-joints have been crippled by a well-earned attack of gout?[7] A pleasant spectacle indeed, except that sometimes such gambling ends in violent quarrels and hence falls into the province of the Furies,[8] not in mine.

But there can be no question at all that another group is entirely enlisted 'under my banner'[9]: those who delight in hearing or telling miracles and monstrous lies.[1] They can never get enough of such

3. Propertius 2.10.6.
4. Cf. Seneca *brev. vit.* 1.1–3.
5. Folly puns on Malea (a promontory dangerous to ships) and "alea" (a die).
6. In ancient times, old men were supposed to be fond of dicing because it required little physical effort (Cicero *sen.* 16.58; Suetonius *Aug.* 71.1–2).
7. Horace *serm.* 2.7.14–18.
8. See above, p. 58, footnote 3.
9. Literally, "of my flour" (*Adag.* 2444; Persius 5.115).
1. Lister refers to More's translation of Lucian's *Philopseudes* (*CW 3*, part 1, 44–77). In his preface, More argues that the satire of a pagan might be used to advantage against the superstition of Christians (*ibid.*, 4–5). Superstitious credulity about ghostly apparitions is the principal target of Erasmus' *Exorcism* (*Coll.*, pp. 230–37).

tales whenever strange horrors are told about apparitions, ghosts, specters, dead souls, and thousands of such marvels as these. And the further such tall tales are from the truth, the more easily they gain credence and the more delicately they tickle the ears of the listeners. Besides, they are not only wonderfully useful in relieving the boredom of the passing hours, but they also produce a fine profit, especially for priests and preachers.[2]

Closely related to such men are those who have adopted the very foolish (but nevertheless quite agreeable) belief that if they look at a painting or statue of that huge Polyphemus Christopher,[3] they will not die on that day;[4] or, if they address a statue of Barbara with the prescribed words, they will return from battle unharmed;[5] or, if they accost Erasmus on certain days, with certain wax tapers, and in certain little formulas of prayer, they will soon become rich.[6] Moreover, in George they have discovered a new Hercules,[7] just as

2. Lister notes how carefully Erasmus has chosen Folly's language here. See below, pp. 157–60.

3. On Polyphemus, see Virgil *aen.* 3.658–59, 664–65, and p. 27, footnote 9, above. Gigantic images of Christopher were commonly placed in churches, especially in the fifteenth century (see Erasmus *Coll.*, p. 301, and É. Mâle, *L'Art religieux de la fin du moyen age*, Paris, 1922, p. 185).

4. A Latin couplet to this effect was often inscribed below Christopher's image.

5. Though St. Barbara was patroness against lightning and explosions, it was also believed that she could grant the favor of not dying without the last sacraments (É. Mâle, *L'Art religieux*, p. 186), which could not normally be received by the soldier dying on the battlefield.

6. St. Erasmus, an Italian bishop, was martyred about 305 after Christ by having his intestines drawn out by a winch. Hence, he was invoked against intestinal ailments and (through a misunderstanding of the winch as a nautical instrument) against tempests at sea. St. Elmo's fire, the static electricity in the shrouds of sailing ships, is derived from his name. Since there is no evidence that he was invoked by those who wished to get rich quick, Erasmus is almost surely making a quiet joke about his own namesake. Erasmus had written with passionate precision against the superstitious worship of the saints in *Enchiridion* (p. 99) and would do so again in his note on *Rom.* 13 : 21 (*Op. 6*, 634C). He defended what he had written about the worship of the saints in his response to Alberto Pio (*Op. 9*, 1162B–63D).

7. St. George was assimilated to Hercules because the hero killed the Lernean

they have found a new Hippolytus.[8] They all but worship George's horse, most religiously decked out in breastplates and bosses, and from time to time oblige him with some little gift.[9] To swear by his bronze helmet is thought to be an oath fit for a king.

Now what shall I say about those who find great comfort in soothing self-delusions about fictitious pardons for their sins, measuring out the times in purgatory down to the droplets of a waterclock, parceling out centuries, years, months, days, hours, as if they were using mathematical tables?[1] Or what about those who rely on certain little magical tokens and prayers thought up by some pious impostor for his own amusement or profit? They promise themselves anything and everything: wealth, honor, pleasure, an abundance of everything, perpetual health, a long life, flourishing old age, and finally a seat next to Christ among the saints, though this last they don't want for quite a while yet—that is, when the pleasures of this life, to which they cling with all their might, have finally slipped through their fingers, then it will be soon enough to enter into the joys of the saints. Imagine here, if you please, some businessman or soldier or judge who thinks that if he throws into the collection basket one coin from all his plunder, the whole cesspool[2] of his sinful life will be immediately wiped out. He thinks all

---

hydra as the saint killed the dragon (H. Delehaye, *Les Légendes Hagiographiques*, Brussels, 1905, p. 194).

8. St. Hippolytus, like the classical Hippolytus (*Adag.* 2565), was destroyed by wild horses (*Acta Sanctorum*, 13 August III, Antwerp, 1737, *36*, 6). The parallel between the two is presented by Prudentius *peristeph.* 11.86–89.

9. This remark was particularly telling in England, where it was not uncommon to place life-size statues of the saint—horse, dragon, and all—in important churches.

1. In a long defensive note, Lister makes it clear that "pardons" refer to indulgences, which (understood precisely) signified the remission of the temporal punishment due to sins already repented and confessed (punishment which must be paid during life on earth or in purgatory after death). They were normally expressed in years and days because they emerged gradually from lists of appropriate or commuted penances assigned in confession. These lists were expressed in terms of the required time of fasting or doing some other penance. As applied to indulgences, the times ceased to have any real referent; they were not intended to represent days spent in purgatory.

2. Literally, "Lernean swamp of evils" (*Adag.* 227).

his acts of perjury, lust, drunkenness, quarreling, murder, deception, dishonesty, betrayal are paid off like a mortgage, and paid off in such a way that he can start off once more on a whole new round of sinful pleasures.

Now who could be more foolish—rather, who could be happier —than those who assure themselves they will have the very ultimate felicity because they have recited daily those seven little verses from the holy psalms? A certain devil—certainly a merry one, but too loose-lipped to be very clever—is believed to have mentioned them to St. Bernard, but the poor devil was cheated by a clever trick.[3] Such absurdities are so foolish that even I am almost ashamed of them, but still they are approved not only by the common people but even by learned teachers of religion.

And then too, isn't it pretty much the same sort of nonsense when particular regions lay claim to a certain saint, when they parcel out particular functions to particular saints,[4] and assign to particular saints certain modes of worship: one offers relief from a toothache, another helps women in labor, another restores stolen goods; one shines as a ray of hope in a shipwreck, another takes care of the flocks[5]—and so on with the others, for it would take far too long to list all of them. Some saints have a variety of powers, especially the virgin mother of God, to whom the ordinary run of men attribute more almost than to her son.[6]

3. A devil appeared to St. Bernard and told him he knew seven verses of the psalms, which, if recited daily, would ensure that a person go to heaven. When the devil refused to tell the saint which they were, St. Bernard replied that he would simply say the whole psalter every day. To avoid the greater good, the devil was forced to reveal the verses. The verses, together with an account of their origin, were included in Thomas More's prayer book (ed. L. Martz and R. Sylvester, New Haven, 1969, p. xxvii) and in many Books of Hours.

4. In L. Réau's *Iconographie de l'art chrétien* (Paris, 1959, vol. 3) the patron saints of countries, provinces, and cities occupy twenty-five pages; the patrons of religious orders, guilds, and trades, twenty pages.

5. Apart from women saints (Folly's pronouns are all masculine), Sts. Medard and Christopher were invoked against toothache; Sts. Leonard and Erasmus, during childbirth; St. Anthony of Padua, against the loss of stolen goods; St. Erasmus, against shipwreck; Sts. Blaise, Anthony, and Bovus, among others, were invoked to protect cattle.

6. In *Coll.* (pp. 289–91) Erasmus gives a list of foolish petitions to the Virgin.

But what do men end up asking from these saints except things that pertain to folly? Just think, among all the votive tablets that you see covering the walls and even the ceilings of some churches, have you ever seen anyone who escaped from folly or who became the least bit wiser? One saved his life by swimming. Another was stabbed by an enemy but recovered. Another, with no less luck than bravery, fled from the battle while the rest were fighting. Another who had been hung on the gallows fell down by the favor of some saint friendly to thieves,[7] so that he could proceed in his career of disburdening those who are sadly overburdened by their riches. Another escaped by breaking out of jail. Another, much to the chagrin of his physician, recovered from a fever. For another, a poisonous potion, because it worked as a purge, was curative rather than fatal, though his wife (who lost her effort and expense) was not exactly overjoyed at the result.[8] Another, whose wagon had overturned, drove his horses home uninjured. Another, buried by the collapse of a building, was not killed. Another, caught by a husband, managed to get away.[9] No one gives thanks for escaping from folly. To lack all wisdom is so very agreeable that mortals will pray to be delivered from anything rather than from folly.

But why have I embarked on this vast sea of superstitions?

> Not if I had a hundred tongues, a hundred mouths,
> A voice of iron, could I survey all kinds
> Of fools, or run through all the forms of folly.[1]

So rife, so teeming with such delusions is the entire life of all Christians everywhere. And yet priests are not unwilling to allow and even foster such delusions because they are not unaware of how many emoluments accumulate from this source. In the midst of all

7. Among the saints who were said to have saved thieves from hanging are Erasmus and Quentin.

8. Ausonius 19.3 (*epigr.* 10).

9. In Erasmus' *Coll.* (pp. 243–44), an adulterer attributes his escape from his mistress' husband to the help of the Virgin.

1. Adapted from Virgil *aen.* 6.625–27 (which is in turn modelled on Homer's *il.* 2.489–90).

this, if some odious wiseman should stand up and sing out the true state of affairs: "You will not die badly if you live well. You redeem your sins if to the coin you add a hatred of evil deeds, then tears, vigils, prayers, fasts, and if you change your whole way of life. This saint will help you if you imitate his life"[2]—if that wiseman were to growl out such assertions and more like them, look how much happiness he would immediately take away from the minds of mortals, look at the confusion he would throw them into!

Of the same stripe are those who prescribe in great detail, while they are still alive, how they wish to be buried,[3] giving exact numbers for the torches, the people in mourning garments, the singers, the official mourners[4] that they want in the funeral procession, as if they could have any awareness of this spectacle or as if the dead would be ashamed unless their corpses were grandly planted in the ground—they seem for all the world like political candidates staging a campaign dinner complete with entertainers.

Even though I am in a hurry, I can hardly pass over in silence those who preen themselves on the empty title of nobility, even though they are no different from the lowliest shoemaker. One traces his ancestry back to Aeneas, another to Brut, another to Arthur.[5] Everywhere they display statues and pictures of their

2. Erasmus often stressed that imitation is the best worship of the Virgin and saints (*Op. 1*, 782C; *5*, 31C–D, 1329B; *9*, 1163E).

3. Wills were often quite detailed and precise about the matters Folly mentions. The sumptuous funeral of Henry VII (who gave instructions for his black marble tomb in his will) took place from May 8 to 10, 1509, not long before Erasmus wrote the *Folly*. In his first will, Erasmus directed that his heir provide for him a funeral neither shabby nor lavish, but even this stipulation disappeared in his second will (*Ep. 6, 503–06; 11, 362–65*)

4. Horace *ars* 431–32.

5. Brutus (Brut), grandson of Aeneas, was the eponymous founder of Britain according to Geoffrey of Monmouth (who is also the prime source for the story of King Arthur). Henry VII and his Tudor successors encouraged the belief that their house was descended from King Arthur (for this very reason the elder brother of Henry VIII, who died in 1502, had been named Arthur). The collocation of three ancient progenitors of the English dynasty makes it unlikely that Erasmus intended "Arcturus" to refer to the star mentioned by Cicero (*nat.* 2.42.110).

ancestors, they count up their great-grandfathers and great-great-grandfathers, they rehearse their ancient family names, while they themselves are not much better than dumb statues, almost inferior to the very symbols they display. And yet this pleasant Selflove[6] enables them to lead an altogether happy life. Nor is there any lack of others, equally foolish, who revere this class of beasts as if they were gods.

But why should I be talking about one group or another, as if such Selflove did not render almost everyone ⟨everywhere⟩ most happy in a variety of marvelous ways? One man who is uglier than any monkey is quite confident that he is as handsome as Nereus.[7] Another, as soon as he can draw three lines with a compass, immediately thinks he is another Euclid. Another, who sounds like an 'ass playing a harp'[8] and who sings no better than the bird that gives the hen uxorious nips,[9] still thinks he is another Hermogenes.[1] But by far the most entertaining kind of madness is the sort which causes some people to boast of any talent among their servants as if it were their own. This was displayed by that twice-blessed rich man in Seneca who always kept servants at hand when he intended to tell an anecdote so that they could prompt him with the names. He wouldn't have hesitated to engage in a fist fight (though he himself was so infirm he was just barely alive) because he relied on the many strapping servants he had at home.[2]

As for professors of the arts, why bother to mention them?—since Selflove is the special prerogative of all of them, so much so that you will sooner find one who will accept the loss of his father's farm than one who will accept second rank in intelligence.[3] But this is especially true of actors, singers, orators, and poets: the more ignorant anyone of them is, the more arrogant his self-complacence,

6. See above, p. 17, footnote 5.
7. See above, p. 35, footnote 4.
8. See above, p. 39, footnote 5.
9. Juvenal 3.90–91; Quintilian *inst.* 9.3.51.
1. A famous singer at the court of Caesar Augustus. Horace *serm.* 1.9.25, 1.3.129–30.
2. Seneca *epist.* 27.4–6.
3. Martial 8.18.9–10.

conceit, and braggadocio. And 'birds of a feather', or like will to like[4]—in fact, the less skillful anything is, the more admirers it obtains, according to the rule that the worst things usually please most people, because the majority of men, as we said, are subject to folly. Therefore, if a man acquires more pleasure for himself and more admiration from others according to the depth of his ignorance, why on earth should he choose real learning? First of all it costs a great deal, and then it will make him more disagreeable and timid, and finally it will please far fewer people.

Then again, I see that Nature has not only given every mortal his own brand of Selflove but has also grafted a sort of communal form of it to particular nations and even cities.[5] Hence it is that the British lay claim above all to good looks, music, and fine food.[6] The Scots pride themselves on their nobility and close blood-ties to the royal house, not to mention dialectical subtlety. The French claim for themselves refinement of manners.[7] The Parisians arrogate to themselves theological learning, to the exclusion of almost everyone else. The Italians lay claim to literature and eloquence, and on one point they all preen themselves most complacently: that, of all mortals, they alone are not barbarians.[8] In this sort of happiness the Romans lead the way, and still dream sweet dreams about that ancient Rome of theirs.[9] The Venetians are happy in their reputation for nobility. The Greeks, as the founders of the various branches of learning, emblazon themselves with the ancient renown of their famous heroes.[1] The Turks and all that scum of the real barbarians claim for themselves the praise due to religion, ridiculing Christians

---

4. *Adag.* 971.

5. See below, p. 146.

6. Cf. *Adag.* 1168.

7. See Erasmus *Coll.*, p. 148.

8. In his letters, Erasmus often notes this Italian arrogance.

9. Erasmus insisted on the superiority of Christian Rome to ancient Rome (*Op.* 7, 771). On his conflict with Roman purists and his double attitude toward Rome itself, see A. Renaudet, *Érasme et l'Italie* (Geneva, 1954), pp. 202–05, 246–47.

1. Cf. Erasmus' note on *Rom.* 1: 14 (*Op. 6,* 561E–F). Cicero calls famous non-military men (e.g., Cato, Plato, and Aristotle) "heroes."

precisely because of their superstitions. But the Jews have it even better, still waiting faithfully for their Messiah and clinging to their Moses tooth and nail even to this day.[2] Spaniards yield to no one in military glory. The Germans pride themselves on their tallness and their knowledge of magic.[3] But, not to run through all of them one by one, you see (I think) how much pleasure Selflove everywhere supplies to individual mortals and to mankind as a whole, and in this function her sister Flattery is almost her equal.

For Selflove is nothing but the soothing praise which a person bestows on himself. If he bestows it on someone else, then it is *Kolakia*.[4] Nowadays flattery is thought of as disreputable, but only by people who are more concerned about words than about things themselves. They judge that flattery is inconsistent with good faith. That the fact is quite otherwise, we can learn even by examples drawn from dumb animals. Is there any animal more fawning than a dog? But then again, is there any more faithful? Is any creature more obsequious than a squirrel? But is any more friendly to man?[5] Unless perhaps you think fierce lions or cruel tigers or treacherous panthers contribute more to man's life! True, there is a certain kind of flattery which is altogether destructive, the kind employed by some unprincipled cynics to ruin their wretched victims. But this Flattery of mine proceeds from a kind disposition and a certain frankness which is much closer to a virtue than the opposite qualities, "sourness" and peevishness, "jangling" (as Horace says) "and dour."[6] This kind of flattery gives a lift to those whose spirits are low, consoles those who mourn, stimulates the apathetic, rouses the dull, cheers the sick, tames the fierce, unites lovers and keeps them

2. Erasmus' attitude toward the Jews is more complex than Folly's (Ep. *1*, 17; *5*, 168; *6*, 489).

3. Two prominent Germans associated with the occult arts were Johann Trittenheim (Trithemius) and Cornelius Agrippa. The first reference to Georg Faust, the shadowy but historical magician who lies behind the Faust legend, occurs in a letter of Trittenheim (20 August 1507).

4. See above, p. 17.

5. Cf. Martial 5.37.12–13.

6. Horace *epist.* 1.18.6.

united. It entices children to learn their lessons,[7] it cheers up old people, it advises and teaches princes under the cover of an encomium, without giving offense.[8] In short, it makes everyone more agreeable and indulgent to himself—and this is surely the chief ingredient of happiness. What is more courteous than for one person to scratch another's back?[9] Not to mention that this flattery plays a large part in that eloquence everyone praises, a larger in medicine, and the largest of all in poetry[1]—in sum, it is the honey and spice of all human intercourse.

But to be deceived, they say, is miserable. Quite the contrary—not to be deceived is most miserable of all. For nothing could be further from the truth than the notion that man's happiness resides in things as they actually are. It depends on opinions. For human affairs are so manifold and obscure that nothing can be clearly known, as is rightly taught by my friends the Academics, the least arrogant of the philosophers.[2] Or, if anything can be known, it often detracts from the pleasures of life. Finally, the human mind is so constituted that it is far more taken with appearances than reality. If anyone wants clear and obvious evidence of this fact, he should go to church during sermons: if the preacher is explaining his subject seriously, they all doze, yawn, and are sick of it. But if that screacher—I beg your pardon, I meant to say preacher—tells some old wive's tale, as they often do, the whole congregation sits up and listens with open mouths. Likewise, if any saint is more legendary or poetic—for example, think of George or Christopher or Barbara—you will see that such a saint is worshiped with far more devotion than Peter or Paul or Christ himself. But such things are out of place here.[3]

---

7. Lister wrote a long note contrasting the kind methods recommended by Horace and Quintilian with the brutal beatings administered by the schoolmasters of his own day.

8. See below, p. 143.

9. Literally, "for one mule to scratch another" (*Adag.* 696).

1. See above, p. 52, footnote 6.

2. Cicero *de or.* 3.18.67, *acad.* 1.3.7–8. Cf. Plato *apol.* 21d.

3. The place they pertain to is above, pp. 63–64.

And then, how much less it costs to gain such happiness! Sometimes it requires a great deal of effort to acquire the real article, even if it is something quite trivial, such as grammar. But to think you have acquired it—nothing could be easier, and yet such an opinion contributes as much or more to happiness. Consider, if someone eats a rotten pickled fish, the mere smell of which would be unbearable to another person, and yet the one who eats it thinks it tastes[4] like ambrosia, what difference does it make to his happiness? Conversely, if some delicacy like sturgeon turns another man's stomach, it will hardly add anything to his happiness. If someone who has an extraordinarily ugly wife still thinks that she could compete with Venus herself, isn't it quite the same as if she were really beautiful? If someone values and admires a canvas daubed with red and yellow, quite convinced that it is by Apelles or Zeuxis,[5] isn't he actually happier than the man who has paid a high price for the real work of those painters but who perhaps takes less pleasure in viewing them than the other man? I know a certain man named after me[6] who gave his bride some imitation gems, assuring her (and he is a clever jokester) that they were not only real and genuine but also that they were of unparalleled and inestimable value. I ask you, what difference did it make to the girl since she feasted her eyes and mind no less pleasantly on glass and kept them hidden among her things as if they were an extraordinary treasure? Meanwhile, the husband avoided expense and profited by his wife's mistake, nor was she any less grateful to him than if he had given her very costly gifts. Surely you don't believe that there is any difference between those who sit in Plato's cave gazing in wonder at the images and

4. In a passage which also mentions the sturgeon, Cicero (*fin.* 2.8.24) puns on the two meanings of "sapere" ("to taste," and "to be wise").

5. On these two famous Greek painters, see Pliny *HN* 35.10.36.79–97 and 61–72.

6. Lister says that Folly seems to be referring to someone named Morus. Though unhistorical anecdotes tended to gather around More, there is no evidence against this account and it has usually been accepted as a more or less factual reference to Thomas More, who married his first wife in 1505. See *CW* 4, 168–69, and above, p. 2, footnote 4.

likenesses of various things—as long as they desire nothing more and are no less pleased—and that wiseman who left the cave and sees things as they really are?[7] Now if Lucian's Mycillus had been allowed to dream forever that rich, golden dream of his, he would have had no reason to wish for any other happiness.[8]

Thus, there is either no difference, or if there is, the lot of fools is clearly preferable. First, because their happiness costs them so little—nothing more than a touch of persuasion. Then too, they enjoy it in common with most other men. And, of course, nothing is really enjoyable without someone to share it with.[9] And who does not know how few wisemen there are—if, in fact, any at all can be found? True, out of so many centuries the Greeks count seven altogether,[1] but if you examine even those very carefully, may I drop dead on the spot if you can find so much as a semi-wiseman, or even a hemi-demi-semi-wiseman.

Now, among the many benefits for which Bacchus is praised, the chief one is held (and rightly so) to be that he clears the mind of its troubles[2]—and that only for a short time, since as soon as you have slept off your little wine-drinking spree, all your anxieties come rushing back to your mind 'posthaste,'[3] as they say. But how much more ample and lasting is the benefit I provide, a sort of continuous inebriation which fills the mind with joy, delight, and exquisite pleasure—and all with no effort from you. Nor do I ever refuse any mortal a share of my gifts, whereas other endowments of the gods are distributed some to one, some to another. It is not every vineyard that produces a noble, mellow wine, one that drives away care, one that enriches us with surging hope.[4] Few have been en-

7. Plato *rep.* 514ab. Cf. Erasmus' *Enchiridion* 15.6, p. 133, and *Educ. Chr. Pr.*, p. 148.

8. Lucian *Somnium sive Gallus* 1 (tr. Erasmus, Amsterdam ed. *1*, part 1, 472.

9. Seneca *epist.* 6.4.

1. See above, p. 30.

2. Homer *il.* 6. 261; Horace *epist.* 1.5.16–20; Tibullus 1.2.1.

3. Literally, "with a team of four white horses" (*Adag.* 321; Horace *serm.* 1.7.8).

4. Horace *epist.* 1.15.18–21.

dowed with delicate beauty, the gift of Venus; even fewer with eloquence, a benefit given by Mercury. Not so very many have received wealth through the good offices of Hercules.[5] Homer's Jupiter has hardly granted everyone political supremacy. Very often Mars favors neither side.[6] Many depart quite disappointed from the tripod of Apollo's oracle. The son of Saturn often hurls his lightning bolt. Phoebus sometimes throws down missiles armed with the plague.[7] Neptune drowns more than he saves. I might also mention in passing such powers as Vejovis, Pluto, Ate, the Poenae,[8] the god of Fever and the like—not really gods, but tormentors. I, Folly, am the only one who embraces everyone equally with such ready and easy generosity. I do not care for[9] vows, nor do I grow angry and demand expiatory gifts if some point of ceremony is overlooked. Nor do I go on a rampage if someone invites the other gods and leaves me sitting at home with no share of the fragrant steam rising from the sacrificial victims.[1] For the other gods are so touchy about such things that it is more advantageous, and even safer, to leave them alone than to follow their cult—just as there are some men who are so hard to please and quick to take offense that it is better to have nothing at all to do with them than to cultivate their friendship.

But no one sacrifices to Folly, they say, and no one has built a temple dedicated to her. Indeed, I myself, as I said, find this ingratitude somewhat surprising. Still, I am good-natured enough to take

5. *Adag.* 73; Persius 2.10–12.

6. *Adag.* 3649 and 663.

7. Homer *il.* 1.9–10 and 43–54.

8. Vejovis was a malicious god, hostile to men; Pluto, the god of the underworld; Ate, the goddess of discord (see above, p. 26, footnote 9); the Poenae, goddesses of punishment.

9. The Latin word for "care for" ("*moror*") is a pun on Folly's name.

1. Eris, the goddess of discord, because she was not invited to the wedding feast of Peleus and Thetis, threw among the guests the apple marked "for the most beautiful" which led to the Trojan war (Lucian *conv. sive Lap.* 35, tr. Erasmus, Amsterdam ed. *1*, part 1, 613). For similar reasons, Diana sent a savage boar to devastate Calydon (Ovid *met.* 8. 279–83).

this also in good part, though I couldn't really want such things anyway. Why should I need a bit of incense or grain or a goat or a hog, when all mortals everywhere in the world worship me with the kind of homage that even the theologians rank highest of all?[2] Unless perhaps I should envy Diana because human blood is sacrificed in her honor![3] I consider that I am being worshiped with the truest devotion when men everywhere do precisely what they now do: embrace me in their hearts, express me in their conduct, represent me in their lives. Clearly this sort of devotion to the saints, even among Christians, is not exactly common. What a huge flock of people light candles to the virgin mother of God—even at noon, when there is no need! But how few of them strive to imitate her chastity, her modesty, her love for the things of heaven! For, in the last analysis, that is true worship, the kind which is by far the most pleasing to the saints in heaven. Furthermore, why should I want a temple, since the whole world, unless I am badly mistaken, is a splendid temple dedicated to me? Nor will there ever be a lack of worshipers, as long as there is no lack of men. Moreover, I am not so foolish as to require stone statues decked out in gaudy colors. For sometimes these are a drawback to the worship of us gods—that is, when stupid numbskulls adore the figures instead of the divinities, and then we are left in the position of those who have been edged out of their jobs by substitutes. I consider that as many statues have been set up for me as there are men who display, sometimes even unwillingly, a living image of me. And so, there is no reason why I should envy the other gods because each is worshiped in his own corner of the world, and on set days too—as, for example, Phoebus is honored at Rhodes, Venus on Cyprus, Juno at Argos,

---

2. That is, by imitation. In his *Summa Theologica*, Alexander of Hales (the irrefragable doctor), writing on the question "How saints should be worshiped," quotes St. Augustine: "We should honor saints for the sake of imitation; we should not make a religion out of their worship" (*CCSL 32*, 256).

3. The people of Tauris sacrificed all those shipwrecked on their coast to a virgin goddess identified by the Greeks with Diana (Strabo 5.3.12[C239]; Herodotus 4.103; Ovid *Pont.* 3.2.51–58 and *trist.* 4.4.63–64).

Minerva at Athens, Jupiter on Olympus, Neptune at Terentum, Priapus at Lampsacus[4]—as long as the whole world in perfect unanimity never ceases to offer me far superior victims.

Now if anyone thinks my claims reveal more boldness than truth, come on, let's examine the actual lives of men for a bit, to make it clear just how much they owe me—throughout all society from top to bottom—and how highly they value me.

But we will not survey the lives of any and all people, for that would take far too long, but only the lives of outstanding personages—from them it will be easy enough to judge the rest. What good would it do to talk about the common people, the mere mob, for there is no question that they all belong to me. Wherever you look they abound in so many forms of folly, and they think up so many new ones from day to day, that a thousand Democritus's would not be enough to laugh at them—though we would need one more Democritus to laugh at the thousand.[5] Indeed, you would hardly believe me if I told you how much laughter, sport, and delight these puny human creatures provide for the gods above. They spend the sober morning hours arbitrating disputes and listening to petitions.[6] But when they are soused with nectar and no longer want to do anything serious, then they take their seats at the place where heaven juts out farthest, and lean forward to watch what mankind is about. Nor could any other spectacle give them more enjoyment. Good lord, what a theater, how manifold the feverish fretting of fools! For I too sometimes take my regular seat in the ranks of the ⟨poetic⟩ gods. One man is head over heels in love with a wench, and the less she responds, the more helplessly he loves her. Another marries the dowry, not the wife. One man sets his own wife to sale. Another is so jealous he watches his wife like a hawk.[7] One man who is in mourning—good grief! what foolish things he says and

---

4. On these local cults, see Strabo 8.3.30(C353–54), 8.6.10(C372), 9.1.16 (C396), 14.2.5(C652), 14.6.3(C682–83); Horace *carm.* 1.28.29; Pliny *HN* 5.32.141; Virgil *georg.* 4.110–11.

5. See above, p. 2, footnote 5.

6. Lister notes that the following passage draws on Lucian *Icaromen.* (tr. Erasmus, Amsterdam ed. *1*, part 1, 410–22).

7. Literally, "like Argus" (see above, p. 32, footnote 2).

does! He even hires professional mourners, like actors, to put on a show of grief. Another weeps at his stepmother's grave.[8] One man spends on his belly whatever he can scrape together only to find himself starving not long afterwards.[9] One man can think of no greater happiness than sleeping and loafing. Some people bustle about minding other people's business, meanwhile neglecting their own. One man thinks he can get rich by refinancing and buying on credit—in no time at all he will be bankrupt. Another thinks the highest pitch of happiness is to impoverish himself in order to enrich his heir. One man skims over all the oceans in search of a trifling (and uncertain) profit, entrusting his life, which no amount of money can buy back, to the wind and the waves. Another would rather seek riches in warfare than lead a safe and leisurely life ⟨at home⟩. Some think the easiest way to get rich is to hunt for the legacies of childless old men.[1] Nor is there any shortage of men who hope to gain the same end by making love to rich old ladies.[2] For the gods watching the spectacle, both types provide the most extraordinary entertainment when the tricksters themselves are outwitted by their victims.[3] The most foolish and the meanest profession of all is that of merchants, since they seek the meanest goal by the meanest methods; even though they tell all manner of lies, perjure themselves, steal, cheat, deceive, still they think they outshine everyone else just because they wear gold rings on their fingers. Naturally, there is no lack of flattering friars who stand in awe of them and openly call them "venerable"—clearly for no other reason than to get a little share of their ill-gotten gain.[4] Elsewhere you can see some Pythagoreans who are so firmly committed to the principle that all goods should be held in common[5] that they

8. A proverbial example of hypocrisy (*Adag.* 810).

9. Cf. Horace *epist.* 1.15.32.

1. Horace *serm.* 2.5.23–26.

2. Juvenal 1.38–39.

3. Horace *serm.* 2.5.55–69; *Adag.* 914.

4. Lister notes condemnations of merchants by Cicero (*off.* 1.42.150) and several church fathers (the latter cited by Gratian *Decrees*, distinction 88).

5. Folly refers to the Pythagorean maxim, "Among friends all things are held in common" (*Adag.* 1).

carry away whatever they find unwatched, just as nonchalantly as if they had inherited it. Some speculators are rich only in wishful thinking; they dream up pleasant pipe-dreams and this they think is enough to keep a man happy.[6] Some are delighted to be considered rich by society at large; but in their own homes they take pains to go hungry. One man can't wait to spend whatever he has; another heaps and hoards by hook or crook. One man campaigns strenuously to win the favor of the voters; another amuses himself quietly by his own fireside. A great many persist in interminable lawsuits, suing and countersuing in an endless tug-of-war, and all to line the pockets of a judge who grants endless continuances and a lawyer who is in cahoots with his opponent. One man agitates to overthrow the government; another labors to carry out some momentous project. Some man will go to Jerusalem, Rome, or St. James of Compostella, where he has no business, abandoning his wife and children at home.[7] In brief, if you could look down from the moon, as Menippus once did, and see the innumerable broils of mortals, you would think you were looking at a great cloud of flies or gnats quarreling among themselves, warring, plotting, plundering, playing, frisking, being born, declining, dying.[8] It is downright incredible what tumults, what tragedies can be stirred up by such a tiny creature, so frail and short-lived. Sometimes even a slight blast of war or plague seizes, scatters, and destroys many thousands at one swoop.

But I myself would be most foolish and a very fitting target for the long and loud laughter of Democritus[9] if I should go on to enumerate the forms of folly and madness among the common people. I shall limit myself to those who have the appearance of wisdom in the eyes of mortals and who pursue, as they say, that golden bough of wisdom.[1]

6. Lucian *nav. sive vota* 18–25, 46.

7. See Erasmus' *Coll.* pp. 285–312.

8. A verbal imitation of Lucian *Icaromen.* 15 (Amsterdam ed. *1*, part 1, 415–16).

9. See above, p. 2, footnote 5.

1. Virgil's golden bough (*aen.* 6. 137) was allegorized by Fulgentius as "the pursuit of learning and knowledge" (*Verg. cont.* M154).

Among these the primacy is held by grammarians. No one could be more wretched, more miserable, more despised by the gods than they would be if I did not soften the hard lot of this most pitiful profession with a certain kind of sweet madness. For they are subject not merely to the πέντε κατάραις (that is, five afflictions) of the Greek epigram[2] but to hundreds of woes. Forever hungry and dirty in their classrooms—classrooms, did I say? no, "think-tanks,"[3] or rather sweat-shops or torture chambers—tending flocks of boys, they grow old in their labors, grow deaf from the noise, waste away in the stink and stench,[4] and yet through my favor they imagine they are the luckiest of mortals—so powerful is their flattering delusion while they terrify the timid band of pupils with threatening words and scowls and beat the poor wretches bloody with rods, switches, and straps, raging wildly with every imaginable sort of arbitrary cruelty, like the Cumaean ass.[5] And all the time that filth seems to them as neat as a pin, that stench smells like oil of marjoram, that most wretched slavery of theirs seems a life fit for a king, so much so that they wouldn't trade their tyrannical rule for the empire of Phalaris or Dionysius.[6] But what makes them even happier yet is a certain strange conviction they harbor about their learning. Though in fact most of them[7] pound nothing but sheer nonsense into the boys' heads, still, by all the gods! how they look down their noses even at Palaemon or Donatus![8] And by some magical trick, I can't imagine how, they manage to make the foolish mothers and stupid fathers take them to be what they claim to be.

2. *Anth. Pal.* 9.173 remarks that the first five lines of the *Iliad* present five calamities.

3. Aristophanes *nub.* 94.

4. Juvenal 7.225–26.

5. At Cumae an ass disguised in a lion's skin played the tyrant until he was exposed (*Adag.* 612 and 266).

6. On Phalaris, see above, p. 12, footnote 9. Lister alludes to the story that Dionysius, the tyrant of Syracuse, became a poor schoolmaster after he was deposed. *Adag.* 1793.

7. The qualification "most of them" was added in 1532.

8. Palaemon was a famous Roman grammarian of the first century after Christ. The *Ars grammatica* of Donatus, St. Jerome's teacher, was the standard Latin grammar until Erasmus' time.

Then, don't forget yet another kind of pleasure they have: when one of them discovers in some moldy manuscript the name of Anchises' mother or some word unknown to the common reader[9]— say, for example, "bubsequa" (neatherd), "bovinator" (tergiversator), or "manticulator" (pickpurse)—or if one of them digs up somewhere a piece of old rock with some fragmentary inscription on it, good lord! what a fuss they make, with rejoicing, triumphs, and encomia fit to celebrate the conquering of Africa or the capture of Babylon.[1] And then, the way they go around displaying everywhere their utterly bloodless and thoroughly insipid verses (which find no lack of admirers); naturally they themselves are quite certain that the inspiring genius of Virgil himself has entered their breast.[2] But the most amusing of all is to see them admiring and praising each other tit for tat, scratching each other's back.[3] But if someone else should make some little slip in diction and one of them who is more sharpsighted just happens by luck to catch it, *by Hercules*! in a flash the air is full of tragical commotions, and they are at each other's throats, hurling insults and invectives! ⟪And if I'm not telling the absolute truth, may all the grammarians join forces against me!

I know a certain *polymath*,[4] who knows Greek, Latin, mathematics, philosophy, and medicine (he is in fact *a physician for a king*), already in his sixties, who has abandoned everything else and for more than twenty years has been tormenting himself and beating out his brains about grammar. He would consider himself perfectly happy if he could live long enough to determine once and for all how the eight parts of speech can be distinguished from each

9. See above, p. 14.

1. The Scipios conquered Africa; Darius captured Babylon. Both events were proverbial for enormous achievements.

2. An allusion to Ennius' dream that Homer's soul had passed into his body (Persius *prol.* 2–3 and 6.10–11; Horace *epist.* 2.1.50–53).

3. *Adag.* 696.

4. This passage probably mocks the grammatical fanaticism of Thomas Linacre (1460?–1524) who became physician to Henry VIII in 1510. When Erasmus added this passage to the *Moria* in 1516, Linacre was almost sixty.

other—something which up to now no one has done to perfection in either Greek or Latin—for all the world as if it would be a sufficient reason to fight a war if someone should assign conjunctions to the province of adverbs. And for this reason, though there are almost as many grammars as grammarians—in fact there are even more, since my friend Aldus alone has issued a grammar more than five different times[5]—he never passes over a single one, no matter how barbarously or wretchedly written, without going through it and examining it, envying everyone who investigates this problem (however ineptly), living in an agony of fear that someone may snatch the glory of this achievement from him, and all those years of labor might be lost.》 Would you rather call this madness or folly? It makes little difference to me, as long as you grant that through my favor a creature who would otherwise be the most miserable wretch imaginable is elevated to such heights of happiness that he would refuse to change places with the kings of Persia.

The poets are less indebted to me, even though they are in fact professed members of my party, since they are classed as free spirits, as the proverb has it,[6] whose whole aim is nothing but to pamper the ears of fools, and to do it with sheer trifles and absurd fables. And yet, relying on such trifles, it is wonderful to see how they promise immortality and a life like that of the gods, not only to themselves but also to others.[7] Beyond all others this group is on intimate terms with *Philautia and Kolakia*, and no other class of mortals worships me with more single-minded fidelity.

As for rhetoricians, though they do indeed put up a false front by their specious alliance with the philosophers,[8] nevertheless it is clear

---

5. Aldus Manutius the elder published his own Latin grammar in 1501, 1508, and 1514. Besides the Greek grammars of Lascaris (1494), Gaza (1495), and Apollonius (1495), Aldus published his own Greek grammar in 1515. On Erasmus' relations with Aldus, see A. Renaudet, *Érasme et l'Italie* (Geneva, 1954), pp. 83–86.

6. "Poets and painters are a free race" (Lucian *imag.* 18). Horace *ars* 9–10. *Adag.* 2048.

7. Horace *carm.* 3.30.1, 4.8.28–29, 9.25–29.

8. Cicero *de or.* 1.15.68–69, 2.36–37 and 152–56. Quintilian *inst.* 10.1.35, 12.2.4–28.

that they too belong to our party, as is shown by many indications, but especially this one: besides many other trivial topics, they have written so much and so meticulously about how to make jokes.[9] In fact, the author who wrote to Herennius about rhetoric, whoever he was, even goes so far as to list folly among the types of wit.[1] And Quintilian, who is clearly the prince of rhetoricians, has a chapter on laughter[2] that is longer than the whole Iliad.[3] Finally, they think so highly of folly as to hold that oftentimes an argument which cannot be refuted in any other way should be glossed over with laughter—unless someone imagines that it is not the prerogative of Folly to provoke horselaughs with funny sayings, and to do it by the book at that.

Of the same stripe[4] are those who strive to win eternal fame by issuing books. All of them owe a great deal to me, but especially those who scribble pages of sheer nonsense. As for those who write learnedly for the judgment of a few scholars and would not hesitate to have their books reviewed by such true judges as Persius or Laelius,[5] they seem to me more pitiable than happy because their work is a perpetual torment to them. They add, they alter; they blot something out, they put it back in. They do the work over, they recast it, they show it to friends, they keep it for nine years,[6] and still they are never satisfied. At such a price they buy an empty reward, namely praise, and that from only a handful. They buy it with such an expense of long hours, so much loss of that sweetest of all things, sleep,[7] so much sweat, so much agony. Reckon up also the loss of health, the spoiling of their good looks, weak eyesight (or even blindness), poverty, envy, the denial of pleasures,

---

9. Cicero *de or.* 2.54 and 217–22, 2.58–71 and 235–91. Quintilian *inst.* 6.3.

1. *Rhet. ad Her.* 1.6.10. In the fifteenth century scholars began to realize that *rhet. ad .Her.* was not actually written by Cicero.

2. *Inst.* 6.3.

3. *Adag.* 3451.

4. See above, p. 62, footnote 9.

5. Cicero *de or.* 2.6.25, *fin.* 1.3.7.

6. Horace *ars* 388.

7. Homer *od.* 7.289, *il.* 1.610. Theocritus 11.22–23.

premature old age, early death, and other things just as bad, if there are any. Such great suffering your wiseman thinks is fully repaid by the approval of one or two blear-eyed readers. But my writer is far more happily deluded, as he writes away without any thought, putting right down on paper whatever he likes, whatever pops into his head, even his dreams. He has nothing to lose but some sheets of paper, for he knows that the more trivial the trifles he writes, the larger his following will be, made up as it is of all the fools and dolts. For what does he care if two or three learned men find his work contemptible—assuming, that is, that they ever read it. What good would it do to win the palm from so few wisemen, since their approval is offset by the jeers of such a huge mob? Even smarter, though, are the writers who publish the work of others as their own, and by such verbal juggling shift to themselves the glory for which someone else has labored long and hard.[8] They do it with full assurance about what will happen: even if they should be exposed as the most shameless plagiarists, still, in the meantime, they will enjoy the credit of the achievement for a while anyway.

It is worth your while to watch how pleased they are with themselves when they are praised by the ordinary reader, when someone points them out in a crowd with "*There is that remarkable man,*"[9] when they are advertised in front of the booksellers' shops, when their full names with all three parts[1] are there to be read on all the title pages—especially when those names are foreign and sound like the strange words of a magician's spell.[2] Good lord! what are they, after all, but names? Then, how very few will know them, if you consider the enormous size of the whole wide world. And even fewer will praise them, since even the ignorant have various tastes and preferences. Then too, even those names themselves are often

8. See Erasmus' note on *Tim.* 1 : 10 (*Op. 6,* 928F).

9. Diogenes Laertius 6.34; Persius 1.28; Horace *carm.* 4.3.22.

1. To the Romans the three names were a sign of nobility (Quintilian, *inst.* 7.3.27; Juvenal 5.125–27). "Desiderius Erasmus Roterodamus" appeared regularly on the title-pages of the early editions of *The Praise of Folly.*

2. The humanists often translated their names literally into Latin or Greek. Thus, Desmarais became Paludanus and Schwarzerd became Melanchthon.

made up or borrowed from the books of ancient writers. One of them is fond of being called Telemachus; another, Stelenus or Laertes; one, Polycrates; another, Thrasymachus[3]—so that it wouldn't make any difference if the books were assigned to "Chameleon"[4] or "Cucumber"[5] or simply designated "A" or "B" in the terminology common among philosophers.[6]

But the most charming thing is to see them praise each other, tit for tat, by exchanging epistles, poems, and encomia, fool praising fool and dolt lauding dolt. One thinks another has come off as well as Alcaeus and is repaid by being dubbed a veritable Callimachus.[7] One thinks another superior to Cicero and in return is called more learned than Plato. Sometimes they also search out an opponent so as to increase their fame by entering the lists against him. Then the uncertain mob is split into opposing camps,[8] until finally each champion has fought so well as to come off winner, and each celebrates the victory. Wisemen ridicule such antics as supremely foolish, and indeed they are. Who denies it? But meanwhile, through my favor, they lead such a pleasant life that they wouldn't exchange their triumphs with the Scipios.[9] Though even the learned, while they find such soul-soothing satisfaction in laughing at these things and enjoy the madness of others,[1] they themselves are more than a little

3. Telemachus was the son of Homer's Odysseus; Laertes, his father. Polycrates and Thrasymachus were Greek rhetoricians (see Cicero *de or.* 3.16.59, 3.22.128, and above, p. 3, footnote 4). "Stelenus" may be an unconscious error for "Sthenelus" (Homer *il.* 2.564, 23.511; and *Op. 1*, 14D), but surely Erasmus and Folly were capable of deliberately formulating a misnomer that has neither real nor literary existence.

4. Proverbial for inconstancy (*Adag.* 2301).

5. See above, p. 60, footnote 4. The cucumber was also proverbially associated with bleary vision (*Adag.* 1076).

6. Letters are often used to designate things in demonstrations by Aristotle (e.g., *an. pr.* 1.2–3) and the mathematicians (e.g., Euclid). Folly does not refer to the practice of using Greek letters to number the books of a poem.

7. Two famous Greek lyric poets (Horace *epist.* 2.2.99–100).

8. Virgil *aen.* 2.39.

9. See above, p. 80, footnote 1.

1. See above, p. 42, footnote 6.

in debt to me—which they can hardly deny, unless they are the most ungrateful wretches imaginable.

Among the learned, the lawyers claim the highest rank, nor could anyone be more self-satisfied than they are as they endlessly roll the stone of Sisyphus,[2] stringing together six hundred laws in one breath—no matter whether they are relevant—piling gloss on gloss ⟨and opinion on opinion⟩ to make their profession seem the most difficult of all.[3] For they imagine that whatever is laborious is automatically also preeminent.

Let us join to them the dialecticians and disputants, a race of men more noisy than 'a steeple-full of brass bells,'[4] any one of whom could be matched in a talking contest with twenty women specially chosen for the occasion. But they would be happier if they were only loudmouthed and not also quarrelsome, fighting to the bitter end over some hair-splitting quibble[5] and, often enough, missing the truth entirely by fighting too much about it.[6] But their self-love places them in such felicity that once they are equipped with two or three syllogisms, they are immediately bold enough to challenge anyone at all to a verbal duel on any subject whatever. But then their persistence renders them invincible, even if their opponent is downright Stentorean.[7]

After them come the philosophers, venerable with their beards[8] and robes, who assert that they alone are wise, all other mortals being mere fleeting shades by comparison.[9] How delightfully they are deluded as they build up numberless worlds; as they measure the sun, the moon, the stars and their orbits as if they were using a ruler and plumb line; as they recite the causes of lightning, winds,

2. *Adag.* 1240; Homer *od.* 11.593-600.
3. Folly has in mind the accretions which gathered for centuries around the legal works of Justinian and Gratian.
4. Literally, "Dodonean bronze" (*Adag.* 7).
5. Literally, "about goat's wool." See above, p. 4, footnote 4.
6. Gellius *NA* 17.14.4; and Macrobius *sat.* 2.7.11.
7. Homer *il.* 5.785-86; *Adag.* 1237.
8. See above, p. 18, footnote 5, and Gellius *NA* 9.2.4-5.
9. Homer *od.* 10.493; *Adag.* 1253.

eclipses, and other unfathomable phenomena, without the slightest hesitation, as if they were confidential secretaries to Nature herself, the architect of all things, or as if they came to us straight from the council chamber of the gods.[1] At the same time, Nature has a grand laugh at them and their conjectures. For that they have actually discovered nothing at all is clear enough from this fact alone: on every single point they disagree violently and irreconcilably among themselves. Though they know nothing at all, they profess to know everything; and though they do not know themselves, and sometimes can't see a ditch or a stone in their path (either because most of them are blear-eyed or because their minds are wool-gathering),[2] nevertheless they claim that they can see ideas, universals, separate forms, prime matter, quiddities, ecceities, formalities, instants[3]— things so fine-spun that no one, however 'eagle-eyed,'[4] would be able, I think, to perceive them. But their arrogant scorn of the unwashed multitude is most notable when they bewilder uneducated people with their triangles, tetragons, and circles, and such mathematical figures, superimposing one on another to produce what looks like a labyrinth,[5] and then lining up series of letters as if in

1. Cicero *nat.* 1.8.18.

2. Aesop (Perry *Aesopica* no. 40); Plato *Tht.* 174A; Cicero *div.* 2.13.30.

3. On "ideas," see above, p. 45, footnote 5. A universal is something characteristic of a whole class of things, so that it can be predicated of all of them. What kind of existence universals have (whether in God's mind, in particular things, or in the mind of a perceiver) was a question much debated by medieval philosophers and became the crux of the opposition between the realists and the nominalists. See *CW* 4, 158/27n. To Aristotle and the scholastics, form was the active, permanent principle of an essence or kind of thing; matter was the passive, limiting, changing principle; prime matter was matter considered as purely potential, not yet informed; a separate form was one existing without matter. Aquinas' identification of the human soul with Aristotelian form stirred up much controversy. A quiddity was the principle which makes a thing what it is, that is, the essence which determines its species. Ecceity was Scotus' term for the principle of individuation which makes a thing this particular member of a species rather than another. "Quiddities, ecceities" was added in 1512. On "formalities" and "instants" (which were added in 1532) see p. 89, footnote 9.

4. Literally, "Lynceus could not see them." See above, p. 46, footnote 8, and *CW* 4, 438.

5. *Adag.* 1951. Lister refers to astrologers, but respectable physicists also used complicated lettered diagrams (e.g., Aristotle *phys.* 262ab, 266ab).

battle lines and repeating them first in one order and then in another. In this group there is also no lack of those who predict the future by consulting the stars and who promise to perform miracles beyond any magician, and they are even lucky enough to find people who believe them.

As for the theologians, perhaps it would be better to pass them over in silence, '*not stirring up the hornets' nest*'[6] and 'not laying a finger on the stinkweed,'[7] since this race of men is incredibly arrogant and touchy.[8] For they might rise up en masse and march in ranks against me with six hundred conclusions and force me to recant. And if I should refuse, they would immediately shout "heretic." For this is the thunderbolt they always keep ready at a moment's notice to terrify anyone to whom they are not very favorably inclined.

Certainly, though no one is less willing than they are to recognize my good will toward them, still these men are also obliged to me for benefits of no little importance. They are so blessed by their Selflove as to be fully persuaded that they themselves dwell in the third heaven,[9] looking down from high above on all other mortals as if they were earth-creeping vermin almost worthy of their pity. They are so closely hedged in by rows of ⟨magistral definitions,⟩ conclusions, corollaries, explicit and implicit propositions,[1] they have so many '*holes they can run to,*'[2] that Vulcan himself couldn't net them tightly enough[3] to keep them from escaping by means of

6. Literally, "not touching the swamp of Camarina." When the nearby inhabitants drained this pestilent swamp against the command of an oracle, the dry land gave easy access to their enemies (*Adag.* 64).

7. *Adag.* 65.

8. Horace speaks of the "touchy race of poets" (*epist.* 2.2.102). By applying the phrase to theologians, Folly turns the tables on them, since they sometimes scorned humanists like Erasmus as mere poets or students of poetry (*Ep. 1*, 462–65). See also More, *Selected Letters*, pp. 28–29.

9. *1 Cor.* 12:2.

1. Belief in explicit propositions was required from all Christians; in implicit, only from the learned (Aquinas *S. T.* 2a-2ae, q. 2. aa. 5–6).

2. Suidas (ed. Adler, Leipzig, 1928–38, *3*, 187). Lucian *eun.* 10; Herodotus 5.24.

3. Homer *od.* 8.273–81.

distinctions, with which they cut all knots as cleanly as the fine-honed edge of 'the headsman's axe'[4]—so many new terms have they thought up and such monstrous jargon have they coined. Moreover, they explicate sacred mysteries just as arbitrarily as they please, explaining by what method the world was established and arranged,[5] by what channels original sin is transmitted to Adam's posterity,[6] by what means, by what proportion, in how short a period of time Christ was fully formed in the virgin's womb,[7] how accidents subsist in the eucharist without any domicile.[8] But such questions are run-of-the-mill.[9] There are others which they think worthy of great and "illuminated" theologians, as they say.[1] If they ever encounter these, then they really perk up. Whether there is any instant in the generation of the divine persons?[2] Whether there is more than one filial relationship in Christ?[3] Whether the following proposition is possible: God the Father hates the Son.[4] Whether God could have taken on the nature of a woman, of the devil, of an ass, of a cucumber, of a piece of flint?[5] And then how the

4. The king of Tenedos held an ax while hearing cases; immediately after he gave judgment he decapitated the convicted party (*Adag.* 829; Cicero *ad Q. fr.* 2.2.2).

5. Peter Lombard *sent.* 2, dist. 12.1–6. Aquinas *comm. in sent.* 2, dist. 12.1–5.

6. Peter Lombard *sent.* 2, dist. 31.1–2. Bonaventure *comm. in sent.* 2, dist. 31.1–2. Aquinas *S.T.* 1a–2ae, q. 81, a. 1, 3.

7. Peter Lombard *sent.* 3, dist. 2.3. Alexander of Hales *S.T.* 3, pars 1, inquis. unica, tr. 1, memb. 2. Aquinas *comm. in sent.* 3, dist. 3, q. 5, a. 2.

8. The question of transubstantiation. Peter Lombard *sent.* 4, dist. 12.1. Bonaventure *comm. in sent.* 4, dist. 12, pars 1, a.1, qq. 1–3. Godefroid de Fontaines *quodlibeta* 11.3. Folly flippantly substitutes "domicile" for "substance."

9. The questions Folly has mentioned are all in Peter Lombard's *Sentences* and hence were discussed by numerous commentators.

1. Doctors "illuminated in the faith by the Holy Spirit" are mocked in *Ep. obscur. vir.* pp. 34, 44.

2. Peter Lombard *sent.* 1, dist. 9.3–4 and 30.1. Aquinas *comm. in sent.* 1, dist. 9, q. 2, aa. 1–2.

3. Alexander of Hales *S.T.* 3, pars 1, inquis. 1, tr. 2, q. 3, cap. 3. Scotus *quaest. quodlib.* 2.11.

4. Among others, Jean Buridan, who taught at the University of Paris when Erasmus was there in the 1490s, discusses this point in *Questiones super decem libros Ethicorum Aristotelis* (Paris, 1513), 8.23, ff. 189–89ᵛ.

5. Except for the devil, the cucumber, and the piece of flint, these questions

cucumber would have preached, performed miracles, and been nailed to the cross? And what Peter would have consecrated «if he had consecrated» during the time Christ was hanging on the cross?[6] And whether during that same time Christ could be called a man?[7] And whether it will be permissible to eat and drink after the resurrection?[8]—taking precautions even now against hunger and thirst.

⟨There are numberless *petty quibbles* even more fine-spun than these, concerning notions, relations, instants, formalities, quiddities, ecceities[9]—things to which no eyesight could ever penetrate, unless it were an 'x-ray vision'[1] so powerful it could perceive through the deepest darkness things that are nowhere. Also throw in those *sententiae* of theirs, so *paradoxical* that those oracular sayings which the Stoics called paradoxes[2] seem downright crude and commonplace by comparison—such as this, for example: it is a less serious crime to murder a thousand men than to fix just one shoe for a poor man on the Lord's day;[3] or it would be better to let the whole world be destroyed—'lock, stock, and barrel,'[4] as they say—than to tell just

---

were actually discussed by scholastic theologians. See my article, "Some Medieval Elements and Structural Unity in Erasmus' *The Praise of Folly*," *Renaissance Quarterly*, 27 (1974), 501, and P. Smith, *Erasmus*, 1923, rpt. 1962, p. 23.

6. Henri de Gand *quodlibeta* 13.4 (Paris, 1518; rpt. Louvain, 1961, ff. 425^v–26).

7. Peter Lombard *sent.* 3, dist. 22.1, and Scotus' commentary thereon (*Op. om.*, Paris, 14 [1894], 754–59).

8. Aquinas *comm. in sent.* 4, dist. 44, q. 1, a. 3.

9. "Notions" sometimes referred to an idea apprehended, sometimes to an apprehension itself. "Relation" is one of the nine Aristotelian categories of accident. On the "instants of nature" which Scotus posited in divine generation and knowledge, see Scotus, *Op. om.* (Vatican City, 4 [1956], 74–75); *Op. om.* (Paris, 22 [1894], 445), and É. Gilson, *Jean Duns Scot* (Paris, 1952, p. 48); Erasmus mentioned disputes about them in his note on 1 *Tim.* 1: 6 (*Op. 6*, 928A). "Formality" usually referred to an accident inherent in a substance. On "quiddity" and "ecceity," see above, p. 86, footnote 3.

1. See above, p. 86, footnote 4.

2. Aristotle *rhet.* 1394ab; Cicero *parad.* 4; and J. von Arnim, *Stoicorum Veterum Fragmenta* (Leipzig, 1903; rpt. 1967), 3, 164–72.

3. Because the one is an offense directly against God; the other, against our neighbors.

4. Cf. Cicero *Quinct.* 15.49.

one, tiny, little white lie.[5] And then these most subtle subtleties are rendered even more subtle by the various "ways" or types of scho-. lastic theology, so that you could work your way out of a labyrinth[6] sooner than out of the intricacies of the Realists, Nominalists,[7] Thomists, Albertists, Occamists, Scotists[8]—and I still haven't mentioned all the sects, but only the main ones.

In all of these there is so much erudition, so much difficulty, that I think the apostles themselves would need to be inspired by a different spirit[9] if they were forced to match wits on such points with this new breed of theologians. Paul could provide a living example of faith, but when he said "Faith is the substance of things to be hoped for and the evidence of things not seen," his definition was not sufficiently magisterial.[1] So too, he lived a life of perfect charity, but he neither distinguished it nor defined it with sufficient dialectical precision in the first epistle to the Corinthians, chapter 13.[2]

5. Gratian (*decret.* 2 pars, causa 22, q. 2, c. 14) quotes Augustine, who says that the perfect spiritual man should not lie, even to save a life, though he may be silent or conceal the truth.

6. See above, p. 86, footnote 5.

7. See above, p. 86, footnote 3.

8. Between 1508 and 1523 Cajetan issued a voluminous commentary on the *Summa theologica* of St. Thomas Aquinas (1225–1274), defending Thomism against the attacks of Scotus, Durandus, Holkot, and others. In the fifteenth century, followers of St. Albert the Great, Aquinas' teacher at Cologne, began to defend Albert's teachings against both Scotists and Thomists, in Paris and Louvain but especially at Cologne. In the fourteenth and fifteenth centuries the nominalism of William Ockham gained more and more followers, especially among philosophers whose primary interest was mathematics or physical science. Among the leading defenders of Scotus was Antoine Syrret, who taught at the University of Paris while Erasmus was there. On the revival and ascendancy of Scotism at Paris during Erasmus' lifetime, see H. Élie, "Quelques maitres de l'université de Paris vers l'an 1500," *Archives d'histoire doctrinale et littéraire du moyen age,* 18 (1950–51), 193–243.

9. *1 Cor.* 2 : 12.

1. A gloss on the *Decretals* of Gregory IX (Venice, 1591, p. 4) objects to Paul's definition because it does not distinguish faith clearly from hope and because it applies only to future events whereas faith applies to both past and present.

2. Probably an exaggerated extension of the fact in the preceding sentence. The schoolmen had no need to quarrel with *1 Cor.* 13: 4–13 as a definition of charity because *Matt.* 22: 37–40 gives a good definition.

Certainly the apostles consecrated the eucharist very piously, but still if they had been asked about the "terminus a quo" and the "terminus ad quem,"[3] about transubstantiation,[4] about how the same body can be in different places,[5] about the difference between the body of Christ as it is in heaven, as it was on the cross, and as it is in the eucharist,[6] about the exact point at which transubstantiation takes place (since the speech through which it is accomplished is a divisible quantity which takes place in a flowing period of time),[7] I don't think they would have responded with a subtlety equal to that of the Scotists when they discuss and define these points. They knew Jesus' mother, but which of them has shown how she was preserved from the stain of Adam's sin as philosophically as our theologians have done it?[8] Peter received the keys, and received them from one who would not have committed them to someone unworthy of them, but still I don't know whether he understood— certainly he never attained sufficient subtlety to understand—how even a person who does not have knowledge can still have the keys of knowledge.[9] They baptized everywhere, but nowhere did they

3. Scotus *comm. in sent.* 4, dist. 10, q. 1, and *quaest. quodlib.* 10 (*Op. om.*, Paris, *17* [1894], 173, 177–78 and *24* [1895], 422).

4. Scotus *comm. in sent.* 4, dist. 11, qq. 1–2 (*Op. om.*, Paris *17* [1894], 318–50). See John Payne, *Erasmus: his Theology of the Sacraments* (Richmond, Va., 1970), pp. 126–54.

5. Scotus *comm. in sent.* 4, dist. 10, q. 2 (*Op. om.*, Paris, *17* [1894], 190–221).

6. In his commentary on Lombard's *Sentences* (Venice, 1520), François Meyronnes discussed "whether Christ's body in the sacrament has as perfect quantity as it does in heaven" and "whether what applies to Christ's body on the cross applies to him in the sacrament, namely, whether he was naked in the sacrament as he was on the cross (*sent.* 4, dist. 10, q. 2, and *sent.* 4, dist. 11, q. 8).

7. Bonaventure *comm. in sent.* 4, dist. 11, pars 1, art. un., q. 5.

8. The debate on Mary's freedom from original sin turned largely on how this could have been done. Scotus' support was an important turning point in the development of the doctrine. On 3 March 1496/97, when Erasmus was in Paris, the Sorbonne declared that all holders of degrees must swear to support the dogma. See Richard Pace, *De fructu qui ex doctrina percipitur* (ed. and tr. R. Sylvester and F. Manley, New York, 1967, p. 61), and More, *Selected Letters*, p. 133.

9. The keys mentioned in *Matt.* 16: 19 were discussed in connection with a priest's power to administer the sacrament of penance. They were explained by

teach what are the formal, material, efficient, and final causes of baptism,[1] nor do they even so much as mention the delible and indelible marks of the sacraments.[2] Certainly they worshiped God, but they did so in the spirit, following no other directive than the one given in the gospel: "God is a spirit and those who worship him should worship him in the spirit and in truth."[3] But it is hardly clear that it was also revealed to them that a charcoal sketch drawn on a wall should be worshiped with the same worship as Christ himself,[4] provided that the picture has two fingers extended, long hair, and three rays in the halo stuck on the back of the skull.[5] For who could perceive these things unless he had spent thirty-six whole years in studying the physics and metaphysics of Aristotle and the Scotists? So too, ⟪the apostles⟫ preach grace very forcefully, but

---

Peter Lombard in his *Sentences* as the key of passing sentence and the key of discrimination or knowledge (*clavis potestatis, clavis scientiae*); he taught that an ignorant priest does not receive the key of discrimination at ordination. Scotus, on the other hand, claimed that an ignorant priest may have the authority (clavis) to discriminate without actually being able to do it (that is, lacking the knowledge itself); thus, a person without knowledge may not rightly use the key of knowledge (the authority to discriminate) though he may have it. Scotus *comm. in sent.* 4, dist. 19, quaest. un., nos. 7–8 (*Op. om.*, Paris, *18* [1894], 610.

1. It was customary to discuss the material and formal causes (matter and form) of all the sacraments, but the efficient and final causes were not always treated. On the matter and form of baptism, see Aquinas *S.T.* 3, q. 66, aa. 3–5; on the final cause, Lombard's *sent.* 4, dist. 3, c. 9. Whether or how the sacraments themselves are efficient causes of grace was hotly contested in Erasmus' time.

2. As Lister notes, an indelible character was assigned to baptism, confirmation, and holy orders to explain why these three sacraments cannot be repeated. Aquinas *S.T.* 3, q. 63, aa. 1–6. Thomas More, *CW* 4, p. 520.

3. *John* 4: 24.

4. The most important theologian who held this position was Aquinas himself (*S.T.* 3, q. 25, a. 3, *comm. in sent.* 3, dist. 9, q. 1, a. 2, sol. 2). In his reply to Alberto Pio, Erasmus gave Scotus' teaching on this point (*Op. 9*, 1160D). The three kinds of worship were latria (for God alone), doulia (for the saints), and hyperdoulia (for the Virgin Mary).

5. Holbein's sketch in the copy of the *Folly* he illustrated matches this description of the work of these sidewalk artists (Froben's 1515 edition, ed. H. A. Schmid, Basel, 1931. sig. O4ʳ).

nowhere do they distinguish between grace "gratis data" and grace "gratificans." They exhort us to good works, without distinguishing "opus operans" from "opus operatum."[6] Everywhere they inculcate charity, without separating infused from acquired charity[7] or explaining whether charity is an accident or a substance, a created or an uncreated thing.[8] They detest sin, but I would stake my life they couldn't define scientifically what it is that we call sin, unless perchance they had been instructed by the spirit of the Scotists. Nor can I bring myself to believe that Paul, from whose learning we may judge that of the others, would so often have condemned questions, disputes, genealogies, and (as he calls them) λογομαχίαι (quarrels about words),[9] if he had been so expert in subtle argumentation, especially since all the quarrels and disputes of that time were coarse and crude by comparison with the supersubtleties of our doctors of theology.

But they are men of the greatest modesty: if the apostles have perhaps written something a bit loosely, without magisterial precision, far be it from them to condemn it; rather, they make the proper allowances in their interpretation, paying at least that much respect to the antiquity of Scripture on the one hand and to the

6. "Gratia gratificans" is the fundamental grace whereby a man is united to God; "gratia gratis data" is a special gift bestowed by God on a person so that he may help in the sanctification of others—e.g., the gift of prophecy (Aquinas *S.T.*, 1ᵃ-2ᵃᵉ, q. 3, aa. 1, 4). "Opus operans" (a phrase which later became "ex opere operantis") refers to the action of the minister or the disposition of the recipient of a sacrament; "opus operatum" refers to the effect of the sacrament itself considered apart from the moral condition of the minister or recipient. The sentence "they exhort . . . operatum" first appeared in 1522.

7. Dionysius Cartusianus *comm. in sent.* 3, dist. 27 (*Op. om.*, Tornaci, *23* [1904], 459). The schoolmen did not place much emphasis on this distinction, but they did normally discuss whether (and how) the supernatural virtue of charity infused at baptism could increase or decrease (Aquinas *S.T.* 2ᵃ-2ᵃᵉ, q. 24. aa. 2–5.)

8. Alexander of Hales *comm. in sent.* 1, dist. 17. Pietro de Falco *Questions disputatées ordinaires*, q. 9, a. 3 (ed. A.-J. Gondras, Louvain and Paris, *2* [1968], 355–56).

9. *1 Tim.* 1 : 4, 2 : 8, 6 : 4, (see Erasmus' note, *Op. 6, 943F*). *2 Tim.* 2 : 23. *Tit.* 3 : 9. *Rom.* 14 : 1.

title of apostle on the other. And lord knows it would be a little unfair to demand from them things about which they never heard a single word from their teacher. But if the same thing happens in Chrysostom, Basil, or Jerome,[1] then they consider it sufficient to write next to it "non tenetur" (untenable). These fathers certainly did confute pagan philosophers and Jews, who are by temperament extraordinarily stubborn, but they did it by the lives they led and the miracles they performed rather than by manufacturing syllogisms. They also convinced people whose minds were completely incapable of following even a single quodlibet of Scotus.[2] But nowadays what pagan, what heretic[3] would not immediately yield to so many fine-spun subtleties, unless he should be too crude to follow them, or so impudent as to make fun of them, or provided with the same snares so that the two sides would be evenly matched,[4] just as if you should match one magician against another or as if one man with a charmed sword should fight against another whose sword was also charmed. For then it would be like the loom of Penelope: weaving and unweaving the same piece of cloth over and over again.[5] So far as I can judge, Christians would be wise if, instead of sending out those regiments of thick-skulled soldiers who have been fighting for so long now without winning a decisive victory, they should send against the Turks and Saracens these most clamorous Scotists and most stubborn Occamists and invincible Albertists,[6] together with the whole band of dialecticians: they would behold, I think, the finest battle imaginable and such a

1. Like St. Basil (329–79, Bishop of Caesarea), St. John Chrysostom (345?–407, Patriarch of Constantinople) was a father of the Greek church. St. Jerome (340?–420) was Erasmus' favorite among the Latin fathers of the church. Erasmus edited the works of all three.

2. A quodlibet was a question (or a series of questions), often somewhat subtle or unusual, posed and discussed at an official public disputation, outside the context of a regular summa or commentary on Lombard's *Sentences*. The *Quaestiones quodlibetales* are among Scotus' later works.

3. The words "what heretic" were added in 1515.

4. Folly employs the argument "divisio" by attempting to decide all possible alternatives in her favor (see Erasmus, *Ecclesiastes*, *Op.* 5, 936B).

5. To put off her suitors, Penelope unwove by night what she had woven by day (Homer *od.* 2.104–05). *Adag.* 342.

6. See above, p. 90, footnote 8.

victory as was never seen before. For who could be so cold as not to be inflamed by their acumen? Who could be so dull as not to be stimulated by the sharpness of their wit? Who so sharp-sighted that they could not pull the wool over his eyes?

But I may seem to be saying all this merely as a joke. No wonder, indeed, since among the theologians themselves there are some better educated men who are disgusted by these theological quibbles, which they consider utterly pointless. There are those who denounce it as a form of sacrilege and consider it the worst sort of impiety to talk in such a tawdry fashion, to dispute with the worldly subtleties of the pagans, to lay down such arrogant definitions, about sacred mysteries which should be reverently contemplated rather than explicated, and to besmirch the majesty of divine theology with words and ideas so bloodless and even squalid.⟩

But meanwhile they themselves are so completely contented and self-satisfied, they even applaud themselves so enthusiastically, that they spend their days and nights in these most delightful trifles and have not a moment to spare to read through the gospel or Paul's epistles even once. At the same time, while they are talking nonsense in the schools, they think they are supporting the universal church, which otherwise would collapse, with their syllogistic props in much the same way that Atlas, in the mythology of the poets, holds up the world on his shoulders.[7] You can imagine how happy a life they lead while they distort and reshape Holy Scripture however they like (just as if it were a lump of wax), while they demand that their conclusions (to which some schoolmen have subscribed) should be more revered than the laws of Solon[8] and more binding than the papal decretals,[9] ⟨while—like moral guardians of the whole world—they demand a recantation of whatever doesn't square 'to a "T" '[1] with their explicit and implicit conclusions,[2] while they

---

7. Virgil *aen.* 4.247; Ovid *met.* 4.661–62.

8. See above, p. 11, footnote 2.

9. The second part of the *Corpus of Canon Law* consists of papal decretals issued by Gregory IX and Boniface VIII and of other regulations by Popes Clement V and John XXII.

1. *Adag.* 490.

2. See above, p. 87, footnote 1.

deliver their oracular pronouncements "This proposition is scandalical," "This one is not sufficiently reverential," "This one gives off a whiff of heresy," "This one does not tinkle true,"[3] so that not even baptism, not the gospel, not Paul or Peter, not St. Jerome or St. Augustine, in fact not even Thomas himself *Aristotelicissimus*,[4] can make someone a Christian unless he has the vote of these bachelors of divinity, so fine-honed is the edge of their judgment. Who would ever have thought that someone who said that the two parts of such paired expressions as "matula putes" and "matula putet" or "ollae féruere" and "ollam feruére" are equally congruent is no true Christian if these wisemen had not taught us about it?[5] Who would ever have delivered the church from the darkness of such

3. Folly's parodic variations on the stock phrases "smacks of heresy" ("haeresim olet" instead of "haeresim sapit") and "does not ring true" ("male tinnit" instead of "male sonat").

4. Giving the epithet "most Aristotelian" in Greek adds an ironic edge because Aquinas knew Aristotle only in Latin. Unlike Colet, Erasmus expressed considerable respect for Aquinas (*Ep.* 1211, ll. 429–41, *Op. 6*, 554E and *9*, 103B).

5. Lister mentions a dispute at Oxford in which a friar was condemned for asserting that the two statements "Socrates currit" ("Socrates is running") and "Socrates curris" ("Socrates, you are running") are equally "perfect" and "congruent." (For the standard phrases, Folly wittily substitutes "the chamberpot stinks" and "chamberpot, you stink.") Folly refers to the intricacies of the speculative or modist grammar which reached its classic formulation in the *Grammatica speculativa* of Thomas of Erfurt in the fourteenth century. To the modists "perfect" and "congruent" meant roughly "complete" and "grammatically correct" (see G. L. Bursill-Hall, *Speculative Grammars of the Middle Ages*, The Hague, 1971, pp. 307–09). "Matula putet" might seem more "congruent" than "matula putes" because in the latter statement a noun (which would ordinarily be third-person) is used either vocatively (leaving the verb without an expressed subject) or as the subject of a second-person verb. The other pair of phrases derives from two different but quite similar verbs meaning "to boil": "ollam fervére" ("that the pot is boiling") is less "perfect" than "ollae férvere" ("the pots are boiling") because the former cannot stand as a complete sentence. On the other hand, "ollae férvere" might seem less "congruent" because it substitutes an historical infinitive for a finite verb. "Olla male fervet" is a proverb meaning "the affair is going badly" (Petronius 38, 13). Also, the proverb "fervet olla, vivit amicitia" (*Adag.* 323) applies to superficial friendship. Cf. Thomas More, *Selected Letters*, pp. 20–24.

grave errors—which, in fact, no one would ever have heard of if they had not read them in pronouncements issued with the great seals of the universities? But aren't they as happy as can be while they do such things?> And also while they depict every detail of the infernal regions so exactly that you would think they had spent several years in that commonwealth. And also while they manufacture at their pleasure new heavenly spheres, finally adding the largest and most beautiful of all just to make sure that the blessed souls would have plenty of room to take walks, to stage their dinner-parties, or even to play ball.[6] With these trifles and thousands more like them their heads are so swollen and stuffed that I don't think Jupiter's brain was any more burdened when he called for Vulcan's axe to give birth to Pallas.[7] Therefore don't be surprised when you see them at public disputations with their heads so carefully wrapped up in swaths of cloth, for otherwise they would clearly explode.[8]

Sometimes I myself have to laugh at them: they think they have finally reached the very acme of theology if they plumb the depths of barbarous and foul language; and when they mumble so badly that only another mumbler could understand them, they call it ingenuity beyond the reach of the ordinary listener. For they assert that it is not consonant with the dignity of sacred writing for them to be compelled to obey the rules of grammar. Wonderful indeed is the majesty of theologians if they alone have the right to speak

6. As in Dante, heaven was sometimes imagined to be in the empyrean, the tenth "sphere" beyond the *primum mobile*. Godefroid de Fontaines discusses the question of extension in the heavenly mansions (*Quodlibeta*, XV, 5, ed. J. Hoffmans, Louvain, *14* [1937], 34).

7. Lucian *deor. dial.* 8. Folly may allude ironically to the fact that, partly because of her birth from Jupiter's brain, Pallas Athene was allegorized as wisdom (Fulgentius *myth.* 2.1.68, and Isidore *etymol.* 8.71–73).

8. The ordinary headgear of a doctor of divinity (or its equivalent, master of theology) was some form of the *pileus*, a close-fitting cap which often covered the ears. Such a cap was a sign of status strictly forbidden to mere bachelors or licentiates of theology. Erasmus, who received a doctorate in theology from the University of Turin, wears such a cap in the portraits of him by Metsys, Dürer, and Holbein.

97

faultily, though they have that in common with many lowly cobblers. Finally, they think they are most godlike whenever they are scrupulously addressed with the title "Magister noster,"[9] for they seem to find in that name something of the same mysterious profundity that the Jews reverenced in the *ineffable four letters of Jahweh*.[1] Hence they say it is quite improper to write MAGISTER NOSTER in anything but capital letters. But if anyone should say it backwards—"Noster magister"—at one stroke he has corrupted the entire majesty of the theological title.

Almost as happy as the theologians are those men who are commonly called "religious" and "monks"—though both names are quite incorrect, since a good part of them are very far removed from religion and no one is encountered more frequently everywhere you go.[2] I cannot imagine how anything could be more wretched than these men, if it were not for the many sorts of assistance I give them. For even though everyone despises this breed of men so thoroughly that even a chance meeting with one of them is considered unlucky,[3] still they maintain a splendid opinion of themselves. First of all, they consider it the very height of piety to have so little to do with literature as not even to be able to read. Moreover, when they roar out their psalms in church like braying asses (counting their prayers indeed, but understanding them not at all), then (of all things!) they imagine that the listening saints are soothed and caressed with manifold delight. Among them are some

9. In a dialogue sequel to *Ep. obscur. vir.* (ed. Edouard Böcking, Leipzig, 1864–69, *1*, 301–16), Erasmus asks Reuchlin how he should address three conservative theologians. Reuchlin replies, "Above all they want to be addressed as 'our masters' ('magistros nostros')." Erasmus: "But what if I don't call them that?" Reuchlin: "They will be angry and will consider you unworthy to speak with them."

1. Literally, the "tetragrammaton," one of God's names in the Bible, an unpronounceable combination of four consonants with no vowels. Lister notes that "by this mystery the letters suggest that God's essence is in every way ineffable." The artificial name "Jehovah" was formed from the tetragrammaton, which is now thought to have been pronounced "Yahweh."

2. "Monk" is derived from the Greek word meaning "solitary."

3. Walther 6769. Cervantes alludes to the same superstition in *Don Quijote*, part II, chap. 58.

who make a great thing out of their squalor and beggary, who stand at the door bawling out their demands for bread—⟨indeed there is no inn or coach or ship where they do not make a disturbance,⟩ depriving other beggars of no small share of their income. And in this manner these most agreeable fellows, with their filth, ignorance, coarseness, impudence, re-create for us, as they say, an image of the apostles.

But what could be more charming than to observe how they do everything by rules, as if they were entering figures in a ledger where it would be a terrible sin to overlook the smallest detail: how many knots to the shoe, what colors and different styles for each garment, of what material and how many straws wide the cincture may be, the cut of the hood and how many pecks it should hold, how many inches long the hair may be, how many hours are allowed for sleep. Who cannot see, considering the variety in physical and mental constitutions, how unequal this equality really is? Nevertheless, because of such trifles, not only do they consider outsiders beneath their contempt but one order scorns another, and men who profess apostolic charity raise a catastrophic uproar about a garment that is belted somewhat differently ⟨or a color that is a little darker.⟩ You can see some of them who are so strictly religious that their outer garments are of coarse goat's hair, but their undergarments are of fine silk; and then again you will see others who wear linen outside, but lamb's wool underneath. Or others who shrink from contact with money as if it were a deadly poison, but at the same time do not refrain from contact with wine and women.[4] In short, they are all amazingly eager to avoid any agreement in their manner of life. ⟨Nor do they strive to be like Christ, but to be unlike each other.⟩

Then too, a great part of their happiness consists in their titles: one order likes to be called Cordeliers, ⟨and among them some are Coletans, others Friars Minor, some Minims, others Bullists.⟩[5]

---

4. Quoting the rule of St. Francis, Lister argues that it does not forbid the touching of money, but the personal control and use of it.

5. Cordeliers and Friars Minor were general names for Franciscans. The other three were reformed branches of the Franciscans.

Then some are Benedictines, others Bernardines; ⟨some are Briget-
tines, others Augustinians; some Williamites, others Jacobites⟩⁶—
as if it weren't enough to be called Christians. ⟨The majority of
them rely so much on their ceremonies and petty human traditions
that they think one heaven is hardly a fitting reward for such merits,
never quite realizing that Christ will scorn all such things and will
require the fulfillment of his own precept, namely charity.⁷ One
will display his barrel-belly, bloated with all kinds of fish. Another
will pour out a hundred pecks of psalms. One will reckon up thousands of fasts and will claim that his belly has almost burst because
he had only one lunch so often. Another will bring forth such a
pile of ceremonies that seven freighters could hardly transport it.
One will boast that for sixty years he never once touched money
unless his fingers were protected by two pairs of gloves. Another
will bring in a hood so filthy and greasy that no common seaman
would consider it fit to put on. One will tell how for more than
five and fifty years he led the life of a sponge, always fixed to one
spot. Another will assert that his voice grew hoarse from continually singing, another that he became almost catatonic from solitude,
another that his tongue atrophied from constant silence. But Christ,
interrupting their boasts (which would otherwise never come to
an end), will say, "Where did this new race of Jews come from?
The only law I recognize as truly mine is the only one I hear nothing
about. Long ago, not speaking obliquely in parables but quite
openly, I promised my Father's inheritance not to hoods, or trifling
prayers, or fasts, but rather deeds of faith and charity.⁸ Nor do I
acknowledge those who too readily acknowledge their own deeds:⁹
those who want to appear even holier than I am can go dwell in the

6. Cistercians were sometimes called Bernardines in honor of St. Bernard of
Clairvaux. The Brigittines were an order of men and women founded by St.
Bridget of Sweden in the fourteenth century. The Augustinian friars were a
mendicant order formally established in 1256. The Williamites were founded
in the twelfth century by St. William of Maleval. Dominicans were sometimes
called Jacobites because the order's house in Paris was established in a hospice
and chapel dedicated to St. James (Jacobus).

7. *John* 15 : 12.

8. *Matt.* 25 : 35–40. The words "faith and" first appeared in 1532.

9. *Luke* 18 : 9–14.

heavens of the Abraxasians[1] if they like, or they can order that a new heaven be built for them by the men whose petty traditions they have placed before my precepts." When they hear this and see sailors and teamsters chosen in preference to them, how do you suppose their faces will look as they stare at each other?

But meanwhile they are happy in their hopes, not without a helping hand from me.⟩ Then too, though these men are cut off from political office, still no one dares to scorn them, especially the mendicants, because they have complete knowledge of everyone's secrets from what they call confession. Of course, they hold that it is wrong to reveal them, except every now and then when they are in their cups and want to amuse themselves with some funny stories, but then they make their point obliquely and hypothetically, without mentioning any names. But if anyone stirs up these hornets,[2] they get their full measure of revenge in their sermons to the people, pointing out their enemy indirectly, so covertly that no one who understands anything at all can fail to understand who is meant. Nor will they ever make an end of barking until you throw 'a sop to Cerberus.'[3]

Tell me now, is there any comedian or pitchman[4] you would rather see than these men when they orate in their sermons, imitating quite absurdly but still very amusingly what the rhetoricians have handed down about the way to make a speech? Good lord! how they gesticulate, how fittingly they vary their tone of voice, how they croon, how they strut, continually changing their facial expressions, drowning out everything with their shouts! And the mysterious secret of this oratorical artistry is passed down personally from one little friar to another. Though it is not lawful for me to know it,[5] I will guess at it anyway and come as close as I can.

First of all, they make an invocation, a device they have borrowed

1. An heretical sect which believed in 365 heavens. The numerical values of the Greek letters in "abraxas" add up to 365. See *CW* 4, 112/3n.

2. *Adag.* 60.

3. Virgil *aen.* 6.419.

4. See p. 10, footnote 8.

5. Lister points out that Folly, as a woman, would not be expected or even allowed to know of such learned matters.

from the poets.[6] Then, if they are going to talk about charity, their exordium has to do with the Nile River in Egypt. ⟨Or if they are going to discourse on the mystery of the cross, they open their sermon very auspiciously with Bel, the dragon of Babylon.[7] Or if they are going to discuss fasting, they open with the twelve signs of the zodiac.[8] Or if they are going to speak about faith, they go through a long prologue about squaring the circle. I myself once heard an eminent fool—I beg your pardon, I mean scholar—who was going to explain the holy Trinity in a sermon before a large audience. To show that his learning was far above the ordinary and to meet the expectations of the theologians among the hearers, he invented a completely new approach—namely, to start with the letters, syllables, and the whole word, then to take up the agreement of noun and verb, adjective and substantive, to the amazement of many listeners, some of whom muttered to themselves that question in Horace "What is he driving at with all this damned nonsense?"[9] He finally came to the conclusion that the rudiments of grammar give such a clear picture of the whole Trinity that no mathematician could make it any plainer by drawing in the dust.[1] And this *theologicissimus* had sweated over this oration for eight whole months, so much so that to this day he is 'blind as a bat,'[2] since all the acumen of his sight was diverted to the sharpness of his wit.[3]

6. See Erasmus *Ecclesiastes* on the rhetoric of preaching (*Op.* 5, 872D).

7. *Daniel* 14.

8. Lister explains how the connection could be made: "They say that during the lenten fast the sun enters Aries, the first sign of the zodiac, so that everything begins to grow warmer and moister at that time, and that the thick humors of the body, which could not be melted during the winter because of the cold weather, begin to be melted at that time, so that the body needs less nutriment, and that therefore the church did well to establish the lenten fast in the springtime. Taking this cue, they babble on in a marvelous fashion about the zodiac and the signs in it so that to the ignorant people they may appear to be learned."

9. Horace *serm.* 2.7.21.

1. See Cicero *nat.* 2.18.48; Livy 25.31.9.

2. *Adag.* 255.

3. Lister points out that the abstract "acumen" ("acies") and the concrete

But the man hardly regrets his blindness and considers it a small price to pay for such glory.

We once heard another preacher, an old man of eighty, so thoroughly theological that you would have thought he was Scotus come back to life. Undertaking to explain the mystery of the name Jesus, he showed with amazing subtlety that whatever could be said on this subject was hidden in the very letters of the name. That it has only three inflectional endings is a clear sign of the Trinity. Then, that the first inflection (Jesus) ends in "s," the second (Jesum) in "m" and the third (Jesu) in "u" conceals an *unspeakable* mystery: namely, the three letters show that He is first (summum), middle (medium), and last (ultimum). He had in store for us an even more recondite mystery: dividing "Jesus" into two equal parts leaves a penthemimer in the middle.[4] Then he explained that in Hebrew this letter is ש, pronounced "sin." Now in the language of the Scots, I think, "sin" means "peccatum." Thus we have a very clear indication that it was Jesus who took away the sins of the world.[5] Everyone was struck with open-mouthed wonder at this novel exordium, especially the theologians, so that they almost

"sharpness" ("cuspis") have been deliberately reversed in their application to "mind" and "sight."

4. In classical prosody, the dactylic pentameter consists of two half-lines separated by a caesura (a "cutting"). Each half-line is a penthemimer consisting of five half-feet. Dividing "Jesus" according to this model (with letters taking the place of feet) leaves a caesura in the middle of the third letter, "s." That is, it takes this letter away in the sense that it cuts it in two, thus crossing it out with a stroke. Folly's friar does not express himself very clearly, since what is left in the middle is not a penthemimer, but the caesura dividing the two penthemimers. The early Greek fathers, influenced by Jewish traditions, had worked out some rather elaborate numerical interpretations of the name Jesus (P. E. Testa, *Il Simbolismo dei Giudeo-Cristiani*, Jerusalem, 1962, pp. 227, 365–70, 379–85, 520–22). Erasmus, like More but unlike some of their humanist contemporaries and forebears, displayed little interest in esoteric numerological symbolism (G. Marc'hadour, *Thomas More et la Bible*, Paris, 1969, pp. 489–90).

5. *John* 1 : 29. "Sin" (or "syn") was equally current in England and Scotland. Perhaps Folly chose Scottish to allude to the homeland of John Duns Scotus. Erasmus condemns stupid etymologies constructed from the letters of a word in *Ep.* 2465, ll. 175–88.

shared the fate of Niobe.[6] But my fate was nearly that of Priapus, that good-for-nothing figwood statue, who, much to his dismay, watched the nocturnal ceremonies of Canidia and Sagana.[7] And certainly with good reason. For when did Demosthenes among the Greeks or Cicero among the Romans ever think up such an *exordium* as this? They considered an introduction faulty if it strayed too far from the subject at hand.[8] As if any swineherd, taught by nature alone, wouldn't have enough common sense to begin with something relevant.⟩ But these learned friars think their preamble (for that's their word for it)[9] will be most exquisitely rhetorical only if it has absolutely nothing to do with the subject matter, so that the bewildered listener mutters under his breath "What is he up to now?"[1]

In the third part, which serves as a narration,[2] they interpret something from the gospel, but fleetingly and as if in passing, though that is the only thing they ought to be doing in the whole sermon. In the fourth section, assuming an entirely new character, they raise some theological question, often enough one that is *'neither here nor there,'*[3] and they think that this too belongs to the art of preaching. Here they really ruffle their theological feathers, quoting solemn doctors, subtle doctors, most subtle doctors, seraphic doctors, cherubic doctors, holy doctors, irrefragable doctors, dinning these grandiose titles into our ears.[4] Then, preaching to uneducated lay people, they put on display their syllogisms, majors, minors, conclusions, corollaries, most jejune hypotheses

6. Niobe was turned to stone by grief at the murder of her children (Ovid *met.* 6.302–05; *Adag.* 2233).

7. Out of fear of the witches, Priapus farted (Horace *serm.* 1.8.44–50).

8. Cicero *de or.* 2.78.315–19, *inv.* 1.15.20, 1.17.23, and 1.18.26; Quintilian *inst.* 4.1.42.

9. "Praeambulum" is a medieval word, not used by the ancients.

1. Virgil *ecl.* 3.19.

2. A "statement of the facts," the second part of a formal oration (Quintilian *inst.* 4.2.2).

3. *Adag.* 444; Lucian *Alex.* 54 (tr. Erasmus, Amsterdam ed. *1*, part 1, 467, l. 4).

4. Scotus was entitled "doctor subtilis"; St. Bonaventure, "doctor seraphicus"; Alexander of Hales, "doctor irrefragabilis."

and utterly pedantic quibbles. There remains now the fifth act, in which it behooves them to perform with the greatest artistry.[5] Here they haul out some foolish folktale, something from the "Speculum Historiale," say, or the "Gesta Romanorum,"[6] and interpret it allegorically, tropologically, and anagogically.[7] In this fashion they put together their chimera, one far beyond what Horace imagined when he wrote "If to a human head, etc."[8]

But they have heard from somebody or other that the beginning of a speech should be quite restrained, not at all loud. And so in the opening they start out so softly that they can't even hear their own voice, as if it did any good to say something that no one can understand.[9] They have heard that exclamations should sometimes be employed to stir up the emotions.[1] Thus, in the middle of a passage delivered in a low voice, every now and then they suddenly raise their voices and shout like crazy men, even when there is no need for it at all. You would think they needed a dose of hellebore,[2] as if it made no difference at what point you raise your voice! Moreover, because they have heard that a sermon should gradually become more and more fiery, they begin the individual parts in a more or less reasonable tone of voice; but then they suddenly burst

5. Folly compares the structure of the sermon to that of a five-act play. Cicero says that the poet ought to be best in the last act (*sen.* 2.5). Cf. *Adag.* 35.

6. *Speculum historiale* is the third part of the *Speculum maius*, an enormous encyclopedia compiled mostly by Vincent of Beauvais (d. 1264). *Gesta Romanorum* is a collection of moralized tales compiled about 1300; by the early sixteenth century it had been translated into German, English, and French.

7. In medieval biblical exegesis, some literal persons or events may be explicated as types or figures of Christ (allegory), as moral lessons (tropology), or as earthly symbols of heavenly reality (anagogy). Aquinas *S.T.* 1, q. 1, a. 10, and Dante's letter to Can Grande (in C. Singleton, "Two Kinds of Allegory," *Dante Studies* 1, *Commedia: Elements of Structure*, Cambridge, Mass., 1957, p. 87). The words translated "allegorically. . . anagogically" were added to the text in 1522. On Erasmus' attitude towards levels of biblical exegesis, see Sr. Geraldine Thompson, " 'Water wonderfully clear': Erasmus and figurative writing," *Erasmus in English*, 5 (1972), 5–10.

8. Homer *il.* 6.180–82; Lucretius 5.905; Horace *ars* 1.

9. Erasmus *Ecclesiastes* (*Op.* 5, 959F).

1. Cicero *de or.* 3.60.224; Quintilian *inst.* 11.3.44–45.

2. See above, p. 59, footnote 7.

out in an incredible vocal barrage, even if the subject is quite dry and abstract, breaking off at last in such a way that you would think they had run out of breath.

Finally, they have learned that the rhetoricians have something to say about laughter[3] and hence they also take pains to sprinkle in a few jokes. But those jokes, (*by all that's refined!*) are so elegant and so appropriate that they would remind you of '*an ass playing a harp.*'[4] Sometimes they are also satirical, but in such a way as to titillate rather than wound. And they never serve up more genuine flattery than when they try hardest to give the impression of *speaking sharply.* In short, their whole performance is such that you would imagine they had taken lessons from some street peddler,[5] except that the friars lag far behind them. Still, they resemble each other so closely that no one can doubt that the friars learned their rhetoric from the peddlers or the peddlers from the friars.

And even so, these preachers, with my help, find people who listen to them with as much admiration as if they were Demosthenes himself or Cicero. This group consists mostly of merchants and fine ladies. The friars devote all their energies to pleasing the ears of these people because the merchants, if they are rubbed the right way, will usually give them some of their booty, a little slice of their ill-gotten gains. The women have many reasons for granting their favor to the friars, but the chief one is that they are accustomed to pour into the sympathetic ear of the friars the grievances they hold against their husbands.

You can see, I think, how much this class of men owes me: though in fact they browbeat mankind with their petty observances and ridiculous nonsense and screaming and shouting, they think they are veritable Paul's or Anthony's.[6] But I am glad to be done with these playactors, whose ungrateful disavowal of my benefits is matched by their ⟨disgraceful⟩ pretense to piety.

3. See above, p. 82, footnotes 9, 1, and 2.
4. See above, p. 39, footnote 5.
5. See above, p. 10, footnote 8.
6. Here and in *Enchiridion* (p. 115), the persons meant are probably not the Egyptian hermits, but the apostle Paul and St. Anthony of Padua, both renowned for eloquent preaching.

For I've long been wanting to say a little something about kings and great courtiers, who pay their respects to me very forthrightly and (in keeping with their honorable station) quite honestly and openly. If these men had an ounce of good sense, what could be more wretched and repellent than the life they lead? No one would think he should commit perjury or parricide to gain regal power, if he stopped to think what an enormous burden rests on the shoulders of the man who wants to be a true prince. If he considered that the man who takes up the reins of government functions as a public servant, not as a private individual, and that he should give no thought to anything except the common good; if he considered that he should not swerve by a hair's breadth[7] from the course prescribed by the laws, which he both enacts and enforces; that he is responsible for the integrity of all officials and magistrates; that he himself is always exposed to public view so that he may either promote the welfare of his people by his spotless character, like a beneficent star, or he may, like a baleful comet, bring disaster upon them; that the vices of others do not make such a powerful or widespread impression; that a prince's status is so high that if he deviates even slightly from the proper course, his offense immediately spreads like a deadly plague, infecting many, many people;[8] and also, since the lot of princes brings with it many inducements to lead him from the right path—such as sensuous delights, freedom, flattery, luxury—if he considered that he must strive all the harder and watch all the more carefully lest even through deception he should fail in his duty; and finally—to say nothing of plots, hatred, and other dangers or fears— if he considered that hanging over his head[9] is the judgment of that king who before long will call him to account even for his slightest misdeed (and the greater the kingdom the stricter the account), if a prince, I say, should reflect seriously on these points and many others like them (and reflect on them he must if he is truly wise), he could neither eat nor sleep, I think, with any enjoyment.

But as it is, through the service I do them, they leave all these

---

7. *Adag.* 406.
8. See *CW* 4, 56/15n.
9. Cicero *tusc.* 5.21.61–62; Horace *carm.* 3.1.17–21; Persius 3.39–43.

concerns in the lap of the gods[1]—their whole concern is to lead a soft life. They will not listen to anyone except those who have learned the knack of saying such agreeable things as will not disturb their minds with any dutiful anxiety. They think they have fulfilled the whole duty of a prince if they constantly ride to the hunt, if they raise thoroughbred horses, if they make a profit by selling appointments to offices and administrative posts, if every day brings with it some newly contrived method of reducing their citizens' wealth and diverting it into their coffers—always, of course, finding suitable pretexts so that downright injustice may at least have some appearance of justice. They make a special effort to throw in some flattery so as to win over, more or less, the hearts of the people. Now imagine, if you please (and there are some who fit the picture), a man ignorant of the law, almost an enemy to the common good, intent on advancing his own private interests, addicted to pleasure, a man who hates learning, who hates liberty and truth, who never gives the least thought to the welfare of the state but measures all things by his own pleasures and his own profit. Then put a gold chain around his neck, a sign of the interlocking agreement of all the virtues. Next give him a crown set with precious gems to remind him that he is supposed to excel everyone in the exercise of all the heroic virtues. Give him a scepter to symbolize justice and a heart completely fortified against the assaults of corruption. And finally, give him a scarlet robe to represent an extraordinary love of the commonwealth. If a prince should compare these accouterments with his own way of life, I cannot but think that he would be thoroughly ashamed of his splendid apparel and would be afraid that some clever wit might make a laughing stock of all this lofty costume.[2]

Now what shall I say about the great lords at court? Although most of them[3] are utterly obsequious, servile, vapid, and degraded, nevertheless they would have us think they are the crème de la crème. Still, in one respect they are the most modest of men: they

1. Horace *carm.* 1.9.9.
2. Erasmus gives the same symbolism in *Educ. Chr. Pr.*, pp. 152, 187, 197–99. The choice of crown, robe, and scepter also suggests *Matt.* 27 : 28–29.
3. In 1522 "most of them" replaced "they."

are content to carry around the bodily burden of gold, gems, robes of royal purple, and the other symbols of virtue and wisdom, yielding to others the endeavor to put those qualities into actual practice. They consider themselves abundantly blessed because they can call the king "my lord," because they can throw in honorary titles such as "Your Serenity," "Your Lordship," "Your Magnificence," because they can put on a bold face,[4] because they can flatter quite elegantly. For these are the arts that befit your true nobleman and courtier. But if you examine their whole style of living more closely,[5] they are nothing but playboys, "suitors of Penelope"— you know how the poem continues, ⟨which I would rather let Echo tell you than say it myself.⟩[6] They sleep till noon.[7] Then some hired flunky of a chaplain, ready and waiting at their bedside, runs through a hasty mass while they are still half asleep. Then off to brunch, which is hardly over before it's time for lunch. After that, dice, chess, drawing lots, buffoons, fools, strumpets, games, crude jokes. Meanwhile, one or two snacks. Then dinner. Afterwards, a round of drinks, and not just one either, by heaven! And in this fashion, without ever feeling the weary burden of living,[8] they let slip by them whole hours, days, months, years, ages. Sometimes I myself feel in finest fettle when I take leave of these cocksure courtiers *strutting their stuff*[9] while each ⟨of the nymphs⟩ imagines that every extra inch of the train she tails behind her makes her that much more divine, while one ⟨great lord⟩ elbows past another to be seen standing nearer the divine majesty, while all of them take pride in themselves according to the weight of the chains they bear

4. *Adag.* 747; Quintilian *inst.* 11.3.160; Pliny *HN* praef. 4.

5. Pliny the younger *epist.* 4.15.13.

6. Horace *epist.* 1.2.28: "the suitors of Penelope, good-for-nothings, the young people of Alcinous." By "how the poem continues" Folly refers especially to "good-for-nothings." She coyly leaves the word with the sting to be spoken by Echo, the nymph who repeats final sounds.

7. Horace *epist.* 1.2.30.

8. See above, p. 21, footnote 1.

9. This Greek compound, which Erasmus seems to have coined, may well mean "great-tailed" where "tail" is to be taken *sensu obscoeno.* The same may be true of the trains (literally, tails) drawn along by the women.

around their necks[1]—as if they were displaying not merely their wealth but also their strength.

Then too, the life-style of princes has long since been diligently imitated, and almost surpassed, by popes, cardinals, and bishops. In fact, if anyone should consider the moral meaning of the linen rochet, so striking because of its snowy whiteness, namely a life innocent in all respects; or the significance of the miter, with its two horns joined by one knot at the top, namely a thorough knowledge of both the Old Testament and the New; or the meaning of hands protected by gloves, namely, administering the sacraments with purity undefiled by merely human considerations; or of the crosier, the most watchful care of the flock entrusted to him; or of the cross carried before him, that is, victory over all human passions;[2] if, I say, anyone should consider these things and others like them, would he not lead a life full of grief and anxiety? But now they do a fine job if they feed themselves. The care of the sheep they either commend to Christ himself or pass on to their brothers, as they call them, and vicars. They don't so much as remember their own name—what the word "bishop" means—namely, painstaking labor and concern.[3] But in casting their nets for money, there they play the bishop, and keep *a sharp enough lookout*.[4]

In the same way, if cardinals realized that they have succeeded in the place of the apostles and are required to perform the same functions; then, if they thought that they are not lords but ministers of spiritual gifts, for every one of which they will soon have to give a most exact account; indeed, if they even gave a little serious con-

1. Golden chains of office, like the one worn by Thomas More in Holbein's portrait of him.

2. These symbolic meanings were traditional. They can all be found in Innocent III's *De sacro altaris mysterio* (PL *217*, cols. 793, 795) or in William Durand's *Rationale Divinorum Officiorum*.

3. The Greek word from which "bishop" is derived means "overseer." For the meaning and its implications, see Isidore *De eccles. officiis* 2.5 (PL *83*, col. 782).

4. Homer *il.* 10.515 and 13.10, *od.* 8.285. This Greek phrase contains the same root "to see" as the Greek word for "bishop." Cf. *Luke* 5 : 4-11.

sideration to their apparel and thought to themselves "What does
the whiteness of this garment mean? Isn't it the most eminent and
flawless innocence of life? What does the scarlet underneath mean?
Isn't it the most burning love of God? And then what is meant by
the scarlet outside, flowing down in such wide undulations and
completely covering the Most Reverend Father's mule?[5]—though,
for that matter, it would be enough by itself to cover a camel.[6]
Isn't it charity reaching out far and wide to help everyone,[7] that is,
to teach, exhort, console, reproach, advise, settle wars, resist wicked
princes, and freely give not merely riches but even life-blood for
Christ's flock—though why should any riches at all belong to those
who act in the place of the poor apostles?"—if they considered these
things, I say, they would not strive to get that office and would
gladly relinquish it, or at least they would lead very laborious and
anxious lives, such as those ancient apostles lived.

Now, as for the popes, who act in Christ's place, if they tried to
imitate his way of life—namely poverty, labor, teaching, the cross,
contemptus mundi—if they thought of the name "pope" (that is,
"father") or of the title "most holy," who on earth could be more
miserable?[8] Or who would spend everything he has to buy that
office? Or defend it, once it was bought, with sword, poison, and
all manner of violence? How many advantages would these men be
deprived of if they were ever assailed by wisdom? Wisdom, did I
say? No, even by a single grain of that salt mentioned by Christ.[9]
So much wealth, honor, power, so many victories, offices, dispensa-

5. The title "your eminence" was not limited to cardinals until the seventeenth century. In Erasmus' time they were addressed as "most eminent and
most reverend."

6. The color symbolism was quite traditional. The "scarlet underneath"
probably refers to a red cassock worn under a white surplice, though it might
refer to the lining of the cappa magna or pluviale worn by cardinals. The
scarlet outside" is the color of the cappa magna itself.

7. Erasmus transfers to the cappa magna the traditional symbolism of the
chasuble (Innocent III, *De sacro altaris mysterio, PL* 217, col. 795).

8. Cf. Erasmus' *Enchiridion*, pp. 154, 156, and *Educ. Chr. Pr.*, p. 197.

9. *Matt.* 5 : 13.

tions, taxes, indulgences, so many horses, mules, retainers, so many pleasures![1] You see what a warehouse, what a harvest, what a 'sea of good things,'[2] I have gathered together. These would be replaced by vigils, fasts, tears, prayers, sermons, studies, sighs, and thousands of such wretched labors. Nor should we neglect another point: so many scribes, copyists, notaries, advocates, ecclesiastical prosecutors, so many secretaries, mule-curriers, stableboys, official bankers, pimps (I had almost added something more delicate,[3] but I am afraid it might sound indelicate to some ears), in short, the huge mass of humanity which weighs down—pardon me, I meant "waits on"— the see of Rome would be turned out to starve. Certainly an inhuman and monstrous crime! And, what is even more abominable, the very highest princes of the church, the true lights of the world,[4] would be reduced to a scrip and a staff.

But as it is now, they leave whatever work there is to Peter and Paul, who have plenty of free time. But the splendor and the pleasures, those they take for themselves. And thus, through my efforts, I have brought things to such a pass that almost no sort of person leads a softer, more carefree life, since they think they have done quite well by Christ if they play a bishop's role with mystical and almost theatrical pomp,[5] with ceremonies, with titles like "your Beatitude," "your Reverence," "your Holiness," with blessings and anathemas. For them, to perform miracles is old-fashioned, outworn, completely out of step with the times; to teach the people is burdensome; to interpret Holy Scripture, academic; to pray, otiose; to pour forth tears, base and womanish; to be in want, degrading; to be conquered, disgraceful and quite unsuitable for one who hardly allows even the greatest kings to kiss his blessed

1. See Erasmus' *Julius Exclusus*, p. 86.

2. *Adag.* 228.

3. Lister says "she seems to mean the perverse love of boys." See Erasmus' *Julius Exclusus*, pp. 54, 76.

4. This phrase is from the original version of the vespers hymn for the feast of St. Peter and St. Paul (June 29). M. Britt, *The Hymns of the Breviary and Missal* (New York, 1922), p. 325.

5. See above, p. 44, footnote 3.

foot; and finally, to die seems disagreeable; to be lifted up on the cross, disreputable.[6]

All that is left are the weapons[7] and sweet benedictions mentioned by Paul,[8] and with such things they are sufficiently liberal: with interdicts, suspensions, formal warnings—denounced and reiterated —solemn excommunications, pictures of vengeance meted out to heretics, and that horrific lightning bolt[9] which they employ with a mere nod[1] to send the souls of mortals to the bottomless pit of perdition. That bolt, however, these most holy fathers in Christ and Christ's vicars on earth hurl at no one more fiercely than at those who, at the instigation of the devil, seek to diminish and gnaw away the patrimony of Peter. Though Peter says in the gospel "We have left all and followed you,"[2] they interpret his patrimony as fields, towns, taxes, imposts, dominions. While they fight for such things with burning Christian zeal and defend them 'with fire and sword,'[3] not without the loss of much Christian blood, they believe this is the very way to defend apostolically the church, the bride of Christ, manfully putting her enemies to flight, as they say. As if the church had any more deadly enemies than impious popes, who allow Christ to fade away in silence, who bind him with mercenary laws, who defile him with forced interpretations, who murder him with the pestilent wickedness of their lives.

Thus, although the Christian church was founded with blood, confirmed with blood, expanded with blood,[4] nowadays they settle everything with the sword, just as if Christ had perished completely and would no longer protect his own in his own way. And

6. See Erasmus' *Julius Exclusus*, pp. 50, 76.

7. There is ironic dissonance between the literal meaning of "weapons" and Paul's metaphoric use of the word (Hudson, p. 145).

8. The "benedictions" mentioned by Paul in *Rom.* 16 : 18 are employed by those who seduce the hearts of the innocent.

9. Excommunication.

1. *Adag.* 3839.

2. *Matt.* 19 : 27. See Erasmus' *Julius Exclusus*, p. 59.

3. *Adag.* 3711.

4. Walther 27490.

although war is so inhuman that it befits beasts, not men, so insane that even the poets imagine that it is unleashed by the Furies,[5] so noxious that it spreads moral corruption far and wide, so unjust that it is normally carried on best by robbers, so impious that it is utterly foreign to Christ, still they neglect everything else and do nothing but wage war. Here you can see rickety old men[6] demonstrate the hardiness of a youthful spirit, not upset by any expense, not wearied by any labors, not the least bit disturbed by the thought of reducing all human affairs, laws, religion, peace, to utter chaos. Nor is there any lack of learned flatterers who call this patent madness by the names zeal, piety, fortitude, having devised a way to allow someone to unsheathe cold steel and thrust it into his brother's guts without any offense against that highest duty of charity which, according to Christ's precept, he owes to his fellow Christian. Indeed, I am still not sure whether the popes have set or followed the example of some German bishops who pay no attention to vestments or benedictions or any such ceremonies but carry on as secular lords, plain and simple, so much so that they consider it cowardly and hardly worthy of a bishop to render up their courageous souls to God anywhere but on the front lines of the battle.

Now the general run of priests, thinking it would be a crime for them to fall behind the holy dedication of their superiors—good lord! how stoutly they fight for their ⟨right to⟩ tithes, with sword, spear, stones, with every imaginable sort of armed force. In this point how sharp-sighted they are in ferreting out of the writings of the fathers anything they can use to intimidate the simple people and make them think they owe even more than a tenth. But at the same time, it never occurs to them how often those writings explain the duties which priests in turn are supposed to perform for the people. They do not even consider what their tonsure means: that a priest is supposed to be free from all worldly desires and ought to meditate on nothing but heavenly matters.[7] But these agreeable

5. Virgil *aen.* 7.324–26.

6. Folly refers to the wars of the aged Pope Julius II who was satirized in Erasmus' *Julius Exclusus.*

7. Isidore (*De eccles. officiis, PL 83,* col. 779–80) gives almost the same significance for tonsure.

fellows say they have fulfilled their duty perfectly once they have mumbled through their office in some fashion or other—as for me, by heaven, I would be amazed if any god either heard or understood such prayers, since they themselves can hardly be said to hear or understand them at the very time their mouths are bawling them out.[8]

But priests have this in common with laymen: they all keep a sharp lookout to harvest their profits, and in that point no one is ignorant of the laws. But if there is some responsibility, they prudently shift that onto someone else's shoulders and pass the buck down the line from one to another. In fact, even lay princes, just as they parcel out the duties of ruling to deputies, and the deputies pass them on to subdeputies, so too they leave ⟨all⟩ the practice of piety, in their modesty, to the common people. The people foist it off on those whom they call ecclesiastics, for all the world as if they themselves had nothing to do with the church, as if their baptismal vows had had no effect whatever. Then the priests who call themselves secular—as if they were united to the world rather than to Christ—pass on the burden to the canons regular, the canons to the monks, the laxer monks to the stricter ones, both groups to the mendicant orders, the mendicants to the Carthusians, and with them alone piety lies buried, hidden away in such a manner that it hardly ever appears. In the same way popes, however diligent in harvesting money, delegate their excessively apostolic labors to the bishops, the bishops to the pastors, the pastors to their vicars, the vicars to the mendicant friars, and they too foist off their charge on those who shear the fleece of the flock.

But it is no part of my present plan to rummage through the lives of popes and priests, lest I should seem to be composing a satire rather than delivering an encomium, or lest anyone should imagine I am reproaching good ⟨princes⟩[9] when I praise bad ones. Rather, I have touched briefly on these matters to make it perfectly clear that no mortal can live happily unless he is initiated into my mysteries and has gained my favor.

8. Innocent III (*De sacro altaris mysterio* 2.62, PL *217*, col. 836): "Whoever does not hear himself is not heard by God."

9. In 1514 "princes" replaced "pontiffs."

Indeed, how could he possibly do so, since even Nemesis,[1] the arbiter of all human affairs, agrees with me so thoroughly that she has always been most hostile to wisemen, whereas she pours her blessings on fools even in their sleep? From this fact Timotheus— you all know about him—derived both his name and the proverb applied to him ('*his net catches for him even while he sleeps*').[2] Then there is that other proverb, '*The owl is flying*.'[3] Quite different are the sayings applied to wisemen: '*born on the fourth day*,' 'he has got Seius' horse,' or 'the gold of Toulouse.'[4] But I will stop *propounding apothegms* lest I seem to have rifled the commentaries of my friend Erasmus.[5]

To get to the point, then, Fortune loves those who are not too bright, who are headstrong[6] and fond of that proverb '*let the die be cast*.'[7] But wisdom makes men into milksops and that is why you always see these wisemen living in poverty and hunger, their hopes gone up in smoke. They are neglected, inglorious, despised, whereas fools are rolling in money, hold high public office, and (in a word) live in the highest style. For if anyone thinks that happiness consists in gaining the favor of great rulers[8] and living on familiar terms with those bejeweled and golden gods, what could be less helpful than wisdom? Indeed, among such men what could be more harmful? If money is the object, how much profit would a merchant

1. Folly distorts the role of the goddess Nemesis (to punish the proud and elevate the humble) by equating her with the goddess Fortuna, who proverbially favors fools (Walther 9847c). See *Adag.* 1538.

2. The reply of Timotheus, an Athenian general, to this proverbial quip was "Imagine what I could do awake" (Erasmus, *Op. 4*, 249B, and *Adag.* 482). Timotheus had the nickname "lucky."

3. "The owl is flying" refers to the luck of the Athenians, to whom the owl, the bird of Athena, was sacred (*Adag.* 76).

4. Labors and griefs were supposed to be the lot of those born (like Hercules) on the fourth day of the lunar month; the owners of Seius' horse or the gold of Toulouse suffered grievous misfortunes (*Adag.* 77, 997–98).

5. Folly refers to Erasmus' *Adagia* (Venice, 1508), the work which first established Erasmus' fame as a scholar.

6. See *Adag.* 145, and above, p. 116, footnote 1.

7. *Adag.* 332.

8. Horace *epist.* 1.17.35.

make if, as wisdom dictates, he had scruples about perjuring himself, if he were ashamed when someone caught him lying, if he cared in the least about all those fine points laid down by wisemen about theft and usury?[9] Then too, if someone is pursuing honor or wealth in the church, any ass or ox will sooner succeed there than a wiseman. If you are after pleasure, girls (who have the biggest parts in that play) are completely devoted to fools and are no less shocked and repelled by a wiseman than by a scorpion. To sum up, whoever wants to live with a modicum of mirth and merriment locks out the wiseman right off and would sooner let in any other creature whatever. In brief, wherever you turn, whether you are dealing with popes, princes, judges, officeholders, friends, enemies, or anyone at all from the top of the social scale to the bottom, you can buy everything with money,[1] and since the wiseman scorns money, it usually does its best to stay out of his way.

But, though there is no bound or limit to my praises, a speech has to come to an end sooner or later. Therefore I will stop—but not before I have devoted a few words to showing that there is no lack of great authorities who have spread my fame both by their writings and their deeds, lest anyone should imagine that I am so foolish as to stand all alone in this high opinion of myself or lest these picayune lawyers should falsely accuse me of giving no evidence. And so I will cite authorities just as they do—that is, *'quite apropos of nothing.'*[2]

First of all, everyone is very familiar with the proverb which admonishes us that in the absence of the reality, the appearance of it is the best thing.[3] Hence, it is quite fitting that among the earliest lessons taught to schoolboys is the verse, "To pretend to be foolish when the case requires it is the highest wisdom."[4] Judge for yourselves what an enormous advantage Folly must be if a deceptive

9. See above, p. 77, footnote 4.
1. See *CW* 4, 102/22n.
2. *Adag.* 445.
3. Cf. Walther 32039.
4. Cato *disticha* 2.18.2.

shadow, a mere imitation of her, has merited such great praise from learned men. But that plump and sleek porker from the herd of Epicurus[5] is much more frank: he enjoins us to mingle folly with our deliberations, although it was not very bright of him to add the qualification, "a little."[6] So too, in another place he says, "It is delightful to be foolish at the proper time and place."[7] Then again, in another passage, he prefers "to seem mad and stupid than to be wise and snappish."[8] Also, Homer's Telemachus, on whom the poet bestows unfailing praise, is sometimes called "*childish*," and the tragic poets readily apply the same epithet to boys and young men as a sign of great promise.[9] But after all, what is the whole subject matter of that revered poem the Iliad but "the broils of foolish kings and the foolish populace"?[1] Then, how unqualified is Cicero's praise, "Everything is full of folly"![2] For who does not know that the more widespread any good thing is, the more excellent it is?[3]

But perhaps the authority of these writers is not highly regarded among Christians. Therefore, if you please, let us support (or as the learned say, "ground") our praises from Holy Scripture, having first begged pardon from the theologians and permission to do so. And then, because we are undertaking a very difficult task and because it would perhaps be unwarranted to call once again on the

---

5. Horace *epist.* 1.4.15–16.

6. Horace *carm.* 4.12.27.

7. Horace *carm.* 4.12.28. "In another place" seems to be a slip on Erasmus' part.

8. Horace *epist.* 2.2.126–28.

9. Folly exploits the ambiguity of the Greek word: simply "child" (in this sense it is applied to Telemachus in *od.* 11.448–49) and "childish, foolish" (e.g., *od.* 9.44). Sophocles uses the word in the sense "child" (*Ion.* 1399, *Andr.* 755, *Heraclid.* 956).

1. Horace *epist.* 1.2.8.

2. Cicero *fam.* 9.22.4. The sentence occurs casually in a discussion of the obscene overtones present in ordinary words.

3. *The Macmillan Book of Proverbs, Maxims, and Famous Sayings*, ed. B. Stevenson (New York, 1968) gives "bonum quo communius eo melius" as an early saying of unknown origin. St. Ignatius Loyola wrote "the more universal good is, the more divine it is" (*Constitutiones*, pars 7, cap. 2).

Muses[4] to make such a long journey from Helicon—especially since the subject is quite foreign to them—perhaps it would be more fitting, while I am playing the theologian and making my way through these thorny thickets, to wish that the soul of Scotus, thornier than any porcupine or hedgehog, might come from the Sorbonne[5] to make a brief sojourn in my breast, after which he may set right out again for wherever he likes—'*to the devil himself*'[6] for all I care. I wish I could change my countenance too and put on the garb of a theologian. But at the same time I am afraid someone might charge me with theft, as if I had secretly rifled the desks of our master-doctors, because I know so much theology. But it ought not to be surprising that, from my long-standing contact with theologians (which has been very close indeed), I have picked up something here and there, since even that worthless figwood god Priapus learned and retained some Greek words from his master when he read aloud.[7] And Lucian's cock, from his long contact with men, learned human speech quite well.[8]

But now, to the point, and the devil take the hindmost![9] Ecclesiastes wrote in his first chapter: "The number of fools is infinite."[1] ⟨When he speaks of an infinite number, doesn't he seem to be including all mortals, except perhaps for some few, and they (so far as I can see) are so rare that hardly anyone has ever laid eyes on them? But Jeremiah professes this belief much more frankly in his tenth chapter: "Every man," he says, "is rendered foolish by his wisdom." Wisdom he attributes to God alone, leaving folly as the lot of all men. And again, a little before, he says: "Let no man boast of his wisdom." And why, O excellent Jeremiah, do you forbid any man to boast of his wisdom?[2] "Indeed," he will say, "for this

4. See above, p. 45, footnote 8.
5. See above, p. 90, footnote 8.
6. *Adag.* 1096.
7. Horace *serm.* 1.8.1–2, *Priap.* 68.3–4.
8. Lucian *gallus* (tr. Erasmus, Amsterdam ed. *1*, part 1, 473, ll. 8–10).
9. Literally, "under favorable auspices." *Adag.* 75.
1. *Eccl.* 1 : 15.
2. *Jer.* 10 : 15, 10 : 7 and 12, 9 : 23.

reason: no man has any wisdom." But I return to Ecclesiastes.⟩
What do you think he meant when he cried out, "Vanity of vani-
ties, and all is vanity"?[3] No more nor less than this (as we said
before)[4]: that all human life is nothing but a stage-play of Folly.
Thus he gives his vote[5] to that eulogy by Cicero, ⟨so rightly celebrated,⟩ which we have already quoted: ⟨"Everything is full of
folly."⟩[6] Again, that wise ⟨Ecclesiasticus,⟩ what did he mean
when he said, "A fool changes like the moon, a wise man is im-
mutable like the sun"?[7] Just this: all mankind is foolish, the title
"wise" applies to God alone. For they interpret the moon as human
nature, and the sun as God, the fountain of all light.[8] The same point
is confirmed by Christ's assertion in the gospel that no one should be
called good except God alone.[9] Thus, if anyone who is not wise is
foolish, and every wiseman must also be good, as the Stoics claim,[1]
then it necessarily follows that all mortals are embraced by Folly.
Again, Solomon says in chapter 15, "The fool delights in his folly,"[2]
thus openly admitting that nothing in life is pleasant without folly.
The same point is also supported by the text, "Whoever gets knowledge also gets suffering, and in much understanding is much
vexation." ⟨Doesn't that remarkable preacher make the same
point quite clearly in chapter 7: "The heart of a wiseman resides
with sorrow; the heart of fools, with joy"? Hence, he did not consider it enough to master wisdom without also gaining a knowledge
of us. And if you place little credence in me, listen to the words he
himself wrote in chapter 1: "I applied my mind to understand wis-

3. *Eccl.* 1 : 2 and 12 : 8.
4. See above, pp. 43–44.
5. *Adag.* 453.
6. See above, p. 118.
7. *Sir.* 27 : 12.
8. Augustine *epist.* 55.8–9 (*CSEL 34*, 177–79); Caesarius *dial.* 2.100 (*PG 38*, 966).
9. *Matt.* 19 : 17.
1. *Stoicorum veterum fragmenta*, ed. J. von Arnim (Leipzig, 1903–24), *3*, 148–49, 164–68.
2. *Prov.* 15 : 21.

dom and knowledge, delusions and folly."[3] Please take note that in this passage folly's praise is enhanced because she is assigned the last position in the sentence. Ecclesiastes wrote it, and you all know that the ecclesiastical order of precedence places the highest dignitary at the end of a procession—mindful, to be sure, in this point at least, of the gospel precept.[4]

Then too, Ecclesiasticus, whoever he was, clearly testifies to the superiority of folly over wisdom in chapter 44.[5] But by heaven, I will not quote his words until you have helped me frame an *introductory context*[6] for them by giving suitable responses, just as the people do who argue with Socrates in Plato. Which is it more fitting to conceal, rare and precious items or common and cheap things? Why do you keep silent? Even if you pretend not to know, the Greek proverb will answer for you: '*The waterjug is left lying in the doorway*'—and lest anyone should be so impious as to reject this proverb, it is reported by Aristotle himself, the god of our master-doctors.[7] Are any of you so foolish as to leave gems and gold lying in the street? Absolutely not, I think. You put them away in the most secret hiding places—even more, in the innermost recesses of the most theft-proof chests. But trash you leave out in the open. Therefore, if what is precious is concealed, and what is cheap is left exposed, is it not perfectly clear that wisdom, which he forbids us

3. *Eccl.* 1 : 18, 7 : 5, 1 : 17.

4. William Durand (*Rationale Divinorum Officiorum* 4.6.15-17, 6.102.3) discusses the order and significance of ecclesiastical processions in detail, but does not refer to the gospel texts about the first and the last. Erasmus' ironical allusion was probably a brilliant invention. *Matt.* 19 : 30, 20 : 16; *Mark* 10 : 31; *Luke* 13 : 30.

5. Erasmus (or the printer, perhaps reading "44" instead of "xx") seems to have mistaken the chapter. *Sir.* 44 contains no support for Folly's viewpoint, and the words to which she refers here (quoted at the end of this paragraph) are from *Sir.* 41 : 18. A very similar sentence appears in *Sir.* 20 : 30.

6. Quintilian *inst.* 5.11.3; Erasmus *Ecclesiastes* (*Op.* 5, 927A, 942E).

7. Erasmus himself interpreted the proverb as Folly does here (*Adag.* 1065, and *Op.* 5, 1047B) though he knew it was defective as reported by Aristotle (*rhet.* 1363a). Modern editors take it to apply to "lost labor"—to break the pitcher after carrying it home.

to hide away, is less valuable than folly, which he commands us to conceal? Now here are the actual words of his testimony: "The man who conceals his folly is better than the man who hides his wisdom."

What about this: Holy Scripture even attributes to the fool a spirit of openminded generosity, while the wiseman thinks no one is as good as he is. For that is how I understand what Ecclesiastes wrote in chapter 10: "As the fool walks along the street, he thinks that, since he himself is stupid, everyone else is also foolish."[8] Isn't it a mark of a certain openminded frankness to take everyone as your equal and, though no one does not have a grand notion of himself, nevertheless to share your praises with everyone else?⟩ Thus, even such a great king was not ashamed of this title, when he says in chapter 30: "I am the most foolish of men."[9] Even Paul himself, the great teacher of the gentiles, ⟨writing to the Corinthians,⟩ is not at all loath to acknowledge the title "fool": "to speak," he says, "as a fool, I am more so"—just as if it were shameful to be outdone in folly.[1]

⟨But now some of these Greeklings will cry out against me, trying (as they do) to 'steal the laurels'[2] of so many modern theologians by throwing dust in others' eyes through their annotations. In this herd, certainly the second place, if not the first, is held by my Erasmus, whom I often mention "honoris causa".[3] A foolish citation, they say, and worthy of Folly herself! The apostle's meaning is worlds away from your fantasies. For he did not employ such language in order to be thought more foolish than others. Rather, when he had said, "Are they servants of Christ? So am I," and had

8. *Eccl.* 10 : 3.

9. *Prov.* 30 : 2. The great king is Solomon, considered to be the author of *Ecclesiastes* and *Proverbs*.

1. *2 Cor.* 11 : 23.

2. Literally, "pecking out the eyes of crows" (*Adag.* 275).

3. Perhaps Erasmus has Folly give himself the second place because his work on the Greek text of Scripture had been preceded by that of Lorenzo Valla or Lefèvre d'Étaples (see below, pp. 171–72). But the self-depreciatory attitude he assumes toward himself is in keeping with the ironical stance he assumes in other places in the *Folly*.

almost boastfully claimed equality with the others in this point too, he added the correction, "I am more so," deeming himself not only equal but even somewhat superior to the other apostles in spreading the gospel. And though he intended this assertion to be taken as true, nevertheless, to keep from offending their ears with arrogant boasts, he guarded his speech by assuming the mask of folly—"to speak without wisdom"—because he knew that only fools have a license to declare the truth without offense.

But I leave it to them to argue about what Paul meant when he wrote these words. Myself, I hold with the great, stout, solid theologians, everywhere most highly regarded, with whom most learned men would rather err, *by Jove*, than be right with these trilingual newcomers.[4] They all consider these Greeklings no better than a flock of grackles,[5] especially since a certain glorious[6] theologian (whose name I prudently refrain from mentioning, lest these grackles should immediately taunt him with that Greek saying *'an ass with a lyre'*),[7] explaining this passage with full magistral and theologial[8] fanfare, made a new heading and added a new break (which he could never have done without consummate skill in dialectic), interpreting it in this fashion (for I will give his own words not only formally but also materially): "To speak less wisely, that is, if I seem unwise in claiming equality with the pseudo-apostles, I will seem to you even less wise in claiming superiority to them." But a bit later he seems to forget himself and take another tack.[9]

4. The three languages are Latin, Greek, and Hebrew. Erasmus played an important part in the founding of the trilingual college at Louvain and remained interested in it throughout his life. See below, pp. 162–64.

5. *Adag.* 622.

6. The Latin "gloriosus" can mean either "famous" or "vainglorious".

7. See above, p. 106, footnote 4. Folly refers to Nicolas de Lyra (d. 1349), a Franciscan whose commentary on the literal (and to a lesser degree moral) sense of Scripture dominated biblical exegesis for two hundred years.

8. In these two modifiers Folly deliberately ridicules the barbarous diction of theologians.

9. In his note on *2 Cor.* 11 : 23 (*Op. 6*, 790–91) Erasmus takes Lyra to task at greater length.

But why should I take so much trouble to defend myself with only one example, since it is the recognized right of theologians to stretch out the heavens—that is, Holy Scripture—like a chamois skin? Even in St. Paul the message of Scripture receives support from some words which, in their original context, do not support it (at least if we have any confidence in *quinquelingual* Jerome).[1] When he happened to notice an inscription on an altar at Athens, Paul twisted it into an argument for the Christian faith: omitting the other words, which would have spoiled his argument, he cut off the last two only—namely these, "to the unknown god"—and even these he changed somewhat. For the whole inscription was as follows: "To the gods of Asia, Europe, and Africa, to the unknown and foreign gods." It is his example, I imagine, which the *scions of theology*[2] nowadays universally follow when they pick out four or five words here and there—distorting them to boot, if need be—and apply them to their purposes, even if what precedes and follows these snippets is completely foreign, or even opposite, to their interpretation. But they carry it off with such felicitous effrontery that sometimes even legal counselors are envious of theologians.

Is there anything at all they cannot bring off, now that the great man (I almost let his name slip, but again I am afraid of the Greek proverb) has squeezed out of Luke's words an opinion about as consonant with the mind of Christ as 'fire is with water'?[3] For, when the final danger drew near, the time when loyal followers devote themselves most wholeheartedly to the defense of their leader and *fight with him shoulder to shoulder*, Christ specifically set out to remove from the hearts of his apostles any reliance on such defense. He asked them whether they lacked anything when he sent them out with so little provision for their journey, with no shoes to protect their feet from thorns and rocks, or knapsacks to keep them from going hungry. When they said they were not short of anything, he

---

1. *Acts* 17 : 23. See Erasmus' note on this text (*Op. 6*, 501). Jerome discusses it in his commentary on *Tit.* 1 : 12 (*PL 26*, 572–73).

2. *Adag.* prol. (*Op. 2*, 10F).

3. *Adag.* 3294.

went on: "But now," he said, "whoever has a purse should take it, and also his pack; and whoever has no sword should sell his coat and buy one."[4] Since Christ's whole teaching stresses nothing so much as gentleness, tolerance, contemptus mundi, how can anyone miss what he means in this passage? Namely, to disarm his messengers even further, so that they might not only have no concern about shoes and a knapsack, but might also part even with their coats in order to undertake their mission of preaching the gospel, unburdened and stripped for action, providing themselves with nothing but a sword—not the kind brandished by robbers and murderers, but the sword of the spirit,[5] which pierces into the very depths of the breast and at one stroke cuts away all desires, leaving nothing but piety in the heart.

But please note how that renowned theologian wrests this passage from its true meaning. He interprets the sword as defense against persecution, the purse as a sufficient amount of supplies, just as if Christ had reversed his position and, lest he should appear to send out his ambassadors without *sufficiently royal pomp and circumstance,*[6] had recanted his former teaching; or as if he had forgotten what he said before, that they would be blessed when they were afflicted with reproaches, scorn, and torments, forbidding them to resist oppression because the meek, not the cruel, are blessed; as if he had forgotten that he had held up before them the example of the sparrows and the lilies,[7] and was now so far from wanting them to set out without a sword that he ordered them to buy one even if they had to sell their coat to get it and would rather see them set

4. *Luke* 22 : 35–36. In his note on this text, Erasmus refutes Lyra's interpretation at length (*Op. 6,* 317C–321F). Commenting on the literal sense, Nicolas does give the interpretation ridiculed by Folly, though he twice qualifies the defense symbolized by the sword as "moderate." Commenting on the moral sense, he adds, "The sword of the spirit is the word of God contained in Holy Scripture," quoting *Matt.* 13 : 45 and *Wisdom* 7 : 9 as parallel texts. See Erasmus' *Julius Exclusus,* p.55.

5. Lister quotes St. Ambrose, *Expos. in Luc.* (*CCSL 10,* 54, 529–36).

6. *Adag.* 1786.

7. *Matt.* 5 : 4–5, 11, and 39–42; 6 : 26–30; 10 : 28–33.

out naked than not girt with a steel blade. Moreover, just as he thinks the word "sword" includes everything necessary to repel force, so too in the notion of "knapsack" he includes all the necessities of life. And thus this interpreter of the divine mind musters the apostles fully equipped with spears, slings, siege-machines, cannons, to preach Christ crucified. He also loads them up with bags, suitcases, and luggage lest they might perchance have to leave the inn without breakfast. This man is not at all disturbed that the very sword which Christ had so urgently ordered to be bought, he soon after severely ordered to be returned to its scabbard[8] and that there is not the slightest report of the apostles fighting the gentiles with sword and shield, as they certainly would have if Christ had intended what this fellow thinks he meant.

There is another, whose name (out of respect) I will not give, but who is of no small reputation, who made the tents mentioned by Habakkuk in the text "The tents of the Medianites will be destroyed" into the skin flayed from Bartholomew.[9] I myself recently attended a theological disputation, as I often do. When someone there had asked what was the scriptural authority for overcoming heretics by burning them instead of converting them by argumentation, a sour old man, whose supercilious look alone was enough to mark him as a theologian, replied very irritably that Paul himself had laid down this law when he said "A heretic should be warned once, and then once again; after that, shun him (devita)." And when he went on thundering out these same words and many were wondering what was wrong with the man, he finally explained that

---

8. *Matt.* 26 : 52, *John* 18 : 11.

9. Lister suggests that this error may be found in the sermons of Jordanus. He probably refers to Jordanus von Quedlinburg (c. 1300–1380), whose sermons were widely known and quite influential in the fifteenth century. In his sermon on St. Bartholomew (*Sermones de sanctis*, Strassburg, 1484, sigs. v2–v3) Jordanus does make some far-fetched connections between Old Testament texts (*Gen.* 3 : 21, *Job* 2 : 4 and 10 : 11, *Mich.* 3 : 3) and the excoriation of St. Bartholomew, but he does not mistakenly take "tents" in *Hab.* 3 : 7 to mean "skin." In a list of sermons which should not be imitated, Erasmus mentions "Sermones Jordanis"; he also gives this same example of a false exordium (*Ecclesiastes, Op.* 5, 857, 863B–C).

a heretic should be removed from life (de vita).[1] Some laughed, but there was no lack of those who thought this explanation thoroughly theological. But when others objected, an irrefragable[2] authority, the 'very last word' (as they say),[3] took his turn. "Here is the solution," he said. "It is written: You shall not allow an evildoer (maleficus) to live.[4] But every heretic is an evildoer; therefore, etc." Everyone marveled at his acuteness and ran roughshod[5] over every objection to clamber onto his bandwagon. It never occurred to anyone that that law applies to diviners and sorcerers and magicians, who are called מְכַשְּׁבִים in Hebrew. Otherwise it would be necessary to punish fornication and drunkenness with death.

But it is foolish for me to run through these things, so numerous that all of them could not be contained in the volumes of Chrysippus and Didymus.[6] I only wanted to make the point that, since such things are allowed to great masters of divinity, allowances should be made for me, a mere *tyro in theology*,[7] if all my citations are not letter perfect.

Now, finally, to get back to Paul.⟩ "How gladly you put up with fools," he says, speaking of himself. ⟨And again, "take me for a fool." And "I speak not according to God, but in my folly, as it were." Again, in another place, "we are fools," he says, "for the sake of Christ."[8] Now you have heard for yourselves such glorious

1. *Tit.* 3 : 10. In his note on this text (*Op.* 6, 973–74), Erasmus remarks that he heard this true story from John Colet, who was present at the council during which it happened (probably the convocation called by Archbishop Warham on 6 February 1511/12 to combat the newly revived Lollard heresy). The false division of "de vita" is an obvious example of the Aristotelian "fallacia accentus" (Peter of Spain, *Tractatus called afterward Summule Logicales*, ed. L. M. De Rijk, Assen, 1972, pp. 128–29).

2. See above, p. 104, footnote 4.

3. Literally, "lawyer from Tenedos." See above, p. 88, footnote 4.

4. *Exod.* 22 : 18.

5. *Adag.* 1612.

6. The philosopher Chrysippus was said to have written seven hundred books (Diogenes Laertius 7.7); the grammarian Didymus, four thousand (Seneca *epist.* 88.37).

7. *Adag.* 685.

8. *2 Cor.* 11 : 16–19, *1 Cor.* 4 : 10

laudation of folly proclaimed by such a noble author.⟩ And what if the same authority goes so far as to urge folly upon his hearers ⟨as especially necessary and thoroughly salutary?⟩ "Whoever seems wise among you, let him become a fool, that he may be wise."⁹

And in Luke, Jesus called the two disciples who joined him on the road "fools."⟩¹ I hardly know whether that is so very suprising, since ⟨that godlike Paul⟩ attributes something of folly even to God himself: "The folly of God is wiser than men."² For Origen in his interpretation will not allow you to say that God is foolish only in the opinion of men, as you can for that other text, "The doctrine of the cross, to those who are perishing, is indeed foolishness."³

⟨But why should I fret uselessly, trying to establish these things through so much testimony from various witnesses, when Christ himself in the mystical psalms openly says to the Father, "You know my folly"?⟩⁴ Nor is it merely an accident that fools are so extremely pleasing to God. I think the reason is simply this: just as great rulers suspect and despise those who are too intelligent (as Caesar did Brutus and Cassius, whereas he had no fear of the drunken Anthony, and as Nero did Seneca, and Dionysius did Plato)⁵ but are delighted with crude and simply minds, so too Christ always despises and condemns those *savants* who rely on their own wisdom. Paul testifies very clearly on this point when he says "What is foolish to the world, God has chosen," and when he says that God

---

9. *1 Cor.* 3 : 18.

1. *Luke* 24 : 25.

2. *1 Cor.* 1 : 25.

3. *1 Cor.* 1 : 18. Erasmus' note on *1* Cor. 1 : 25 *Op.* 6, 665) and Origen, *Homilies on Jeremiah*, tr. St. Jerome (*PL* 25, 630–32). See C. H. Miller, "Current English Translations of *The Praise of Folly*: Some Corrections," *Philological Quarterly*, 45 (1966), 730–31.

4. *Ps.* 68 : 6. As Lister notes, Folly distorts the text since Christ was traditionally understood to speak here not for himself but as the mouthpiece of his members, sinful Christians (Augustine, *CCSL* 39, 910–11; Cassiodorus, *CCSL* 97, 608; Nicolas de Lyra).

5. Plutarch *Iul. Caes.* 72 (*vit.* 737C); Tacitus *ann.* 15.62 and 65; Cicero *Rab. Post.* 9.23.

was pleased to save the world through folly because it could not be redeemed by wisdom.[6] Indeed, God himself makes the same point clear enough when he cries out through the mouth of the prophet, "I will destroy the wisdom of the wise and the prudence of the prudent I will reject,"[7] and again when he gives thanks that the mystery of salvation has been hidden from the wise and revealed to the simple, that is, to fools. ⟨For the Greek for "simple" is νηπίοις, which he contrasted with σοφοῖς (wise).⟩[8] Relevant here, too, are his attacks everywhere in the gospel against the scribes and pharisees and doctors of the law, whereas he carefully protected the ignorant populace. ⟨For isn't "Woe to you, scribes and pharisees"[9] equivalent to "Woe to you, wisemen"?⟩ But he seems to have taken the greatest delight in simple people, women, and fishermen. In fact, even on the level of animal creatures, Christ is most pleased with those who are farthest removed from the slyness of the fox. Hence he preferred to ride on an ass,[1] when if he wished he could have mounted on a lion's back with impunity. And the Holy Spirit came down in the shape of a dove,[2] ⟨not an eagle or a hawk.⟩ Moreover, throughout Holy Scripture, harts, young mules, and lambs are frequently mentioned.[3] Consider also that he calls his own followers, destined for immortal life, sheep.[4] No other animal is more stupid, as is quite clear from the Aristotelian proverb '*a mind like a sheep's,*' which (as he informs us) is derived from that animal's stupidity and is frequently leveled at blockheads and dolts as an insult.[5] But, of such a flock as this, Christ professes to be the shep-

---

6. *1 Cor.* I : 21 and 27.

7. *1 Cor.* I : 19, referring to *Is.* 29 : 14.

8. *Matt.* 11 : 25, *Luke* 10 : 21. See above, p. 118, footnote 9.

9. *Matt.* 23 : 13–27, *Luke* 11 : 42–43.

1. *Matt.* 21 : 1–7.

2. *Matt.* 3 : 16.

3. "Lamb" occurs well over one hundred times in the Bible; "hart," over twenty times; "young mule" (*hinnulus*), only five times. Folly hides the false evidence in the midst of the true.

4. *John* 10 : 1–27, *Matt.* 25 : 32–33.

5. Aristotle *hist. an.* 610b; *Adag.* 2095.

herd. Even more, he himself delighted in the title "lamb," as when John pointed him out with, "Behold, the lamb of God," which is also frequently mentioned in the Apocalypse.[6]

Do not all these witnesses cry out with one voice that all mortals are fools, even the pious? And that even Christ, though he was the wisdom of the Father,[7] became somehow foolish in order to relieve the folly of mortals[8] when he took on human nature and appeared in the form of a man?[9] Just as he became sin in order to heal sins.[1] Nor did he choose any other way to heal them but through the folly of the cross, through ignorant and doltish apostles.[2] For them, too, he carefully prescribed folly, warning them against wisdom, when he set before them the example of children, lilies, mustard seed, and sparrows[3]—stupid creatures lacking all intelligence, leading their lives according to the dictates of nature, artless and carefree—and also when he forbad them to be concerned about how they should speak before magistrates,[4] and when he enjoined them not to examine dates and times,[5] so as to keep them from relying on their own wisdom and make them depend on him heart and soul. To the same effect is the prohibition of God, the architect of the world, that they should not eat any fruit from the tree of knowledge,[6] as if knowledge would poison their happiness. For that matter, Paul openly condemns knowledge as dangerous because it puffs men up.[7] St. Bernard, I imagine, was following Paul when he interpreted the

6. *John* 1 : 29 and 36, *Apoc.* chap. 5–7.
7. *1 Cor.* 1 : 24.
8. In 1516 "the folly of mortals" replaced "our folly."
9. *Phil.* 2 : 7. See below, p. 157.
1. *2 Cor.* 5 : 21.
2. *1 Cor.* 1 : 18–23, *Gal.* 5 : 11.
3. Children: *Matt.* 18 : 3, *Mark* 10 : 15, *Luke* 18 : 17. Lilies: *Matt.* 6: 28, *Luke* 12 : 27. Mustard seed: *Matt.* 13 : 31 and 17 : 19, *Mark* 4 : 31, *Luke* 13 : 19 and 17 : 6. Sparrows: *Matt.* 6 : 25 and 10 : 29, *Luke* 12 : 6.
4. *Matt.* 10 : 18–19, *Mark* 13 : 11, *Luke* 12 : 11–12 and 21 : 14.
5. *Acts* 1 : 7.
6. *Gen.* 2 : 17.
7. *1 Cor.* 8 : 1.

mountain on which Lucifer established his throne as the mountain of knowledge.[8]

⟨Perhaps we ought not to omit the argument that folly is pleasing to the powers above because it alone can win pardon for mistakes, whereas a knowledgeable man is not forgiven. Hence, those who pray for forgiveness, even if they sinned knowingly, still employ folly as a pretext and defense. For this is the way Aaron prays to avert the punishment of his sister in The Book of Numbers, if I remember correctly: "I beg you, Lord, do not hold us responsible for this sin, which we have committed in our folly."[9] So too Saul begged David to forgive his offense, saying, "For it is clear that I acted in my folly."[1] Again, David himself coaxes the Lord in these words: "But I beg you, Lord, to take away the iniquity of your servant, because we have acted in our folly,"[2] as if he would not obtain pardon unless he pleaded folly and ignorance as excuses. But what is even more compelling, when Christ on the cross prayed for his enemies, "Father, forgive them," the only excuse he made for them was their ignorance: "for they do not know," he said, "what they are doing."[3] In the same way Paul, writing to Timothy: "For this reason I obtained mercy from God, because I acted ignorantly, as an unbeliever."[4] What does "I did it ignorantly" amount to but "I did it in my folly, not with malice?" What does "For this reason I obtained mercy" mean but that he would not have obtained it if he had not been recommended by the patronage of folly? Our case is also strengthened by that mystical psalmist, who did not occur to us in the proper place:[5] "Do not remember the sins of my youth

---

8. *In ascensione domini sermo IV* (*PL 183*, 310–12).

9. *Numb.* 12 : 11.

1. *1 Sam.* 26 : 21.

2. *2 Sam.* 24 : 10.

3. *Luke* 23 : 34.

4. *1 Tim.* 1 : 13.

5. Since this text is from the psalms, it probably should have come to mind at p. 128 (footnote 4) above. Lister remarks that forgetfulness is appropriate to Folly; she also renounces memory at the end of her speech.

and my stupidities."[6] You hear the two excuses he makes: namely, youth, to whom I am a regular companion, and stupidities—and in the plural at that, so that we may understand the full force of his folly.⟩[7]

And now, to stop running through endless examples and to put it in a nutshell, it seems to me that the Christian religion taken all together has a certain affinity with some sort of[8] folly and has little or nothing to do with wisdom. If you want some proof of this, notice first of all that children, old people, women, and retarded persons are more delighted than others with holy and religious matters and hence are always nearest to the altar, simply out of a natural inclination. Moreover, you see how those first founders of religion were remarkably devoted to simplicity and bitterly hostile to literature. Finally, no fools seem more senseless than those people who have been completely taken up, once and for all, with a burning devotion to Christian piety: they throw away their possessions, ignore injuries, allow themselves to be deceived, make no distinction between friend and foe, shudder at the thought of pleasure, find satisfaction in fasts, vigils, tears, and labors, shrink from life, desire death above all else—in short, they seem completely devoid of normal human responses, just as if their minds were living somewhere else, not in their bodies. Can such a condition be called anything but insanity? In this light, it is not at all surprising that the apostles seemed to be intoxicated with new wine[9] and that Paul seemed mad to the judge Festus.[1]

But now that we have taken on our shoulders 'the mantle of this task,'[2] let us go on with it and explain a further point: namely, that the happiness which Christians strive for with such great effort is no more than a certain kind of madness and folly—don't get the

6. *Ps.* 24 : 7.

7. Erasmus *Copia*, p. 26. In his note on *Rom.* 12 : 1 (*Op. 6*, 628), Erasmus reports Origen's opinion about the use of a plural form for emphasis.

8. "Some sort of" first appeared in 1522.

9. *Acts* 2 : 13.

1. *Acts* 26 : 24.

2. *Adag.* 266.

wrong idea, but consider the facts carefully.[3] First of all, Christians essentially agree with Platonists that the mind is buried and bound in bodily chains and that it is prevented by the body's grossness from contemplating and enjoying things as they truly are.[4] Thus, he defines philosophy as a meditation on death, because philosophy frees the mind from visible and bodily things, just as death itself does.[5] Now the mind is called sane as long as it properly controls the bodily organs. But when the links are broken and it strives to attain its own freedom, concentrating (as it were) on escape from its prison, that condition is called insanity. If such a thing happens because of disease or some organic defect, then everyone is quite agreed that it is insanity. And yet we see such men also predict future events, know languages and literatures that they never studied before, and generally have a sort of divine aura about them. The reason for this is quite clear: the mind, being now a little freer from the contagion of the body, begins to exercise its own inborn powers. For the same reason, I imagine, something similar happens to persons in the final throes of death, so that they too utter some amazing things, as if they were inspired.[6]

Now if such a thing happens from the pursuit of piety, perhaps it is not the same kind of insanity, but it is so close to it that most people would judge it to be insanity pure and simple, especially since these few negligible stragglers conflict in their whole life-style with the entire company of mortals. Thus they share the fate of those who, in the myth thought up by Plato, I believe, are bound in a cave, wondering at the shadows of things, and of that prisoner who escaped but returned to the cave to tell them he had seen things as they truly are and that they were very much deceived in thinking that nothing else exists except those wretched shadows. For this wiseman pitied and lamented the insanity of those in the grip of

3. See below, p. 159.

4. In *Ep. 4*, 289, Erasmus explains in what sense he used the phrase "things as they truly are" by referring to Plato's myth of the cave, Aristotle's *Metaphysics*, and *2 Cor.* 4 : 18. See above, p. 73, footnote 7.

5. Plato *Phaedo* 64a, 80e. Erasmus *Enchiridion*, p.68.

6. Plato *apol.* 39c.

such a grave error. They, in turn, laughed at him as quite mad and threw him out.[7] Just so the ordinary run of men regard with the greatest wonderment those things that are most corporeal; they think, in effect, that only such things really exist. But pious persons, on the other hand, the closer anything comes to the body, the less they regard it: they are completely taken up with the contemplation of invisible things. The others place most stress on riches, and next on bodily comforts, and last of all on the mind,[8] which most of them don't really think exists anyway, because they do not see it with their eyes. Quite unlike these, the pious strive with all their hearts to reach God himself, who is purest and simplest of all; this world takes second place, and even here they place most stress on what comes closest to him, namely the mind; they pay no attention to the body, they contemn and avoid money as so much trash. Or, if they are forced to deal with such things, they do so with reluctance and aversion—they have as if they did not have, they possess as if they did not possess.[9]

In single details, too, they work on quite different levels. First, among the senses, though all have some relation to the body, still some of them are more gross, such as touch, hearing, sight, smell, taste. Some are more removed from the body, such as memory, intellect, will.[1] And so, where the mind concentrates its energies, there it becomes proficient.[2] Since pious people direct their mental energy at things which are furthest removed from the grossest senses, these lower powers harden and atrophy, as it were. On the other hand, in ordinary people these perceptions are highly developed; the higher ones, hardly at all. This is the explanation for what we have heard has happened to some godly men—that they drank oil instead of wine.[3]

7. Plato *rep.* 514a–17a. See above, p. 73, footnote 7.

8. Aristotle *eth. Nic.* 1098b12–16, *pol.* 1323a23–1323b21. Cicero *fin.* 3.13.43.

9. *1 Cor.* 7 : 29–30.

1. Aristotle *an.* 429a10–429b2. The Augustinian division of man's mind into memory, intellect, and will was well known to scholastic theologians (e.g. Aquinas *S.T.* I, q. 59, a. 1; q. 79, aa. 6–7).

2. Cf. Aquinas *S.T.* 1ª–2ªᵉ, q. 37, a. 1.

3. The story is told of St. Bernard in the *Legenda aurea* (ed. Graesse, Breslau, 1890, p. 531).

Then again, among the desires of the mind, some have more to do with the grossness of the body, such as lust, a passion for food and sleep, anger, pride, envy.[4] With these the pious war unceasingly, but ordinary men can't imagine life without them. There are some intermediate feelings, which are in a sense natural, such as patriotism, or love of children, parents, friends. Ordinary men have some regard for these, but the pious strive to root out even these from their minds, except insofar as they can be assimilated to that highest part of the mind,[5] so that a father is no longer loved simply as a father (for what did he beget except the body?—though even that too is owing to God, the father of all), but as a good man whose personality projects a shining image of that highest mind of all, to which alone they give the name "highest good" and apart from which they teach that nothing is to be loved or sought.

By the same rule they measure all the other duties of life, treating what is visible, if not with complete contempt, at least as far less valuable than what cannot be seen. Even in the sacraments, they say, and in religious observances, a bodily and a spiritual dimension can be found. Thus in fasting, they do not think it amounts to much to abstain from flesh and food—ordinary people think this is all that fasting is—unless a person also restrains his passions somewhat, controlling his anger and his pride better, so that his spirit, less burdened with the weight of his body, may strive to taste and enjoy the comforts of heaven. So too in the eucharist, although the ceremonies with which it is administered are not to be scorned, still in themselves, ⟨⟨they say,⟩⟩ they are not very profitable and may even be harmful, unless what is spiritual is also present, namely, what is re-enacted by these visible signs. For what is re-enacted is the death of Christ, which mortals ought to express by taming, extinguishing, and burying (as it were) bodily passions so that they may rise up into renewed life and can be one with him and also one

4. The list includes all of the seven capital sins except avarice.

5. Lister notes that Erasmus took the tripartite division (body, soul, spirit) from St. Paul, as interpreted by Origen (e.g., Origen's commentary on *Rom.* 1 : 9 and 13 : 1, *PG 14*, 856 and 1226). See Erasmus' argument to his commentary on *Rom.* and his note on *Rom.* 13 : 1 (*Op. 6*, 550 and 634); *Enchiridion*, pp. 78–79.

among themselves. This, then, is what the pious man does; this is what he thinks about. The ordinary person, on the other hand, thinks the sacrifice means no more than to be present before the altar—as near as possible, at that—to hear the mumbling of the words, and to be a spectator at such trifling kinds of ceremony.

Not in these matters only, which I have given simply as examples, but in absolutely every activity of life, the «pious man» flees from whatever is related to the body and is carried away in the pursuit of the eternal and invisible things of the spirit. Hence, since these two groups are in such utter disagreement on all matters, the result is that each thinks the other is insane—though that word applies more properly to the pious than to ordinary men, if you want my opinion. This will be much clearer if, according to my promise, I devote a few words to showing that their supreme reward is no more than a certain insanity.

First, therefore, consider that Plato had some glimmer of this notion when he wrote that the madness of lovers is the height of happiness.[6] For a person who loves intensely no longer lives in himself but rather in that which he loves,[7] and the farther he gets from himself and the closer to it, the happier he is. Moreover, when the mind is set on leaving the body and no longer has perfect control over the bodily organs, no doubt you would rightly call this condition madness. Otherwise what is the meaning of such common expressions as "he is out of his wits," "come to your senses," and "he is himself once more." Also, the more perfect the love, the greater and happier is the madness. What, then, is that future life in heaven for which pious minds long so eagerly? I'll tell you: the spirit, stronger at last and victorious, will absorb the body. And it will do so all the more easily, partly because it is in its own kingdom now, partly because even in its former life it had purged and refined the body in preparation for such a transformation.[8] Then the spirit will be absorbed by that highest mind of all, whose power is

6. Plato *Phaedr.* 244a–45b. Cf. Plato *Io.* 533e–34e, *Men.* 99c–d.

7. P. O. Kristeller ("Erasmus from an Italian Perspective," *Renaissance Quarterly, 23* [1970], 11) notes here a "clear echo of Ficino's commentary on the Symposium."

8. Erasmus *Enchiridion*, p. 103.

infinitely greater, in such a way that the whole man will be outside himself, and will be happy for no other reason than that he is located outside himself, and will receive unspeakable joy from that Highest Good which gathers all things to Himself.

Now, although this happiness is not absolutely perfect until the mind, having received its former body, is endowed with immortality, nevertheless it happens that, because the life of the pious is nothing but a meditation and a certain shadow (as it were) of that other life, they sometimes experience a certain flavor or odor of that reward.[9] And this, even though it is like the tiniest droplet by comparison with that fountain of eternal happiness, nevertheless far surpasses all pleasures of the body, even if all the delights of all mortals were gathered into one. So much beyond the body are the things of the spirit; things unseen, beyond what can be seen. This, indeed, is what the prophet promises: "Eye has not seen, nor ear heard, nor has the heart of man conceived what things God has prepared for those who love him."[1] And this is Folly's part, which shall not be taken from her[2] by the transformation of life, but shall be perfected. Those who have the privilege of experiencing this (and it happens to very few) undergo something very like madness: they talk incoherently, not in a human fashion, making sounds without sense.[3] Then the entire expression of their faces vacillates repeatedly: now happy, now sad; now crying, now laughing, now sighing—in short, they are completely beside themselves.[4] Soon after, when they come to themselves, they say they do not know where they have been, whether in the body or out of it,[5] whether waking or sleeping. They do not remember what they

9. Erasmus defends this passage in *Ep.* 843, ll. 575–627.

1. *1 Cor.* 2 : 9, where Paul cites *Is.* 64 : 4.

2. *Luke* 10 : 42. Folly's "Moriae pars" echos "Mariae pars." Mary and Martha were traditionally allegorized as contemplation and action (Gregory the Great, *epp.* 5 and 25, *PL 77*, cols. 449, 877). St. Bernard's description of Mary's ecstasy (*PL 184*, col. 1004) resembles what Folly says here.

3. Virgil *aen.* 10.640.

4. Lister remarks that this ecstatic vacillation can be understood better if one consults Origen's commentary on *Cant.* (*PG 13*, 178–81) and the life of St. Elizabeth (*PL 195*, 136–38, 181–83).

5. *2 Cor.* 12 : 2.

heard or saw or said or did except in a cloudy way, as if it were a dream. All they know is that they were never happier than while they were transported with such madness. Thus, they lament that they have come to their senses and want above all else to be forever mad with this kind of madness. And this is only a faint taste, as it were, of that future happiness.

But I have long since forgotten myself and '*have gone beyond the pale.*'[6] If you think my speech has been too pert or wordy, keep in mind that you've been listening to Folly and to a woman. But also remember that Greek proverb '*Often a foolish man says something to the point*'[7]—unless, perhaps, you think it doesn't apply to women.

I see that you are waiting for an epilogue,[8] but you are crazy if you think I still have in mind what I have said, after pouring forth such a torrent of jumbled words. The old saying was '*I hate a drinking-companion with a memory.*'[9] Updated, it is '*I hate a listener with a memory.*' Therefore, farewell, clap your hands,[1] live well, drink your fill, most illustrious initiates of Folly.

Finis

6. Plato *Cratyl.* 413a. Lucian *gallus* 6 (tr. Erasmus, Amsterdam ed. *1*, part 1, 475, l. 6). See below, p. 160.

7. *Adag.* 501; Gellius *NA* 2.6.9.

8. According to Erasmus (*Op.* 5, 950E) an epilogue may have three purposes: 1) to refresh the hearers' memory; 2) to give a unified view of the whole speech; 3) to dispose of some loose ends. The epilogue of an encomium was often a summing up of the life under discussion and an appeal to others to imitate the virtues it illustrates; such an epilogue might appropriately end with a prayer (Theodore C. Burgess, *Epideictic Literature*, p. 126).

9. *Adag.* 601. Plutarch *mor.* 1. 612c. Martial 1.27.7. Lucian *conv.* 3 (tr. Erasmus, Amsterdam ed. *1*, part 1, 605, ll. 5–6).

1. A formula spoken by an actor at the end of a play.

ERASMUS' LETTER
TO MARTIN DORP (1514)

From Erasmus of Rotterdam,
greetings to the distinguished theologian Martin Dorp.

Your letter has not yet been delivered, but at Antwerp a friend, who had somehow gotten a copy of it, showed it to me.[1] You are dismayed at the rather unfortunate publication of the "Folly," you heartily approve my efforts to amend and edit Jerome, and you strongly urge me not to publish the New Testament. I am so far, my dear Dorp, from being offended by this letter of yours that it has made you much dearer to me, though you have always been most dear. You advise so frankly, admonish so amicably, rebuke so lovingly. To be sure, Christian charity, even when it is most severe, retains the flavor of its natural sweetness. Every day I receive many letters from learned men who call me the glory of Germany, who make me into a sun[2] or a moon, who do not so much laud me as load me with splendiferous titles. But may I be struck dead if any

---

1. Dorp's letter, written c. September 1514 (*Ep. 2*, 10–16), was first printed (with this reply from Erasmus) in October 1515 at Antwerp. Both letters appeared together again in Badius' edition of the *Moria* (Paris, 24 June 1524) and in the most important editions of the *Moria* during the rest of Erasmus' lifetime.

2. *Ep. 2*, 38 and 49.

of them has ever given me such pleasure as that reproachful letter from my friend Dorp. What Paul says is true, charity never sins: when it flatters someone, it does so to improve him; when it grows angry, the intent is exactly the same.[3] I wish that I had leisure enough to answer your letter so as to satisfy fully such a dear friend. I am most eager that you should approve whatever I do, for I have such a high opinion of your almost divine intelligence, your preeminent learning, your superlatively acute judgment that I would rather have Dorp alone on my side than a thousand others. Though I am still queasy from the sea voyage and weary from the following horseback ride, and on top of that occupied in getting my baggage together,[4] I thought it better to reply as best I can than to leave a friend holding such opinions—whether you thought of them yourself or others instilled them and instigated you to write that letter so that they could accomplish their aim from behind the scene.[5]

First of all, then, to tell the truth, I am almost sorry myself that the "Folly" was published. That little book did bring me some glory, or (if you prefer) notoriety. But I care nothing for glory joined with odium. Besides, by all that's holy, what popularly goes under the name of glory is nothing but an empty relic of paganism. A good deal of such paganism has survived among Christians: thus they say that immortality is fame left behind among their posterity and virtue is the study of literature of whatever sort. In publishing all my books my single goal has been to provide by my efforts something profitable to readers, or if I could not do that, at least not to publish anything injurious. We see some men, even great ones, misusing their writings to divulge their passions: one celebrates his silly love affair in verse, another flatters those he intends to entrap, another who has been provoked by some injury strikes back with the pen, another blows his own horn and in singing his own praises far outdoes any Thraso or Pyrgopolinices[6]

3. *1 Cor.* 13 : 4–7.
4. Erasmus wrote at Antwerp, on his way from England to Basel.
5. In his reply to Dorp, More assumes that Dorp expressed not so much his own opinions as those of others (*Selected Letters*, pp. 63–64).
6. Braggart soldiers in Terence *eun.* and Plautus *mil. glor.*

whatsoever. But I have always used my meager intelligence and the very little learning I have for one purpose: to help if I can and, if not, at least not to hurt anyone. Homer satisfied his hatred of Thersites by composing a devastating poetical sketch of him.[7] How many does Plato censure by name in his dialogues! Could anyone escape the reprimand of Aristotle, who spared neither Plato nor Socrates?[8] Demosthenes had his Aeschynes, against whom he turned his pen with wild rage. Cicero had his Piso, his Vatinius, his Sallust, his Antony.[9] How many does Seneca ridicule and revile by name![1] Or if you consider more recent writers, Petrarch used his pen as a weapon against some physician; Lorenzo, against Poggio; Politian, against Scala.[2] Can you name me any writer at all who was so moderate that he never wrote with the least bitterness against anyone? Even Jerome, pious and serious as he was, could sometimes not restrain himself from fiery outbursts against Vigilantius, fierce tirades against Jovinian, bitter attacks on Rufinus.[3] Learned men have always been in the habit of committing their griefs and joys to paper,[4] as if to a faithful friend into whose bosom they pour all the fiery turbulence of their minds. You can even find some authors who undertake to write books for no other reason than to give vent to their own feelings indirectly and thus transmit them to posterity.

But for my part, in the many volumes I have already published, in which I have praised many men quite openly, can you tell me of

7. *il.* 2.215–20. The word translated "sketch" signifies a rhetorical device (Quintilian *inst.* 9.2.40).

8. Aristotle frequently refuted positions held by Plato or Socrates, but always respectfully.

9. Demosthenes and Cicero attacked these political enemies in their orations. The diatribe against Sallust, however, was wrongly attributed to Cicero.

1. See above, p. 3, footnote 8.

2. About 1355 Petrarch wrote his *Invective against a Certain Physician*, in which he defends poetry and attacks medical quackery. In the first half of the fifteenth century Lorenzo Valla had locked horns with Poggio on philological questions, as did Politian and Bartolomeo Scala in the last half of the century.

3. St. Jerome attacked these three because of their unorthodox views on ascetic practices, virginity, and the theology of Origen.

4. Horace *serm.* 2.1.30–31.

one person whose reputation I have ever blackened? Have I ever stained anyone's character with the least spot? Have I ever reproached any nation, any class, any man by name? If you only knew, my dear Dorp, how often I have been provoked to do so by intolerable insults! But I have always suppressed my grief and given more weight to what posterity will think of us than to what their malice deserved. If others had known the truth of the matter as I myself did, no one would have considered me mordant but rather quite just, moderate, and temperate. But I thought to myself, what do others care about our personal feelings? How can our affairs even be known to those living in distant lands or in times to come? I shall have done what is owing not to their malice but to my own dignity. Besides, no one can be so unfriendly to me that I would not hope to make him my friend, if at all possible. Why should I block that possibility? Why should I write against an enemy things that I may vainly wish were never written when he is my friend? Why should I blot his good name, which I can never restore, even when he deserves it? I would rather err on the side of praising the unworthy than of disparaging the worthy. For if you praise someone who does not deserve it, it will be attributed to your generosity. But if you paint a villain in his own colors, however accurately, it will be ascribed not to his deeds but to your own morbidity. To say nothing of this: just as wrongs perpetrated and revenged over and over again sometimes lead to full-scale war, so too insults hurled back and forth have been known to result in a very dangerous outburst of passion. Moreover, just as it is hardly Christian to repay wrong with wrong, so too it is hardly gentlemanly to seek revenge for your pain by loud abuse in the manner of women.

Such reasons as these have led me to keep my writings from doing harm or drawing blood and have prevented me from defiling them with the name of any wicked person. In the "Folly" I had no other aim than I had in my other writings, but my method was different. In "The Enchiridion" I propounded the character of a Christian life in a straightforward way. In my little book "On the Education of a Christian Prince" I suggest explicitly the subjects in which a prince ought to be well versed. In that work I write openly and clearly, but my purpose was exactly the same in "The Panegyric of Philip the Duke of Burgundy," where I proceeded indirectly and under the guise of praise.[5] And in the "Folly," under the appearance of a joke, my purpose is just the same as in "The Enchiridion." I intended to admonish, not to sting; to help, not to hurt; to promote morality, not to hinder it. Even such a grave philosopher as Plato approves of drinking rather freely at parties because he thinks that the merriment generated by wine can dispel certain vices which could not be corrected by sternness.[6] Horace also believes that a humorous admonition may be just as profitable as a serious one:

"There is nothing," he says, "to prevent you from telling the truth, as long as you do it with a smile."[7]

Of this the wisest men of ancient times were quite aware: they preferred to deliver the most wholesome rules of conduct in humorous and (to all appearances) childish fables because the truth, which is in itself somewhat forbidding, penetrates more readily into the minds of mortals when it comes recommended by the allurement of pleasure. Indeed, this is the honey which, according to Lucretius, doctors who are treating children smear on a cup of wormwood.[8] For the same purpose princes in ancient times introduced licensed fools into their courts so that their freedom of speech might expose and correct certain lesser faults without offending anyone. Perhaps it is not proper to add Christ's name to the list. But supposing that some sort of comparison can be drawn between the heavenly and the human, surely His parables have some affinity with the fables of the ancients. And the truth of the gospel enters

5. The *Enchiridion* (*Handbook or Hand-weapon of the Christian Soldier*), Erasmus' first full statement of his program for religious and theological reform, was published in 1503. *The Education of a Christian Prince*, written or at least begun in the spring of 1515, was published a year later. Erasmus defended his *Panegyric of Philip* (1504) against charges of flattery by claiming that it was an inoffensive way of presenting ideals and criticizing faults indirectly (*Ep. 1*, 397, 399).

6. *Leg.* 649b–50b, 671a–73e. Macrobius *sat.* 2.8.4–10.

7. *Serm.* 1.1.24–25.

8. 1.936–41.

the mind more pleasantly and remains more firmly fixed if it is recommended by such inducements than if it were propounded abstractly, as St. Augustine explains at length in his work "On Teaching Christian Doctrine."[9] I saw how the ordinary run of mortals in every walk of life were deluded by most foolish beliefs, and that a remedy was more to be desired than expected. And then I thought I had found a way to take the minds of spoiled men by surprise, as it were, through this artistic technique and even to cure them by means of pleasure. I had often observed that this humorous and witty manner of admonition worked very well for many persons.

But if you reply that the role I assumed was so undignified that I should not have adopted it for the discussion of serious matters, perhaps I will admit to this fault. I am not much concerned to deny the charge of indecorum, but I do deny any bitterness. Actually I could offer a good defense even against indecorum, if on no other grounds, then at least by the example of the many serious writers I mentioned in my brief preface to the work.[1] After all, what was I to do? At that time, I had just returned from Italy and was staying with my friend More.[2] For several days I was confined with a kidney ailment. My library had not yet arrived. And even if I had had all the books I wanted, my illness would not have allowed me to apply myself intensely to serious studies. To pass the time I began to amuse myself with an encomium on Folly, not with any intention of publishing it but simply to relieve the discomfort of the disease by a diversion, as it were. After I had begun it, I gave some close friends a taste of it, to improve the joke by letting more share in it. They were extraordinarily taken with it and urged me to go on with it. I agreed to do so and spent about seven days finishing it—certainly longer, I thought, than was warranted by the importance of the subject matter. The same persons who urged me to write it arranged to have it taken to France and printed—though the printer's copy was not only full of errors but also defective.[3]

9. 2.6 (*CCSL 32*, 35–36).
1. See above, p. 3.
2. See above, p. 1, footnote 1.
3. More than once Erasmus asserted that he was not responsible for the first

How much it was disliked is sufficiently clear from the fact that within a few months it was printed more than seven times, and also in various places.[4] I myself wondered what everyone liked about it. If you call this a lapse of judgment, my dear Dorp, I plead guilty, or at least make no defense. In this fashion, for the sake of amusement and at the urging of friends, I went beyond the bounds of propriety—and I did so just this once in my whole life. Who, after all, can live every minute wisely?[5] Then too, you yourself admit that my other discourses are such that they are fully endorsed by the holy and the learned. Who are these strict judges, or rather these Areopagites,[6] who cannot see their way clear to allow a man even one offense against decorum? How extraordinarily morose they must be to strip a writer of all the favor he has won by his previous labors, simply because they are offended by one facetious little book! How many improprieties—and those far more improper, by all odds, than mine—could I cite from others, even from great theologians, who think up contentious and insipid questions and then fight 'tooth and nail' over the most trifling trifles. And these silly tales, these more than vaudevillian farces,[7] they propound in their own person. I at least had the modesty to shield myself with the mask of folly when I set out to do something improper; just as Plato's Socrates covers his face when he proclaims the praises of love,[8] so too I assumed a mask to play this part.

You write that even those who are displeased by the subject matter approve of the wit and the learning and the eloquence but are offended by the free-ranging and biting satire. But these critics give me more credit than I want. In fact, I care nothing about such praise, especially coming from people who in my judgment have neither wit nor learning nor eloquence. If they did, you can be sure, my dear

---

edition (Paris, 1511). No doubt, he could have prevented publication if he wished, but there is no evidence whatsoever that he instigated the first printing.

4. By October 1512, it had been printed five times (in Paris, Strassburg, and Antwerp).

5. Pliny *HN* 7.40.131.

6. Members of an ancient Athenian court, proverbial for severity.

7. Literally, "Atellan farces." See above, p. 27, footnote 2.

8. *Phaedr.* 237a.

Dorp, they would not be offended by jests which are wholesome rather than witty or learned. I ask you by all the Muses, what sort of eyes or ears or taste can they bring to bear on it if they are offended by biting satire in that book? First of all, how can there be any biting satire in it at all, since it censures no one by name except me? Why did they not think of the point Jerome insists on so often: when a discussion of vice is general, it casts no aspersions on any individual.[9] But if anyone is offended, he has no reason to protest against the writer. If he likes, let him bring a libel action against himself, because he has betrayed himself by proclaiming that something applies particularly to him whereas it was stated in such a way as to apply to everyone and therefore to no one, unless somebody should willingly claim it for himself. Surely you can see that in the whole work I have not only refrained from giving the names of individuals but have also avoided sharp criticism even of particular countries. Thus, in the passage where I survey the kinds of self-love characteristic of particular nations,[1] I ascribe military glory to the Spanish, literary culture and eloquence to Italy, fine food and good looks to the English, and so forth to the others, attributing such qualities as everyone would willingly acknowledge if they were assigned to him or at least would hear them with a smile. Moreover, although the plan of the subject matter I chose required that I should make my rounds through all the classes of mankind and satirize the vices of each one, where, I ask you, do you encounter the least bit of filthy or vitriolic language? Where do I dip into the cesspool of vice? Where do I stir up that hidden, 'noisome swamp'[2] of human life? Everyone knows how much could be said against evil popes, wicked bishops and priests, vicious princes, in short, against every rank of society, if (like Juvenal) one were not ashamed to express in writing what many are not ashamed to put into action. All I did was to recount such things as are entertaining and laughable rather than foul, and I recounted them in such a way as to suggest indirectly some ideas on major issues which it is very important for people to know.

9. *Epist.* 125.5 (*PL 22*, col. 1074–75; *CSEL 56*, 122).
1. See above, pp. 69–70.
2. See above, p. 87, footnote 6.

I know that you have no time for such trifles. But if you happen to have a free moment, examine those silly jests of Folly more attentively. I am sure you will find that they correspond to the teachings of the evangelists and apostles much better than do some people's disputations, however splendid (as they imagine) and worthy of great masters. In your letter you admit that most of what I wrote in the "Folly" is true.[3] But you also think that it does no good "to grate on tender ears with harsh truths."[4] If you think that no one should ever speak freely or reveal the truth except when it offends no one, why do physicians heal with bitter medicines and place *aloe sacra*[5] among their most highly recommended remedies? If they do so in healing the ills of the body, is it not much more fitting for us to do the same in curing the diseases of the mind? "Entreat," says Paul, "reprove, upbraid, in season and out of season."[6] The apostle wants us to attack vice in every possible way, and do you really not want us even to touch a sore spot? Not even when it is done with such moderation that no one could ever be hurt by it unless he went out of his way to hurt himself? Now if there exists any way to cure human vices without offending anyone, this surely is the most suitable way of all, for these reasons: it mentions no names; it excludes whatever would be shocking to the ears even of good men (for just as in tragedies some things are too horrible to be presented to the view of the spectators but are narrated instead, so too in human behavior some things are so obscene that it offends modesty even to narrate them); and finally, what it does narrate is presented under a laughable persona with such sportive wit that the humorous language prevents any possible offense. We have all seen how effective an appropriate and timely jest can sometimes be, even when the object of it is a grim tyrant. I ask you, could entreaties, could a serious speech have placated the wrath of the king as easily as the soldier's joke? "Yes indeed," he said, "if we had had a bottle, we would have said far worse things about you." The king laughed

---

3. *Ep. 2*, 12.
4. Persius 1.107–08.
5. The Greek name means "holy bitters."
6. 2 *Tim.* 4 : 2.

and forgave them.[7] Surely there is a good reason why the two supreme rhetoricians, Cicero and Quintilian, devote so much attention to laughter.[8] A graceful, charming style can be so effective that we find delight in well-turned witticisms even when they are aimed at ourselves—as is recorded about Julius Caesar.[9] And so, if you admit that what I wrote is the truth, that it is entertaining rather than obscene, what method could be more suitable for curing the ordinary ills of mankind? First, pleasure attracts the reader, and once attracted keeps him reading. For in other respects, various men pursue various goals, but all alike are allured by pleasure, except for those who are so insensitive that they are completely impervious to the pleasures of literature.

Those who are offended where no names are mentioned seem to me not very far removed from the silly attitude of women: if something is said against wicked women, they are as agitated about it as if the insult applied to every individual woman; but, if some praise is bestowed on worthy women, they are as pleased with themselves as if the praise given to some one woman or other applied to all women. I should hope that men would never sink to such foolishness, much less learned men, and least of all theologians. If in some passage I come across an accusation of which I am not guilty, I am not offended but rather congratulate myself that I am exempt from vices to which I see many others fall victim. But if it touches some sore spot and like a mirror lets me see myself as I am, even then there is no reason why I should take offense. If I am prudent, I will pretend not to be aware of it; I will not come forward and give myself away. If I am upright, I will heed the warning and take care that the charge which is here made with no names should not at some later time be thrown up to me under my own name. Why do we not at least grant this little book the same freedom which the uneducated allow in popular comedies?[1] In them how frequent and

7. Plutarch *Pyrrhus* 8.5, *mor.* 184d.
8. See above, p. 82, footnotes 9 and 2.
9. Suetonius *Jul. Caes.* 73.
1. Erasmus may well have had in mind the *sottie*, a kind of satiric skit performed by the *sociétés joyeuses* at Paris and other cities during his lifetime.

free are the insults hurled at kings and priests and monks and wives and husbands—indeed, who is safe? But yet, because no one is attacked by name, everyone laughs and either frankly admits to his fault or prudently dissembles it. Even the most savage tyrants put up with their buffoons and court fools, who sometimes taunt their masters with open insults. The emperor Flavius Vespasian took no revenge on the courtier who charged him with having a face like that of a man straining his bowels.[2] And who, pray tell, are these thin-skinned critics who cannot put up with Folly herself as she makes fun of human life in general, branding no individual by name? The Old Comedy would never have been driven from the stage if it had refrained from mentioning the names of famous men.[3]

But in fact, most noble Dorp, from what you write one would almost believe that this little book on Folly has turned the entire body of theologians against me. "What need was there," you say, "to assail the whole theological profession so bitterly?" And you lament my own lot: "Formerly," you say, "everyone read your works avidly and were very eager to see you in person. Now Folly, like Davus, is ruining everything."[4] I know that there is no malice or deceit in what you write, and I will not put you off with evasions. I ask you, do you consider that the theological profession has been attacked whenever something is said against foolish and wicked theologians, persons quite unworthy of the name? But by that rule whoever says anything against vicious men would make the whole human race his enemy. Was there ever a king so shameless that he would not admit that some kings are wicked and unworthy of regal honors? Was there ever a bishop so arrogant that he would not admit the same about his state of life? Is the theological profession the only one which contains, among so many practitioners, not a single blockhead, not a single dunce, not a single wrangler? Are

2. Suetonius *Vesp.* 20.

3. See above, p. 2, footnote 1.

4. *Ep. 2*, 12–13. Davus was a name often given to slaves in Roman comedy (Terence *Andr.* 663). In Horace *serm.* 2.7, a slave named Davus, taking advantage of the freedom of speech allowed during the Saturnalia, tells his master quite frankly and insultingly what he thinks of him.

they all Pauls, Basils, and Jeromes? Quite the contrary, the more noble a profession is, the fewer there are who can fulfill its requirements. You will find more good ship captains than good kings, more good physicians than good bishops. But this fact casts no aspersions on the profession but rather magnifies the praises of those few who in a most noble profession have conducted themselves most nobly. Tell me, if you please, why theologians should be any more offended (if, indeed, any are offended) than kings, noblemen, magistrates, bishops, cardinals, popes? Or than merchants, husbands, wives, lawyers, poets—for Folly omitted no class of mortals—except, of course, that these people are not so stupid as to imagine that a general indictment of the wicked is directed at themselves as individuals. St. Jerome wrote a book on virginity for Eustochium and in it he depicted the morals of wicked virgins so clearly that Apelles[5] himself could not have painted them more vividly.[6] Was Eustochium offended? Was she angry with Jerome for disparaging the whole class of virgins? Not in the least. And why? Because she was a wise virgin who did not imagine that what was said against the wicked applied to her. Indeed, she was glad to have good virgins admonished lest they should degenerate into bad ones. She was glad to have bad virgins admonished so that they might cease to be bad. Jerome wrote to Nepotianus on the life of the clergy.[7] He wrote to Rusticus on the life of monks.[8] How vividly he portrays, how wittily he reproaches the vices of both groups! Those to whom he wrote were not offended because they knew that what was said did not apply to them. Why was William Mountjoy,[9] a nobleman and courtier of no mean stature, not offended by all the fun that Folly pokes at noblemen and courtiers? For this reason: since he himself is most worthy and wise, he thinks, and rightly so, that whatever is said against wicked and foolish noblemen has nothing to do with

5. See above, p. 72, footnote 5.
6. *Epist. 22*, 13–14 (*CSEL 54*, 143–211).
7. *Epist. 52.5* (*CSEL 54*, 413–41).
8. *Epist. 125.16* (*PL 22*, col. 1081–82).
9. William Blount, Lord Mountjoy, a pupil and patron of Erasmus, first brought him to England in 1499.

him. How often does Folly poke fun at wicked and worldly bishops? Why was the Archbishop of Canterbury not at all offended by this?[1] For this reason: since he is perfect in all kinds of virtue he judges that it has nothing to do with him.

But why should I go on mentioning the names of the noblest princes or other bishops or abbots or cardinals or men famous for their learning—none of whom, so far as I am aware, has been the least bit estranged from me because of the "Folly." Nor can I be brought to believe that any theologians are irritated by this book, except perhaps some few who are incapable of understanding it, or envious of it, or so ill-tempered that they never approve anything at all. For it is well known that some who belong to the ranks of the theologians are from the outset so deficient in intelligence and judgment that they are not fit to pursue any kind of learning, least of all theology. When they have learned a few trifling rules of Alexander of Villedieu,[2] they proceed to acquire a smattering of pointless sophistry. Then they master ten propositions from Aristotle, and even those they do not understand. Finally, when they have learned the same number of questions from Scotus or Ockham,[3] they are content to seek out the rest from the Catholicon or Mammetrecton or some such dictionary as if from a horn of plenty.[4] They strut and ruffle their feathers in the most wonderful way—for nothing is more arrogant than ignorance. These are the people who scorn St. Jerome as a mere grammarian, because they do not understand him. These are the people who ridicule Greek, Hebrew, and even Latin literature, and though they are more stupid than any sow and do not have even ordinary common sense, they think they have reached the very pinnacle of wisdom. They pass judgment on everyone, condemning, pronouncing sentence, never in doubt,

1. WilliamWarham, an admirer and patron of Erasmus.

2. A thirteenth-century grammarian whose versified Latin grammar was enormously popular for almost three centuries.

3. See above, p. 90, footnote 8.

4. The *Catholicon* or *Summa grammaticalis* by Giovanni Balbi and the *Mammetrecton* by Marchesinus de Reggio are thirteenth-century compendia, grammatical and lexical, designed as tools for biblical exegesis.

never hesitating, never ignorant of anything. And yet these few men often make the greatest uproar. For what can be more shameless and stubborn than ignorance? They conspire most zealously against good literature. They are ambitious to attain status among theologians, and they are afraid that if the world comes to its senses and good literature is reborn, it will be apparent that those who hitherto were commonly believed to know everything actually know nothing. These are the ones who cry out, who make such an uproar, who plot against men devoted to good literature. These are the ones who do not like the "Folly" because they do not understand it, neither the Greek nor the Latin. If some sharp words are directed against such theologians, or rather pretenders to theology, what does that have to do with the most glorious profession of worthy theologians? If these critics are motivated by a love of piety, why have they singled out the "Folly" as the object of their anger? How much that is irreverent, filthy, or noxious did Poggio write? But everyone has taken him to their hearts as a Christian writer, and he has been translated into almost all languages.[5] How insultingly and scurrilously does Pontano attack the clergy?[6] yet he is read for his elegance and wit. How much obscenity is there in Juvenal?[7] And yet some think he may even be useful to preachers. How abusively did Cornelius Tacitus write against Christians! With what hostility Suetonius wrote against them! How irreverently Pliny and Lucian ridicule the immortality of the soul![8] And yet they are read everywhere for the sake of learning, and rightly so. Folly alone cannot be tolerated because her sportive wit is directed not against good theologians and those worthy of the name but rather against the

5. In his *Facetiae*, Poggio (d. 1459) wittily and scurrilously satirized priests and monks. By 1500 the work had been translated into English, French, Italian, and Spanish. See above, p. 141, footnote 2.

6. Giovanni Pontano (d. 1503), president of the Academy at Naples, wrote witty Lucianic dialogues containing anti-clerical satire.

7. See above, p. 5.

8. Tacitus *ann.* 15.44. Suetonius *Nero* 16. Pliny *HN* 7.55.188–90. Lucian *dial. mort.* 374, 404–05, *Peregrinus* 10–15.

petty, trifling questions of ignorant theologians and their ridiculous title of "magister noster."[9]

One or two of these rascals, masquerading as theologians, have tried to stir up hatred against me, on the pretext that I have injured and estranged the whole body of theologians. For my part, I have such a high regard for theological learning that I ordinarily reserve the name "learning" for it alone. I respect and revere the theological profession so much that in it alone have I enlisted, to it alone would I wish to belong.[1] But shame keeps me from assuming such a noble title, since I am all too aware how gifted in learning and virtuous living a theologian ought to be. In a sense, the profession of theology is above the reach of man. Such a dignity rightly belongs to bishops, not to someone like me. It is enough for me to have learned from the teaching of Socrates that I know nothing at all[2] and to work as hard as I can to promote the studies of others. I certainly cannot imagine where these two or three god-like theologians who, according to your letter, are not very well disposed toward me can be hiding. I have lived in several places since the "Folly" was published. I have resided in many universities, in many large cities. I was never aware of any theologian who was angry with me, except one or two from that contingent which is hostile to all literary culture. And even these never registered their protest by speaking directly to me. What they mutter against me behind my back is of no concern to me because I rely on the judgment of so many good men. If I were not afraid, my dear Dorp, that I would appear more boastful than truthful, I could give you a long list of theologians, men celebrated for their holy lives, men of extraordinary learning and of the very highest standing, some of them even bishops, who were never more fond of me than after the "Folly" was published and who were far more pleased with that little book than I myself. I would list them here individually by name and title if I were not

9. See above, p. 98, footnote 9.

1. Erasmus received a doctorate in theology from the University of Turin in 1506.

2. See above, p. 36, footnote 4.

afraid that because of the "Folly" even men as great as these would fall into disfavor with those three theologians—actually only one, I think, was the cause of all this uproar among you, for from certain hints I can guess how it was.[3] As for him, if I cared to paint him in his true colors, no one would be surprised that such a man would dislike the "Folly." Indeed, I would not like it myself unless such people disliked it. Actually I do not like it, but certainly I dislike it all the less for the very reason that such minds do not like it. I attach far more importance to the judgment of wise and learned theologians, who are so far from censuring me for being too caustic that they actually praise me for the temperate and candid way in which I handle a basically licentious subject with no license and write entertainingly on a humorous subject with no bitter barbs. And so to respond to the theologians only—from what I hear they are the only ones offended—everyone knows how much is openly spoken against the morals of bad theologians. This sort of thing Folly never touches on. She only makes fun of their pointless, petty disputations, and even them she does not reject absolutely. She only condemns theologians who think that such disputations constitute the whole of theology, 'from stem to stern,'[4] so to speak, and who are so taken up with these wars of words, as St. Paul calls them,[5] that they have no time to read the evangelists, prophets, and apostles.

And would that there were fewer, my dear Dorp, who are open to this reproach. I could bring forward some of them over eighty who have wasted all those years with such nonsense and never once read through the whole text of the gospel—as I discovered for myself and they afterwards confessed. I did not dare, even under the persona of Folly, to say what I often hear many theologians deplore, true theologians, that is, men of integrity, dignity, and learning who have assimilated the teaching of Christ by drinking deep from the very springs themselves. Such men, whenever they are in company where they may speak their minds freely, lament that this

3. Allen (*Ep. 2*, 100) suggests John Briard. Olin (Erasmus, *Selected Writings*, p. 71) suggests James Latomus. Both were theologians at Louvain.
4. *Adag.* 8, and Cicero *fam.* 16.24.1.
5. *1 Tim.* 6 : 4.

modern sort of theology ever came into the world and long for the ancient kind. Nothing could be holier than this ancient theology, nothing more majestic. Nothing has such a savor of those heavenly teachings of Christ, nothing can recall them so well. As for modern theology, I pass over the base monstrosities of its barbarous and factitious language. I pass over its complete lack of literary culture, its ignorance of languages. But it is so contaminated with Aristotle, with trifling ideas thought up by men, even with secular laws, that I hardly see how it can preserve the true savor of Christ, who is pure and uncontaminated. For what happens is this: while it looks aside too often, gazing on man-made traditions, it is less able to follow its archetype, Christ. Hence it is that more intelligent theologians are often forced to say things to the people which they do not really agree with in their hearts and which they would not say among close friends. And sometimes they have no answer for those who consult them because they see clearly that Christ taught one thing and human traditions command something else. What connection is there, I ask you, between Christ and Aristotle? or between sophistical quibbles and the mysteries of eternal wisdom? Where will these labyrinths of questions get us? How many of them are pointless! How many are downright noxious, by the very fact that they breed quarrels and dissension. Of course, some points must be investigated, some points must be decided. I quite agree. But on the other hand, there are many points which it is better to pass over than to examine (and it is a part of knowledge not to know some things). There are many points concerning which it is more salutary to remain in doubt than to make a decision. Finally, if a decision must be made, I would like to see it done reverently, not arrogantly, and based on Holy Scripture, not on some trifling reasons fabricated by men. But nowadays there is no end to the quibbling questions. And also in discussing them there is endless dissension among various sects and factions. Every day decree after decree is issued, one begetting another. In short, things have gotten so bad that the chief point in any affair will not depend on Christ's command but on the definitions of the scholastics and the power of the bishops, no matter what their qualifications may be. Everything is now so entangled with these questions and decrees that we dare not even hope to call the world back to true Christianity.

These troubles and many others are clearly perceived and deeply lamented by men of great piety and learning, who find that the principal cause of all of them is the irreverent effrontery of modern theologians. O my dear Dorp, if only you could silently read the thoughts in my mind! Then, surely, you would understand how much I leave unspoken here out of prudence. But Folly never touches on such things, or at least only very lightly, for I wished to avoid giving offense. And I exercised the same caution at every point; I carefully avoided writing anything obscene or harmful to morals or prejudicial to civil order or anything that might even remotely appear to cast aspersions on some particular class of men. If something is said there about the worship of the saints, you will always find some added qualification which makes it quite clear that the only thing censured is the superstition of those who do not worship the saints in the right way. So too, if something is said against princes, bishops, or monks, I always add something to show that I am not attacking any profession as a whole but only corrupt practitioners, unworthy of the profession, for I had no wish to slander any good man while attacking the vices of the wicked. Moreover, while I satirized them, I gave no names, thus doing my best not to offend even the wicked. Finally, by presenting the whole content of the book with wit and humor and under a fictional and comic persona, I tried to ensure that even gloomy and sour readers would take it in good part.

But then, you write, it is censured not as too biting but as impious. For you say, "how can pious ears bear to hear you say that the happiness of the future life is a species of madness?"[6] I beg you, my dear Dorp, tell me who has taught a man of your sincerity this sly form of false accusation? or (what I think is more likely) what crafty manipulator has taken advantage of your simplicity in order to accuse me falsely? This is the usual trick of these wretched slanderers: to pick out a couple of words and give them quite isolated and sometimes also changed a bit, leaving out everything that might

6. *Ep. 2*, 12.

qualify and explain the otherwise harsh words. In his "Institutes" Quintilian points out and recommends a similar trick: that we should present our own arguments in the very best light, adding proofs and whatever might mitigate, extenuate, or in any way help our case; our opponent's arguments, on the other hand, we should present without any of these additions and also in the most lurid language we can command.[7] These perverters of the truth did not learn this trick from the precepts of Quintilian, but from their own malice. That is why it often happens that a passage that would have been very well received if it were presented as it was written gives great offense because it is misrepresented. Read the passage again, I beg you, and pay close attention to the stages of the argument and the gradations of language leading up to the statement that heavenly happiness is a species of madness. Also, notice the words I use to express that idea. You will see that, far from giving any offense, what is written there would actually delight truly pious ears. The stumbling-block is in your rendition, not in my book.

For when Folly set out to show that all sorts of occurrences are included in the designation "folly" and was demonstrating that the whole sum and substance of human happiness depends on folly, she made her way through all the classes of mankind until she came to kings and supreme pontiffs. Then she went on to the apostles themselves and even to Christ, for we find a certain folly attributed to them in Holy Scripture. Not that there is any danger that someone will think the apostles and Christ are really fools, but rather that they too have a certain infirmity, a sort of concession to our emotions, which, by comparison with the eternal and pure wisdom of God, might seem something less than wise. But it is this very folly that conquers all the wisdom of the world. So too the prophet compares all human justice to a woman's soiled menstrual rag.[8] Not that the justice practised by good men is polluted, but because whatever is most pure among men is somehow impure compared to the ineffable purity of God. And just as I set forth a wise folly, so too I propound a sane insanity and a sagacious madness. And to

7. 5.13.25–28.
8. *Isa.* 64 : 6.

palliate what I say about the fruition enjoyed by the saints, I first present the three kinds of madness according to Plato, of which the happiest sort, the madness of lovers, is clearly nothing but a sort of ecstasy. But the ecstasy of holy persons is a taste, as it were, of that beatitude to come, when we shall be completely absorbed into God and will have our existence more in Him than in ourselves. But according to Plato, such a state is madness, when a person is carried out of himself into that which he loves so that he can fully enjoy it. Can't you see how a little later I carefully distinguish the different kinds of folly and madness so that no unsophisticated readers might be led astray by my words?[9]

"But I have no quarrel with the meaning," you say, "but the language itself is abhorrent to pious ears." Why are such ears not offended when they hear Paul say "the folly of God" or "the folly of the cross"?[1] Why do they not call St. Thomas to account when he describes Peter's ecstasy in this way: "With pious folly, he begins to speak of tabernacles."[2] He calls his holy and beatific rapture, folly. And yet these words are sung in church. Why did they not indict me before when I wrote a prayer in which I called Christ both a magician and an enchanter?[3] St. Jerome calls Christ a Samaritan,[4] though in fact he was a Jew. Paul calls him sin, as if to express more than "sinner" would have.[5] He also calls him "cursed."[6] What a blasphemous insult if a person wished to misinterpret it! What a holy eulogy if it is understood as Paul intended. Similarly, if someone called Christ a robber or an adulterer or a drunkard or a heretic, wouldn't all good men hold their hands over their ears? But if these ideas are expressed in appropriate language so that in the course of

9. See above, pp. 136–37.

1. *1 Cor.* 1 : 23, 25.

2. From a sequence (hence sung in church) for the feast of the Transfiguration (*Analecta Hymnica 54*, 168–70, No. 110). The author is unknown; only Erasmus connects it with St. Thomas.

3. *Op.* 5, 1213A.

4. In his translation of Origen's homilies on Luke (No. 34, *PL 26*, cols. 292–93).

5. *2 Cor.* 5 : 21.

6. *Gal.* 3 : 13.

the speech the reader is gradually led almost by the hand, as it were, to the notion that by his triumphant death on the cross Christ brought back to His father the spoils he had taken from hell, that he joined himself with the synagogue of Moses, like the wife of Uriah,[7] that from it might be born the people of peace, that He was drunk with the new wine of charity when he offered himself up for us, that he introduced a new sort of doctrine, quite different from the tenets of all others, both wise and foolish alike—who, I ask, could be offended, especially since we sometimes find these words used in Holy Scripture in a good sense? In the "Adagia," now that I think of it, I called the apostles Sileni; what is more, I called Christ himself a sort of Silenus.[8] If a malicious critic should come forward and interpret these words in a scanty and perfunctory fashion, in order to put them in the worst possible light, they would be absolutely intolerable. But if a holy and fair-minded man should read what I wrote, he would approve of the allegory.

I am also surprised that these critics have not noticed how cautiously I expressed these ideas and how carefully I guarded them with qualifications. This is how I present them: "Now that we have taken on our shoulders *the mantle of this task,*' let us go on with it and explain a further point: namely, that the happiness which Christians strive for with such great effort is no more than a certain kind of madness and folly—don't get the wrong idea, but consider the facts carefully!"[9] Do you hear what I say? First of all, because Folly is discussing a profound subject, I soften the inconsistency with the proverb about putting on the mantle of this task. Nor do I mention simply "folly and madness" but rather "a kind of folly and madness," so that you may understand a holy folly and a blessed madness, according to the distinction which I make a little later. Not

---

7. It was traditional to interpret David's adulterous liaison with Bathsheba, the wife of Uriah (*2 Sam.* 11 and 12) as a figure or type of Christ's union with the Jews under the old law. From the union sprang Solomon (the "peaceful one"), a type of the Christian church. See Gregory, in the *Glossa ordinaria* (*PL 113*, col. 572), and Rabanus Maurus (*PL 109*, cols. 100–01).

8. *Erasmus on his Time*, pp. 79–80. See above, p. 43, footnote 1.

9. See above, pp. 132–33.

satisfied with this, I add "a certain" kind to make it clear that the language is figurative, not literal. Still not satisfied, I guard against any offense that might arise from the sound of the words themselves by admonishing my readers to pay more attention to what is being said than to the words in which it is said. And all these precautions I take in the very first statement of the idea. As for my development of it, is there anything at all which is not expressed with piety and prudence and with even greater reverence than is suitable to Folly? But in this passage I preferred to be a little negligent of decorum than to fall below the dignity of the subject matter. I preferred to offend against rhetoric than to violate piety. And finally, when I have finished the argument, lest anyone should be disturbed because I present such a comic figure as Folly speaking about such a sacred subject, I seek to exonerate myself from this fault in these words: "But I have long since forgotten myself and have 'gone beyond the pale.' But if you think my speech has been too pert or wordy, keep in mind that you've been listening to Folly and to a woman."[1]

You see how I strove continuously to remove all possible occasions of offense. But such measures mean nothing to persons whose ears admit nothing but propositions, conclusions, and corollaries. What about the preface with which I guarded the book in an attempt to preclude any slanderous interpretations?[2] I have not the slightest doubt that it was enough to satisfy all fair-minded men. But how can you satisfy those who are either too obstinate to let themselves be satisfied or too stupid to know what satisfaction is? For just as Simonides said that the Thessalians were too obtuse to be deceived by him,[3] so too you sometimes see people too stupid to be appeased. Then too, it is no wonder that someone who is looking for nothing but slander should discover something slanderous. If someone read the books of St. Jerome in the same spirit, he would come across hundreds of clearly slanderous passages, and even in this most Christian of all doctors of the church there would be no lack of places which such readers could call heretical—to say nothing

1. See above, p. 138.
2. See above, pp. 1–5.
3. Plutarch *mor.* 15d.

of Cyprian, Lactantius,[4] and other such writers. Finally, who ever heard of a humorous piece being called to the attention of theologians? On that principle, why don't they scrutinize the writings and jeux d'esprit of modern poets with the same diligence and by the same rules? There they would find plenty that is obscene or redolent of ancient paganism. But since these poems are not taken seriously, no theologian considers that he need have anything to do with them.

But from such precedents as these I would not wish to seek a defense for myself. I would not want anything that I have written, even in jest, to detract from Christian piety in any way whatsoever—provided I have a reader who understands what I have written, provided he is fair and impartial, provided he does not desire merely to cavil but strives to understand. But if a writer should take into account first of all readers who have no intelligence and even less judgment, then those who have no literary competence at all, since their education—or rather, deformation—lies only in the foul and muddied waters of their own teachings, and finally those who are enemies to everyone who knows anything of which they are ignorant, and whose whole purpose is to distort what little they may chance (somehow or other) to understand, certainly a writer faced with such readers cannot afford to write anything at all if he wishes to avoid being slandered. And then too, some of these people are led to slander others by a desire for glory. For no one is more eager for glory than an ignorant man who thinks he knows something. And so, because they have a passionate longing for fame and cannot achieve it by legitimate means, rather than live without it they choose to imitate the young man of Ephesus who gained his reputation by burning the most famous temple in the whole world.[5] And since they themselves cannot publish anything worth reading, all their efforts are directed at picking to pieces the writings of celebrated men.

4. Christian apologists of the third and fourth centuries.
5. The name of the young man who sought fame by burning the temple of Diana in 356 B.C. is recorded (Plutarch *Alex.* 3; Valerius Maximus 9.14.5; Gellius *NA* 2.6).

I am speaking of others, not myself, for I do not count for anything at all. As for my little book on Folly, I set no great store by it and would not want anyone to think I am greatly upset by this whole affair. No one should be surprised if men like the ones I have just described pick out certain isolated statements from a long work, labeling some as giving scandal, some as irreverential, some as having a bad sound, some as lacking piety and smacking of heresy— not that they have found such evils in the statements themselves, but rather that they have projected their own deformities onto them. How much more peaceable and compatible with Christian sincerity it would be to foster and support the labors of learned men and, if someone chances through inadvertence to make a mistake, to overlook it or to interpret it in the best light instead of going on the attack, seeking out something to find fault with, playing the part of a backbiter rather than a theologian. How much happier we would be if we collaborated in teaching or learning, and (to use Jerome's words) if we could exercise on the playing fields of Scripture without fear of injury.[6] But it is amazing how these men never take a middle position. Some authors they read so favorably that even when they encounter an obvious error they defend it with some feeble pretext. Towards others they are so hostile that even the most circumspect statements cannot escape their malicious attacks. Instead of doing this, instead of slashing and being slashed, instead of wasting their own time and that of others, how much better it would be for them to be learning Greek or Hebrew or at least Latin, which are so important to the study of Holy Scripture that I cannot see how anyone who is ignorant of them can have the gall to claim the title of theologian.

Therefore, my dear Martin, because of my affection for you, I shall not cease to exhort you, as I have often done before, to supplement your studies with a knowledge of Greek. You are happily endowed with rare intellectual gifts. Your literary style, which is firm and energetic, fluent and copious, shows that your mind is not only sound but also fertile. You are not only unimpaired by age,

6. *Epist.* 115 (*CSEL* 55, 397).

you are in the very prime and bloom of youth.[7] And you have already completed with distinction the ordinary course of studies. Believe me, if you put the finishing touches on these splendid beginnings by learning Greek, I would venture to predict, both to myself and to everyone else, that you will achieve something quite extraordinary, something which no modern theologian up to this time has ever accomplished. But if you are of the opinion that the love of true holiness makes all human learning contemptible, if you think that we can reach such wisdom more quickly by transforming ourselves, as it were, into Christ, and that everything else worth knowing can be perceived more fully in the light of faith than in the books of men, I am quite willing to agree with you. On the other hand, as matters now stand, if you think you can get a true knowledge of theology without skill in languages, especially in that language in which almost all of Holy Scripture has come down to us, you are completely 'off the track.'[8]

I only wish I were as able as I am eager to persuade you on this point, for my eagerness is no less than my love for you and my interest in your studies, and my love is as strong as my interest is boundless. If I cannot persuade you that what I say is true, I wish that these entreaties from a friend might win from you at least this much, that you should try it and see. I will bear any punishment whatever if you do not confess that my advice was that of a trustworthy friend. If my love for you has any merit in your eyes, if the homeland we share has any weight with you, if you attach any significance, I will not say to my learning, but at least to my diligent application to the study of literature, if you place any importance on my age[9] (for, so far as years are concerned, I am old enough to be your father), let me win this one thing from you, if not by my arguments, then by my affection or my authority. I will not believe I have any claim to eloquence, which you are always attributing to me, unless I persuade you to do this. If I succeed, we will both re-

---

7. Dorp was thirty years old.
8. *Adag.* 48; Terence *eun.* 245.
9. Erasmus was almost fifty years old.

joice—I that I gave the advice, you that you followed it; and though you are now the dearest of all to me, you will be even dearer because I shall have rendered you dearer to yourself. If I fail, I am afraid that when you are older and more experienced you will come to approve of my advice and condemn your present opinion and then, as it usually happens, you will understand your error when it is too late to correct it. I could list the names of very many men who in their gray hairs became schoolboys once more to learn Greek because they had finally come to understand that without it scholarship is lame and blind.

But on this point I have already said more than enough. To return to your letter, you think that the only way for me to placate the hostility of the theologians and regain the favor I once had with them is to counterbalance my "Praise of Folly" with a praise of wisdom as a sort of 'retraction', and you implore me and beseech me most urgently to do so.[1] As for me, my good Dorp, since I hold no one in contempt but myself, and since I would wish, if it were possible, to be on good terms with all mankind, I would not be reluctant to undertake such a task except that I see what would happen: whatever ill-will has arisen among a few unjust and ignorant men would not only not be extinguished but would actually be more inflamed. Hence, I think it better 'not to disturb sleeping dogs[2] and not to stir up such a fetid swamp as Camarina'.[3] It will be better, I think, to let this poisonous serpent die with the passing of time.

Now I come to the second part of your letter. You heartily approve of my effort to restore Jerome and you urge me to undertake such tasks as this. You spur on a willing horse.[4] What this project needs is not so much encouragement as assistance, so difficult is the task. But may you never believe anything I say after this if you do not discover that I am telling the truth on this point: those who were so offended by the "Folly" will never approve of the edition

1. *Ep. 2*, 13.
2. Sophocles *Oed. Col.* 510.
3. See above, p. 87, footnote 6.
4. *Adag.* 146–47.

of Jerome. Nor are they much better disposed toward Basil, Chrysostom, and Gregory Nazianzen[5] than they are toward me, except that they rail against me more freely. Sometimes, though, in their more heated moments, they do not hesitate to blurt out their insults even against such great luminaries as these. They are afraid of good scholarship and fearful for their own tyranny. And so that you may know that I am not simply making wild guesses about them, consider this: when the work was first undertaken and the news of it spread abroad, certain important men (for so they are considered to be) and outstanding theologians (for so they consider themselves to be) hurried to the printer and implored him by all that is holy not to allow any Greek or Hebrew to be mixed in the edition because (they said) writings in those tongues are dangerous, fruitless, and designed merely to satisfy idle curiosity. Moreover, some time ago when I was living in England, I happened to be drinking with a certain Franciscan, a Scotist of the first water.[6] In the judgment of the common people he knows a great deal; in his own judgment, he knows all there is to know. When I explained to him what I was trying to do with Jerome, he expressed the greatest surprise that there could be anything in his works that was not already known to theologians—a man so abysmally ignorant that I would be surprised if he rightly understood three lines in all of Jerome's writings. This obliging personage added that if I had any problems with Jerome's prefaces, the Breton commentator had explained everything very clearly.[7]

Now I ask you, my good Dorp, what can you do for such theologians, what can you ask for them in your prayers, except perhaps a trustworthy physician, to heal their brains? And yet it is men of this stripe who sometimes roar the loudest in the assembly of theologians. Such men as these make pronouncements about Chris-

---

5. Greek fathers of the Church who lived in the fourth century.

6. Perhaps Henry Standish (*Ep. 3*, 21n).

7. Gulielmus Brito (William of Brittany), a thirteenth-century Franciscan, wrote commentaries on Jerome's prefaces to his biblical commentaries. William's commentaries had been printed at least twice before 1500.

tianity. They fear as dangerous, they avoid like the plague the very knowledge which St. Jerome and Origen (even in his old age)[8] acquired with much toil in order to become true theologians. Augustine, on the other hand, when he was already a bishop, already of advanced age, lamented in his "Confessions" that as a young man he had been averse to learning that very literature which could have been of great assistance to him in interpreting Holy Scripture.[9] If there is any danger in such studies, I will willingly take the risk which such wise men embraced wholeheartedly. If there is any idle curiosity, I have no desire to be holier than Jerome—I wonder how well Jerome is served by those who lump everything he did under the heading "idle curiosity," but that is their problem. There is a very old decree, issued by a papal council, which sets up public lectureships on certain languages,[1] whereas there is not the slightest provision for chop-logic or for mastering Aristotle's philosophy, except that in canon law some question arises whether they should be studied at all.[2] And in fact many great writers do reject them. Why then do we neglect what has been commanded by the authority of the pope and embrace only what is doubtful or actually disapproved? But even in the study of Aristotle the same thing happens as in their handling of Holy Scripture. Everywhere they encounter their Nemesis, who takes revenge on their contempt for language: with Aristotle, as with all the others, they wander in a fog, they dream, they bump into things blindly, they produce nothing but monstrosities.[3] To these extraordinary theologians we owe it that out of all those writers listed by Jerome in his catalogue[4]

8. Erasmus had Jerome's authority for the belief that Origen learned Hebrew in his old age (*De vir. illust.* 54, *PL 23*, col. 665).

9. *Confessions* 1.13–14.

1. The *Constitutions* of Clement V, issued after the Council of Vienne (1311–12) provided that two teachers for each of the three languages, Hebrew, Arabic, and Chaldaean, should be appointed at the universities of Paris, Oxford, Bologna, and Salamanca (*Ep. 1*, 411).

2. *Decretum Gratiani* 37, *Corpus Iuris Canonici*, ed. A. L. Richter & A. Friedberg, Leipzig, 1879 (repr. 1922), I, 135–40.

3. Cf. More, *Selected Letters*, pp. 53–54.

4. *De vir. illust.* (*PL 23*, cols. 607–719).

so few have survived, simply because our master-doctors could not understand what they wrote. To them we owe it that we have Jerome in such a corrupt and mutilated form that others have to take almost as much trouble restoring his works as he did in writing them.

But now for the third point. What you write about the New Testament makes me wonder what has happened to you. Where have you misdirected that most clear-sighted mind of yours? You do not want me to change anything, unless perhaps something is expressed more meaningfully in the Greek; and you deny that there are any defects in the edition we commonly use. You think that it is impious to undermine in any way an edition that has been sanctioned by the consensus of so many centuries and approved by so many councils. I beg you, most learned Dorp, if what you write is true, why do Jerome, Augustine, and Ambrose so often quote scripture in a different form than the one we read? Why does Jerome censure and correct many specific errors, which we still find in our edition? What will you do when many of these sources agree—that is, when the Greek codices have a different reading, when Jerome cites according to the Greek readings, when the oldest Latin manuscripts also have the same as the Greek, when the Greek readings also make better sense in context? Will you simply scorn all these and follow your own codex, which has perhaps been corrupted by some scribe? Neither is anyone asserting that there is any falsehood in Holy Scripture, since you also brought up that charge, nor do any of the points over which Augustine and Jerome contended have anything to do with the matter. The facts of the case make it abundantly clear—'clear enough for a blind man to see it,'[5] as they say—that the Greek has been badly translated, whether from the translator's lack of skill or from his carelessness, and that often the original and true meaning has been corrupted by ignorant copyists (as we still see happening today), or else, as sometimes happens, changed by half-educated, unattentive scribes. Who promotes the cause of falsehood, the person who restores the correct

5. *Adag.* 793.

reading or the one who would rather see an error added than taken away? For it is the very nature of such corruptions for one to breed another. And most of the changes I have made pertain to the emphasis rather than the meaning itself, although the emphasis often constitutes a large part of the meaning. But not infrequently the translation is completely 'off the track.'[6] When that happened, where (I ask you) did Augustine, Ambrose, Hilary, and Jerome look for a solution except in the Greek sources? And though this method has been endorsed by ecclesiastical decrees, you evade it and seek to refute it, or rather to elude it by splitting hairs.

You write that in the age of the fathers the Greek codices were more correct than the Latin but that now the reverse is true, and that we should not have any faith in the books of those who have broken away from the Roman church. I can hardly bring myself to believe that you intend this to be taken seriously. Well, now! Are we not to read the books of those who have broken away from the Christian faith? Why then do they place so much stock in Aristotle, a pagan who never had the least contact with the faith? The whole nation of the Jews broke away from Christ; shall the psalms, then, and the prophets, written in their language, carry no weight with us? Come, list for me all the points on which the Greeks differ from orthodox Latins; you will not find anything which has its origins in the words of the New Testament or has anything to do with this question. The only disputed points are the word "hypostasis," the procession of the Holy Spirit, the ceremonies of consecration, the poverty of priests, and the power of the pope. But they do not support any of these points with falsified copies. And what will you say when you see that Origen, Chrysostom, Basil, and Jerome give the same interpretation? Did someone falsify the Greek codices even in their time? Who has ever found a single place where the Greek codices were falsified? Finally, why should they want to falsify them, since they do not use them to support their dogmas. Moreover, Cicero himself admitted that in all branches of learning the Greek codices were superior to ours, though in other respects he was no friend to the Greeks.[7] For the differences between the

6. *Adag.* 48, Terence *eun.* 245.
7. Cf. *Ad Q. fratr.* 3.5.6.

letters, the accent marks, and the very difficulty of writing it make it harder to make a mistake and, if one occurs, easier to correct it.

Now, when you write that we should not depart from the Vulgate because it has been approved by many councils, you are acting like the ordinary run of theologians: whenever anything has somehow crept into public use, they always attribute it to the authority of the church. Show me just one council in which this edition was approved. How could it approve a work the author of which no one knows? For that it is not Jerome's can be established by Jerome's own prefaces. But suppose that some council did approve it. Did they approve it in such a way as to rule out completely any corrections from Greek sources? Did they approve all the errors which could have slipped in in various ways? Was the decree of the council fathers couched in such terms as this: "We do not know the author of this version, but we nevertheless approve it. We intend this approval to stand even if the Greek codices have different readings, no matter how carefully these codices may have been corrected, even if Chrysostom or Basil or Athanasius or Jerome give different readings, even if those readings correspond better to the sense of the gospel. And yet in other matters we heartily approve of those same authors. Furthermore, we approve with the same authority whatever errors, corruptions, additions, and omissions may be made in the future, in whatever manner, whether by ill-educated and rash correctors or by ignorant, drunken, or sleepy copyists. And we forbid anyone to change a reading once it has been introduced into the text." A silly decree, you say. Yet such a decree as this would be necessary if you are to deter me from my task by the authority of a council.

Finally, what are we to say when we see that all of the copies of the Vulgate itself do not agree with each other? Did the council approve of this disagreement too, seeing ahead of time, as it were, the changes that would be made? How I wish, my dear Dorp, that the Roman Pontiffs had enough leisure time to issue wholesome regulations on these points, providing that the works of good authors should be corrected and that corrected copies should be prepared and preserved. But at such a council I would not seat these so-called theologians—theologians in name only—whose only object is to ensure that their sort of learning be the only sort held in high regard. And what is their sort of learning but a jumble of pointless nonsense? If these men had absolute sway, the best authors would grow outworn and the world would be forced to treat their insipid trifles as if they were pronounced by an oracle. Their nonsense has so little true learning that I would actually rather be an ordinary shoemaker than the most prominent among them—so long as they acquire no better learning. These are the men who want nothing in the text restored, lest it might seem that there is something they do not know. These are the men who throw up to us the fictitious authority of councils. These are the men who exaggerate the great danger to the Christian faith. These are the men who preach about the crisis in the church, which they (of course) prop up with their shoulders (which might more properly uphold some farm wagon), and throw up such smoke screens among the ignorant and superstitious mob. Since the mob considers them to be theologians, they do not want to lose any of their reputation. They are afraid that when they cite Holy Scripture wrongly—which they often do—the true meaning, based on the authority of the Greek or Hebrew, will be thrown in their teeth, and what was presented as an oracular pronouncement will soon enough appear to be merely a dream. St. Augustine, a very great man and a bishop to boot, did not disdain to learn from a little boy only a year old.[8] But these men would rather bring everything to rack and ruin than to give anyone the least occasion to believe that they are ignorant of anything that pertains to full and perfect learning, though I don't see anything in this dispute which is very relevant to the purity of the Christian faith. And even if it were quite relevant, there would be all the more reason to redouble our efforts.

Nor is there any danger that everyone will immediately fall away

8. Perhaps *Conf.* 8.12.29. Or Erasmus may be referring to the well-known apocryphal story about the child Augustine met on the beach as he was meditating on the trinity. Asked why he was carrying water in his cupped hands from the sea to a hole in the sand, the child replied by asking the saint why he was trying to make the boundless mystery of the trinity fit the capacity of the human mind. See *Ep. 2*, 270.

from Christ if they should happen to hear that a place had been found in Holy Scripture which some ignorant or drowsy scribe has miscopied or some translator has rendered wrongly. The danger arises from other causes, which for the moment I pass over in prudent silence. How much more Christian it would be if all strife should cease, if everyone would freely contribute what he can to the common store and with no affectation would master the whole store himself, learning without arrogance what he does not know and teaching without envy what he does. But if some are too illiterate to be able to teach anything rightly and too proud to be willing to learn anything, let us send them on their way, since there are so few of them, and turn our attention to good or at least promising minds. Some time ago I showed my annotations, still in rough form and 'hot from the forge,' as they say, to some irreproachable men, superb theologians, most learned bishops. These men confessed that they found my notes, however rudimentary, threw considerable light on Holy Scripture and helped them to understand it.

Now what you mention about Lorenzo Valla, that he undertook this task before me, I already knew, since I was the first one who saw to it that his annotations were published.[9] I have also seen Jacques Lefèvre's commentary on the epistles of Paul.[1] I only wish that they had finished the task so completely that my labors would no longer be necessary. Certainly I consider Valla a man who deserves the highest praise. Though he was more a rhetorician than a theologian, he studied Holy Scripture so diligently that he compared the Greek with the Latin, whereas there are not a few theologians who have never read the whole testament straight through. Still, I differ from him in some places, especially on matters that pertain to theology. As for Jacques Lefèvre, he was already engaged on his commentaries when I undertook this work. Unfortunately, as it turned out, it did

---

9. Having discovered a manuscript of Lorenzo Valla's (1406–57) annotations on the New Testament, Erasmus published it at Paris in 1505. Valla also showed that the Donation of Constantine, the supposed basis of the pope's tenure of the papal states, was a forgery.

1. In 1509 and 1512, Jacques Lefèvre d'Étaples (1455–1537) published annotated editions of the psalms and the epistles of St. Paul.

not occur to either of us, even in the most intimate conversations, to mention the project he was working on. I had no idea what he was doing until the printed book appeared. I heartily approve of his efforts although in a few places I also disagree with him, quite reluctantly because I would very much like to be *of one mind* with such a friend on all points, except that we must rate the truth higher than a friend,[2] especially when dealing with Holy Scripture.

But it is still not sufficiently clear to me why you present these two men as an objection to my work. Surely it was not to deter me from the task because it was already undertaken by someone else? Even though I am following in the footsteps of such great men, it will be clear that I had ample reason to undertake it. Or did you mean this, that their efforts have not received the approval of theologians? Certainly I do not see that it increased that long-standing hatred of Lorenzo. I hear that everyone approves of Lefèvre. Are you aware that our projects are not entirely similar? Lorenzo annotated only some places, and that, it would seem, in haste and grazing only lightly over the surface,[3] as it were. Lefèvre published commentaries only on Paul's epistles, and translated them in his own fashion; then, if there was any discrepancy, he annotated it in passing. I have translated the whole New Testament from Greek copies, with the Greek text on the opposite page for convenient comparison. I have added notes separately in which I show—partly by evidence, partly by the authority of ancient theologians—that my emendations were not made lightly, in order to gain credence for my corrections and to make it harder for emended passages to be corrupted once again. I only wish that my achievement could have matched my unremitting efforts. As for the bearing of this project on the church, I will not be afraid to dedicate these poor products of my sleepless nights to any bishop, or cardinal, or even pope, as long as he is like the one we have now.[4] Finally, though

2. Aristotle *eth. Nic.* 1096.

3. *Adag.* 327.

4. In 1513 the humanist Leo X succeeded the bellicose Julian II on the papal throne. In his Greek New Testament (1516) Erasmus wrote a preface to Leo, to whom he also dedicated (with Leo's permission) his edition of St. Jerome's letters (1516).

you now seek to discourage me from publishing this work, I have no doubt you too will congratulate me when it is actually published, provided that you have acquired some small taste of that literature without which it cannot be truly judged.

Notice, my good Dorp, how you have earned a two-fold regard from a single service: from those theologians on whose behalf you have most diligently carried out your mission; and also from me, since I find in your friendly admonition increased evidence of your love for me. In return, you should take my equally frank explanation in good part. And if you are wise, you will follow my advice, since I have only your welfare at heart, rather than that of men whose only aim is to draw your superb intellect to their side so that they can strengthen their forces with the addition of such a great leader. Let them mend their ways, if they can; if not, you at least should follow the best course. And if you cannot make them better —and I would certainly wish you to try—at least take care that they do not make you worse. And do this too: present my case to them as faithfully as you have reported theirs to me. You will placate them, if that is at all possible, and you will convince them that I did what I did not out of scorn for those who are ignorant of this literature but for the common good, which is open to all who wish to make use of it and makes no demands on those who do not. Finally, you will show them that my attitude is this: if anyone comes forward who is able or willing to teach more correct doctrines, I would be the very first to renounce and abrogate my own teachings and subscribe to his.

Give my best wishes to Jean Desmarais, whom you should inform of this quarrel about the "Folly" because the commentary on it was dedicated to him by our friend Lister.[5] Give my warmest regards to the most learned Jean de Nève[6] and to the very kind Nicholas of Burgundy,[7] Lord of Beveren and Provost of St. Peter's. For your

5. Desmarais (Johannes Paludanus) was Public Rhetor and Scribe to the University of Louvain. He wrote a prefatory letter for More's *Utopia*. Lister's commentary first appeared in 1515 (*Ep. 1*, 398; *2*, 407–08).

6. Regent of the Collège du Lis and Rector of the University of Louvain (*Ep. 2*, 1).

7. The illegitimate son of the powerful Anthony of Burgundy. Nicholas'

sake I love and revere the Abbot Meynard,[8] upon whom you have lavished the most splendid eulogies (and coming from someone as trustworthy as you, I have no doubt they are quite true). I will not fail to make favorable mention of him in my writing when the proper occasion arises. Farewell, my friend Dorp, dear to me beyond all others.

Antwerp, 1515

---

sister-in-law Anne had been a somewhat uncertain patroness of Erasmus around the turn of the century (*Ep. 1*, 208, 229, 341).

8. Meynard Mann (d. 1526), abbot of Egmond near Alcmar, a patron of Dorp.

INDEX

Scripture, 93, 118; exegesis, 95,
103 *n*, 105, 124–25, 159; neglected by popes, 112, 169;
mentions harmless animals,
129; basis of theology, 155; attributes folly to Christ and apostles, 157; should be studied
without quarrels, 162, 171;
should be studied in Greek,
162–63, 166, 167–68; badly
copied or translated, 167–68,
171; Vulgate version, 169. *See
also* Acts of the Apostles;
Apocalypse; Daniel;
Ecclesiastes; Ecclesiasticus;
Exodus; Daniel; Genesis;
Habakkuk; Isaiah; Jeremiah;
John, Saint; Luke, Saint; Mark,
Saint; Matthew, Saint; Num-
bers; Paul, Saint; Proverbs;
Psalms
Sejanus, 116
Select gods, 15
Selflove, 34, 68–70, 87, 146
Seneca the younger, xi, 45, 128,
141; *Apocolocyntosis,* 3;
Oedipus, 20; *Epistles,* 68, 73
Sermon joyeux, xix, xx
Sermons, 101–04
Sertorius, 40
Seven wisemen, 30, 73
Shakespeare, xviii, xxii
Sileni of Alcibiades, xv–xvi, xxii,
43, 159
Silenus, 27
Simonides, 160
Sin, 103
Sirach. *See* Ecclesiasticus
Sirens, 41
Sisyphus, 85
Sociétés joyeuses, xix, 148 *n*
Socrates, 36, 37, 39, 40, 57, 121,
145, 153
Solomon, 120, 122. *See also*

Ecclesiastes; Proverbs
Solon, 11, 95
Sophists, 10–11
Sophocles, 19, 164
Sorbonne, xi, xiii, 119
Sorites, 31 *n*
Spanish, the, 146
Speculative grammar, 96 *n*
Speculum Historiale, 105
Standish, Henry, 165 *n*
Stelenus, 84
Stentorean, 85
Stoics, 18, 19, 57, 89 *n;* definition
of wisdom of, 28; reject all emo-
tion, 45; paradoxes of, 46, 89;
wiseman of, 46, 120; fine-spun
arguments of, 54
Strassburg, x, xiii
Stunica, Jacobus, xii
Suetonius, 2 *n,* 148 *n,* 149, 152
Suidas, 87 *n*
Superstitious tales, 62–63
Sutor, Petrus, xii
Synesius, 3

Tacitus, Cornelius, 152
Tantalus, gardens of, 45
Tarentum, 76
Telemachus, 84, 118
Tenedos, king of, 88 *n*
Terence, 46, 140, 149
Tetragrammaton, 98
Thamus, 50 *n*
Themistocles, 40
Theocritus, 32
Theologians, 87–98; genuine, 95,
154, 155; barbarous language
of, 97, 155; titles of, 104; ignor-
ance of, 151; misinterpret Scrip-
ture, 170
Theology, 153, 155
Theophrastus, 37
Thersites, 35 *n,* 141
Thessalians, 160